GUIDE TO SUPPLY CHAIN MANAGEMENT

OTHER ECONOMIST BOOKS

Guide to Analysing Companies
Guide to Business Modelling
Guide to Business Planning
Guide to Economic Indicators
Guide to the European Union
Guide to Financial Management
Guide to Financial Markets
Guide to Investment Strategy
Guide to Management Ideas and Gurus
Guide to Organisation Design
Guide to Project Management
Numbers Guide
Style Guide

Book of Obituaries
Brands and Branding
Business Consulting
Business Miscellany
Coaching and Mentoring
Dealing with Financial Risk
Economics
Emerging Markets
The Future of Technology
Headhunters and How to Use Them
Mapping the Markets
Marketing
Successful Strategy Execution
The City

Essential Economics: an A–Z Guide
Essential Investment: an A–Z Guide
Essential Negotiation: an A–Z Guide
Essentials for Board Directors: an A–Z Guide

For more information on these books:
www.bloomberg.com/economistbooks

GUIDE TO SUPPLY CHAIN MANAGEMENT

David Jacoby

Bloomberg Press
New York

THE ECONOMIST IN ASSOCIATION WITH PROFILE BOOKS LTD

This edition published in the United States and Canada by Bloomberg Press
Published in the U.K. by Profile Books Ltd, 2009

Printed in Canada

1 3 5 7 9 10 8 6 4 2

Library of Congress Cataloging-in-Publication Data on file

ISBN 978-1-57660-345-1

Contents

List of figures

Appendix

List of tables

Acknowledgements

I would like to thank the companies which have given permission for their experiences in supply chain management to be used in this book, including: American Honda, APL, APM Terminals, Atherton Trust, BASF, Beretta, BNSF, Boston Warehouse Trading Company, Brown Shoe, Cabur, Carolina Biological, Charles River Laboratories, CLP Power, Cochlear, CSX, CVS, Dana Farber, DB Schenker, Dreams, DSTS/Grupo CTT, FedEx, FMC, Fulham, Futuris Automotive, General Motors, Hasbro, IBM, Incyte Corporation, Interswitch, Iron Mountain, JDA Software, John Deere, Life Fitness, M&C Specialties Co, MacGregor, MTR Foods, Netflix, New York City Housing Authority (NYCHA), Nypro, Plaxo, Popular Telephony, Port Said, Qatar Fuel, Road Runner Sports, Royal Ahold, Royal Philips, Saudi Aramco, Savi Networks, Siemens, Stanley Works, Sydney Airport, Thoresen Thai Agencies Public Company, Tiffany & Co, Volvo China, Wikipedia and Wilhelmsen Ships Service. In addition, Alcoa, Cabot, Cabur, Galeries Lafayette, Georgia Pacific, Jabil Circuit, McDonald's, Nokia, PepsiCo and Qualcomm are some of the companies that contributed to white papers and briefings I have written for the Economist Intelligence Unit, on which this book draws.

I would also like to express my gratitude to a number of authors for allowing the reproduction of their charts, citations and examples, including: Lewis Dartnell, University College London; James Greene, Purdue University (who sadly passed away while the book was being written); Robert Handfield, North Carolina State University; Douglas Lambert, Ohio State University; Michael Maccoby, The Maccoby Group; John Mentzer, University of Tennessee; John Sterman and Stephen Miles, Massachusetts Institute of Technology (MIT); Charles Poirier, CSC; and Robert Rudzki (Greybeard). Thanks also to Janelle Heineke, Department of Operations Management, Boston University, and Jerry Wind, Wharton School, for their advice, clarifications and permissions.

Thanks are also owed to those at the following institutions for their contributions to the body of knowledge: APICS (the Association for Operations Management), the Institute for Supply Management, the Council of Supply Chain Management Professionals, the Supply Chain Council and the American Society for Transportation and Logistics. Several organisations have helped stimulate debate about important supply chain ideas through their conferences, and for this recognition is due to Transport Events, IQPC Worldwide and the International Air Transport Association (IATA).

Special thanks go to consultants at Boston Strategies International who supported my effort to write this book despite their already full workload. Fei Rong gathered and analysed numerous benchmarks; Matt Fixler analysed survey data; Erik Halbert and Luis Gondelles researched and organised case-study material; Betul Altintas, Rob Casper, Bruna Figueiredo, Katy Weener and Patrick Yang provided much appreciated encouragement.

Finally, Jessica, Weston, Brent, Camille and my extended family deserve enormous credit for their tireless patience, understanding and support of this and other projects that compete for my time.

If you have suggestions for improvements to future editions of this guide, please send them to me at djacoby@bostonstrategies.com.

Introduction

The term "supply chain management" (SCM) entered the public domain when Keith Oliver, a consultant at Booz Allen Hamilton, used it in an interview with the *Financial Times* in 1982.[1] The term was slow to take hold and the lexicon was slow to change. It gained currency in the mid-1990s, when a flurry of articles and books came out on the subject. In the late 1990s it rose to prominence as a management buzzword, and operations managers began to use it in their titles with increasing regularity.

The Council of Logistics Management hotly debated changing its name to the Council of Supply Chain Management in 2002, but rejected the idea at the time because many experts disagreed on the definition of SCM. Joel Sutherland, the board chair of the organisation at the time, said: "Surveys turned up hundreds of definitions." He pointed out that the term was too broad and unclear, and could not be managed or measured. He said: "Logistics is part of the supply chain process as the Earth is part of the universe." While we know the weight, the speed of rotation and the composition of the Earth, Sutherland pointed out that the universe is infinite in size and is expanding, and that 95% of it is made of a type of matter or energy that we cannot see or understand. After spending two more years developing an acceptable definition of SCM and deciding on a new name, the Council of Logistics Management ended up renaming itself in 2005 the Council of Supply Chain Management Professionals (CSCMP), but its official definition of SCM left many ambiguities unresolved by describing the set of disciplines that are evoked by the term rather than defining exactly what SCM is.[2]

Other professional associations – for example, APICS (the Association for Operations Management)[3] and ISCEA (the International Supply Chain Education Alliance) – have since developed certification programmes in SCM. APICS' certification is called the Certified in Supply Chain Practitioner, or CSCP, and ISCEA's certification is called the Certified Supply Chain Manager (CSCM). Another, the Institute for Supply Management, is developing one called the Certified Practitioner in Supply Management (CPSM). However, since the CSCP and the CPSM certifications require practical experience as a prerequisite for certification, one may mistakenly infer that SCM must be learned on the job, like a trade, and cannot be codified into a clear body of knowledge that can be learned by students and general managers.

As of the writing of this book, there is no succinct definition of SCM, nor (more importantly) is there a definitive formula for executives and managers desiring to create shareholder value from the supply chain. So, while a new breed of companies such as Wal-Mart and Dell have demonstrated that managers can indeed use SCM for competitive advantage, most companies have found it difficult to replicate such success because the available resources fail to accurately and clearly provide a clear recipe for doing so. To most business people, SCM is still a broad term that covers many functions, including but not limited to purchasing, logistics, production, sales, customer service and engineering.

Conflicting definitions and interpretations

Use of the phrase "supply chain" has become widespread. According to Ohio State University's 2004 career pattern survey in logistics, 27% of the respondents had the words "supply chain" in their title.

Yet many practitioners use key words like logistics, procurement, transportation and supply chain interchangeably and without a consistent hierarchy, confusing the supply chain's role with respect to the other functions, and implying that everybody who works in any of those fields is a supply chain practitioner.

Academics have written extensively on the subject, but their definitions have at times been unclear or evasive. For example, one book defines supply chain management as "the integration and management of supply chain organizations through co-operative organizational relationships, effective business processes, and high levels of information sharing to create high-performing value systems that provide member organizations a sustainable competitive advantage."[4] Another sidesteps a definition in favour of an unquantifiable goal: "to achieve linkage and co-ordination between the processes of other entities in the pipeline".[5] Many others amalgamate principles from lean management, re-engineering, quality and manufacturing,[6] which raises questions about whether SCM is part of these movements or something separate, and if so, where the overlap is.

Practitioners' books are typically biased towards the functions in which the author has the deepest experience. Consultants' books usually offer best practice models that characterise the stages that companies must pass through in order to attain supply chain excellence, but provide managers with little guidance regarding the payback to be expected from the efforts, leaving the business case shaky.

None of the books makes clear a business case for the value of SCM to the "C suite", which describes senior executives whose job title begins with the word "chief" or "chair". Sitting at the highest level in the organisation, these executives ultimately make the largest budgetary decisions. Hierarchically, the next level down is usually called director, and below that is a manager. "C"-level leaders have to make change happen, usually under time pressure from the stockmarket and their boards of directors. They frequently operate under circumstances of high expectations, where ambiguity or uncertainty can consume precious time and organisational goodwill. Senior management is increasingly aware of the importance of SCM, but lacks a definitive formula or roadmap for creating shareholder value from it.

Purpose of this book

The purpose of this book is to distil the essential supply chain concepts into a convenient reference for chief executives. It is designed to be clear, objective, relevant and effective (CORE) in helping executives achieve rapid results. It seeks to clarify the ambiguities surrounding the concept of SCM and its relationship to the functions from which it stems. It will be objective, not biased towards the viewpoint of logistics, manufacturing or any other traditional related function. It will concentrate on what is most relevant by eliminating and subordinating minor concepts that are not essential to getting shareholder value from SCM. The strategies outlined in the book have proved to be effective in achieving significant financial results in companies worldwide.

Clarity means no ambiguity, and to be unambiguous the content is mutually exclusive and exhaustive (MECE). Clarity also means that the key concepts can be reduced to numbers. As with so many concepts, their strength and durability can be tested by whether or not they can ultimately be quantified, because numbers do not allow for ambiguity or overlap. Whether or not a financial business case can be made for supply chain practices or technologies can be the litmus test between concepts that should be taught and implemented, and those that should fall off the bottom of the agenda.

Objectivity means the book draws on experiences in all the functional areas that touch SCM, without bias towards one function. This author's experience represents a variety of functional areas, including transportation, logistics, procurement, manufacturing and customer service, which provides a unique platform for formulating SCM strategies.

Relevance means addressing service industries as well as manufacturing and materials-based industries, new economy as well as old economy. It also means integrating examples, case studies and data analysis from around the globe, so this book attempts to give equal emphasis to the experiences, successes and failures of companies worldwide based on primary and secondary research, analysis and four passports' worth of management consulting experience. It is important to reiterate to some readers that in its search for relevance to corporate strategy the book does not contain information on operational topics that might typically be found in a book on SCM; concepts such as, for example, barcode symbologies, EDI transaction sets, replenishment mechanisms (lot-for-lot compared with EOQ), detailed forecasting methods (historical, heuristic, causal, and so on), or logistical processes such as picking and packing. Furthermore, the definitions provided in the text and in Appendix 4 are written to be easy to understand rather than technically accurate; therefore they may be shorter and simpler than those found in texts for operational managers.

Effectiveness means being able to measure results and compare them with benchmarks and standards. Many authors have focused on the soft side of operations management, emphasising that the right people and the right team dynamics are the secret to supply chain success.[7] While people are a necessary condition for the success of any business initiative, that is not enough to assure supply chain success. This book provides specific supply chain strategies and methods to financial results and targets. As W. Edwards Deming, the guru of the lean movement, is widely credited to have said, "In God we trust; all others must bring data."

To be effective, strategies must be able to be reduced to essential guideposts. Therefore, this book explains SCM in the context of discrete strategies. While supply chain *management* is frequently used to describe internal improvements to existing processes within the context of current, actual situations and constraints, the supply chain *strategy* realises the intent to create a sustainable competitive advantage by wisely using those operational resources and tactics. Whereas supply chain management is about constraints, the corresponding strategy is about realising opportunities. While supply chain management is often about highly structured tangible processes and information management systems at the middle and lower levels of companies, the supply chain strategy is about results-focused activities at the highest levels of companies.

Overall, this book provides an accurate and durable roadmap to help executives leading ambitious, cross-functional SCM initiatives. It blends operational experience with the perspective of a financial decision-maker, so as to show the way to lead with precision and confidence, even under adverse conditions, such as extreme time demands and resistance from diverse functional areas that so often act in unco-ordinated silos. It is the executive's guide to SCM.

1 A historical perspective on industry, trade and transport

Before the Industrial Revolution, production scheduling was typically done manually. Since volumes were low and lead times were long by today's standards, there was little need for formal planning, scheduling, or information management systems. Shop foremen made most production-related decisions by intuition, and most products were consumed close to where they were produced.

The Industrial Revolution

The Industrial Revolution changed the medieval model by introducing repetitive manufacturing. With repetitive manufacturing, foremen gave way to production managers who needed to make decisions on complex variables such as production runs, lot sizes and inventory levels. Henry Gantt, creator of the Gantt chart that maps the critical path in a set of project activities, introduced the concept of formal scheduling in 1916.

Early tools for determining the optimal solutions for mathematical decisions such as production runs, lot sizes and inventory levels were

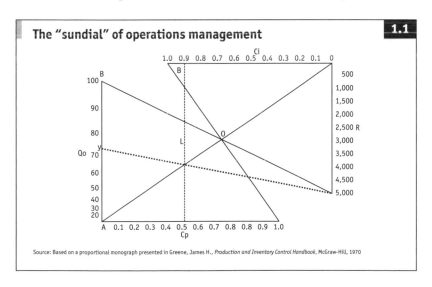

The "sundial" of operations management **1.1**

Source: Based on a proportional monograph presented in Greene, James H., *Production and Inventory Control Handbook*, McGraw-Hill, 1970

based on trigonometric equations and graphs. Figure 1.1 on the previous page shows a graphical representation of the economic order quantity (EOQ) algorithm – a formula that was used to determine the optimal reorder amount for about 100 years, and is still in widespread use today. By showing the relationship between each of the key variables (R = annual usage, C_p is the cost of preparing an order, C_i is the interest rate, plotted on three different axes and connected each to the other via a line), the square root formula Qo = EOQ = square root of ((2 × annual usage × ordering cost ÷ order) ÷ (carrying cost % × unit cost)) was plotted on the fourth axis and connected to the annual usage. The EOQ was approximated by estimating proportional distances on the chart, cross-multiplying the ratios, and solving the resulting equation.

Mass production

Initially, visual scheduling tools ("loading boards") became common in factory environments to assist in co-ordinating labour and machinery to the optimal production lot sizes and inventory levels determined by the algebraic methods.

As factories became larger and factor inputs (labour, capital and methods) became more sophisticated, it was natural for operations managers to turn to the computer to automate hitherto manual processes. According to James H. Greene's *Production and Inventory Control Handbook*[1] roughly 60% of most production control activities were manual in 1970, including: order entry; customer delivery, quantity and timing of production orders; preparation of detailed schedules for manufacturing; follow-up reporting; inventory records for finished, work in process, raw materials; and machine loading. By 1966, over half of companies processed order entry and inventory management manually. About a quarter used punch cards, and only 5–10% used desk calculators.

Labour and unionisation

As production and shipment volume increased faster than the pace of technology, transportation became more labour-intensive and operations management became synonymous with union issues. Labour management and collective bargaining became staples of the distribution, logistics and materials management professions. Robert Lieb, a professor at Northeastern University, chronicled the advent of labour-intensive transportation and logistics operations in his book *Labor in the Transportation Industries*,[2] in which he cited numerous work stoppages at rail companies, airlines and ports.

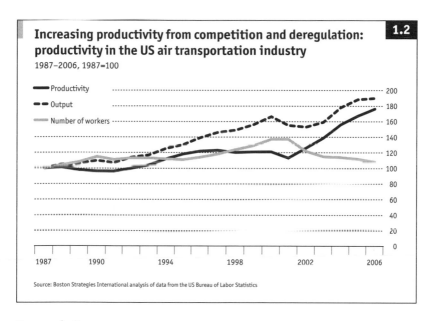

1.2

Increasing productivity from competition and deregulation: productivity in the US air transportation industry

1987–2006, 1987=100

Source: Boston Strategies International analysis of data from the US Bureau of Labor Statistics

Deregulation

After the Staggers Act deregulated the US rail and trucking industries in the 1970s, freight rates became much more competitive. This allowed shippers to ship freight much longer distances at the same cost, which increased the output per person (see Figure 1.2). Waves of privatisation spread around the world, increasing productivity and making transportation and logistics more of a profession than a trade.

The science of logistics gained prominence as distribution became a source of cost savings and a dimension for service level differentiation. Publications in 1993[3] showed logistics as including transportation, warehousing, packaging, inventory and customer service.

Globalisation and long supply chains

Perhaps the most significant catalyst to the growth of SCM was the growth of long supply chains as a result of globalisation. For thousands of years, world trade was minimal compared with today's levels. Between the 1950s and 2000, world trade grew at an average of 5–6% per year.[4] Then between 1990 and 2000, the rate of growth accelerated to 8–9%, and from 2000 to 2008 it doubled again to 17–18%.[5]

Trade between Asia and the rest of the world has been the biggest change. Exports through the port of Shanghai grew by 20–30% a year

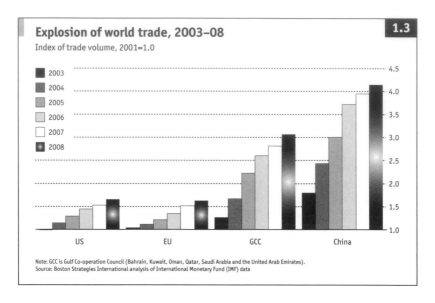

Explosion of world trade, 2003–08   `1.3`

Index of trade volume, 2001=1.0

- 2003
- 2004
- 2005
- 2006
- 2007
- 2008

US   EU   GCC   China

Note: GCC is Gulf Co-operation Council (Bahrain, Kuwait, Oman, Qatar, Saudi Arabia and the United Arab Emirates).
Source: Boston Strategies International analysis of International Monetary Fund (IMF) data

between 1994 and 2006, except in 2001 when it was 13%.[6] Trade between the Middle East and the rest of the world also expanded rapidly (Figure 1.3), even when adjusted for the price of oil, since oil has been decreasing as a share of exports from countries like the United Arab Emirates (UAE) as the local and international economies have grown. Trade between the UAE and other countries more than doubled between 2002 and 2007, and in anticipation of a continued trade boom the country is investing $300 billion in infrastructure between 2007 and 2012, almost five times as much as the Marshall Plan cost, and more than twice what it cost to put a man on the moon.

The number of parties involved in buying or selling goods increased dramatically as world trade grew. Whereas in the historically insular world, most transactions took place between two regionally proximate parties, the explosion of world trade triggered not only a boom in international transportation, but also a proliferation of agents, brokers and forwarders connecting the original shipper with the overseas consignee. Before the growth of global third-party logistics companies, there were sometimes close to a dozen parties taking title to, or in some other way handling, international multi-modal shipments.

The advent of shipping in standard containerised units accelerated global trade, and in the opinion of some it was singlehandedly responsible for the growth of globalisation. Malcolm McLean, the chairman of an American shipping company US Lines, created a revolution when he started taking what had traditionally been shipped via break-bulk (loose cargo loaded and unloaded by manual labour) and packed it into containers that could be loaded and unloaded from ships to trucks almost totally mechanically. Containerisation increased dramatically, to the point where today 108m cargo containers move worldwide each year and 90% of manufactured goods move by container.[7] Areas where containerisation is not prevalent, such as Africa, are on track to catch up with the rest of the world in the early 2010s.

The growing length of supply chains and the increased number of parties in the transaction created the perfect recipe for a bullwhip effect: the amplification of changes in order volume as one progresses from the origin of the variation towards the ultimate source (see Chapter 2 for more details). The large number of intermediaries and intermediary stocking locations created surplus inventories in some places and shortages in others. The large number of actors in the journey from the source to the customer created divergences and time lags between each party's knowledge and estimates of what product was coming and when it would be there. People had to anticipate what was going to happen and plan in advance. Without good tools to do that, many, even most, estimates were wrong. Frequently, by the time products got to where they were supposed to be, they were not needed any more. The global nature of the interactions added language, cultural and time-zone barriers that exacerbated these problems. The result was excess inventory, shortages, overordering and obsolete inventory. Costs ballooned and sales prices fluctuated while inventory was in transit. Jay Forrester, a professor at MIT, cleverly expressed these problems in an interactive game in the 1950s.[8] The so-called "beer game" simulates beer distribution in a multi-echelon distribution system. Participants play the roles of manufacturers, wholesalers, distributors and retailers of beer. Invariably, most participants overorder and lose money, thereby learning the challenges of managing the flow of goods through a long and multi-tier supply chain.

Information shifts power to the customer

The dynamics of making supply meet demand changed dramatically in recent years. Thanks to technology – specifically the ability of retailers to capture point-of-sale data – customers began to dictate which product should move through the chain and when it should start its journey. Consumers' purchases of bottles of shampoo began triggering the manufacture and shipment of replacement bottles all the way from the source.

Technology played a key role in facilitating this transfer of power to the customer. Point-of-sale information provided instantaneous knowledge of product or service sales. Global positioning systems (GPS) on delivery trucks provided real-time access to the status of in-transit inventory, which allowed goods to be diverted to where consumption was greatest. Electronic data interchange (EDI) replaced fax machines as the primary ordering mechanism, which made ordering instantaneous and reduced ordering errors. Internet ordering allowed consumers to bypass the entire set of traditional wholesalers and distributors, thereby reducing the delivery time and the cost of the product.

Companies' knowledge of their customers and of potential customers expanded exponentially. Retailers used data warehousing and other database technologies to gather information on their customers' buying history by recording their purchases and enriching the transaction data with data that could be gleaned from other databases about those customers. Customer relationship management (CRM) and sales force automation (SFA) software provided tools that could query that information and provide useful information to facilitate up-selling and cross-selling. SCM applications allowed them to match incoming orders with available inventory, and compensate for gaps before the store shelves ran empty. One technology built on another to accelerate the trend. Over less than a decade, retailers increased their power in the supply chain by exploiting information. Retailers that applied these technologies and customer management strategies gained market share and had healthy cash flows. The information advantage allowed some retailers to strengthen their positions in the overall supply chain by developing and marketing their own private labels, which increased their profit margins and allowed them to compete with the companies that supplied them high-volume, relatively inexpensive packaged goods, called consumer packaged goods, or CPG. Those that did it poorly lost ground and got bought by the others, fuelling a consolidation trend in retail.

Knowledge of customers has allowed, and to some extent forced, CPG companies and retailers to customise, differentiate and personalise their offering. Mass customisation, the idea of running small lots of customised product through a relatively high-volume production or assembly process, and even the idea of making each product to order within bands of commonness, became popular in the early 2000s under the name of flexible manufacturing. While many companies have begun to customise their offering, finer differentiation within narrow customer groups has become the new marketing goal.

Natural extensions of customisation are personalisation and individual auto-replenishment:

- ◢ Personalisation. If companies could develop and deliver individually tailored products and services, they would increase the chances of sale as well as the value to the customer. Personalisation, as it is called, allows the user to customise the product in a way that satisfies his or her unique needs. For example, Tesco, a large UK retailer, allows its customers who choose home delivery to specify the day and time they want the items delivered.
- ◢ Individual auto-replenishment. For over a decade, retail grocers have viewed home delivery as a vision. It seems to have all the right ingredients. It allows individual customer service and data collection, thereby increasing customer retention and loyalty, and is hopefully a way to simultaneously increase their razor-thin margins. It avoids the need to stock shelves in the store, thereby cutting out one of the most costly components of the grocery value chain. So far, grocery home delivery has had more failures (for example, Webvan, Streamline and Netgrocer) than successes, but ultimately may succeed as retailers refine the delivery model.

Four modern supply chains

To help clarify what supply chains are, below are examples of four supply chains. They describe the flows from the first supplier, which is usually a farmer or extractor of some kind, to the end-customer, which is often the consumer.[9]

Beer and wine supply chain

For thousands of years beer was manufactured, sold and drunk in the same city, primarily because the taste of the beer degraded during the transit and storage time required to ship it. Beer and wine are still brewed and sold locally in some markets. French wine may make only one stop on its way from the vineyard to the dinner table, and the increasingly popularity of microbreweries, where the beer is brewed at the pub itself, has kept beer and wine distribution local in some areas. However, consider this global supply chain for one major US brewer. The company buys its malted barley from Canada and its hops from Germany to make its lagers. It trucks the barley and airfreights the hops to its brewery in the United States. It then mixes the hops and barley with water and yeast at the brewery, and trucks kegs and six-packs to regional distributors in full-truckload quantities. The regional distributors maintain the right amounts of stock to serve local needs. The regional distributors make local deliveries to retail outlets in less-than-truckload quantities. The retailers stock the right amount of each variety of beer to serve local tastes and to meet needs.

Cereal supply chain

Breakfast cereal originates from grain grown in rural areas. Grain is trucked from the grower to storage facilities, then it is shipped by rail to the cereal plant. For example, in North America spring wheat grown in rural Kansas and red winter wheat grown in rural Arkansas and Canada are shipped to grain-storage elevators in trade centres in Topeka or Kansas City (cereal processing plants consume intense amounts of energy, so they are usually located near waterways to cool the machinery needed for grinding). The cereal plants process and mix the grains with other ingredients such as sugar, nuts and dried fruit. The mixture is then shaped or assembled into its final form and packaged. The processor shapes the grains into flakes or chunks. The packaged cereal is trucked to distribution centres, where it is sorted by type of cereal and ultimate destination. From the distribution centres, it is trucked to retail stores.

The voyage from the farm to the home can take a whopping 110 days,[10] due in part to rapid consolidation in the processing industry, which has increased the physical distance between the growers and the households that consume the end product. In response, the Home Grown Cereals Authority (HGCA) worked with the Cereals Industry Forum to foster better communication between farmers, storage, marketing and trading companies, primary and secondary processors, and transporters with the objective of accelerating the flow of product through the pipeline.[11]

Automotive supply chain

Automobile manufacture used to be carried out by a small number of national car companies in their domestic plants, but globalisation has transformed that model dramatically. Today steel coils are produced in Japan and exported to other countries worldwide. For example, US automakers import steel coils to New Orleans, and then ship them by rail and truck to Chicago, Indianapolis and Detroit. Steel slitters and metal stampers make parts out of them and deliver them to auto assembly plants in places such as Lordstown, Ohio, which also receive components like engines and transmissions from other suppliers. Once the finished vehicles are complete, they are sent by rail to mixing centres, where they are regrouped by destination and trucked to dealers nationwide. As the vehicle requires service parts, automakers operate networks of stocking centres that provide parts as rapidly as needed. In Europe, service parts are distributed by truck to distribution centres or in some cases airfreighted, for example from manufacturing plants in continental Europe to distribution centres or service centres in the UK or Ireland.

Chemical supply chain

The journey from crude oil to a white wall involves many steps, at least if you use oil-based paints. Crude oil is shipped from places such as the Arabian Gulf to ports where extensive petroleum processing facilities are located. In the United States, many of these facilities are located in Texas and Louisiana, and Europe has similar capabilities at ports such as Antwerp (Belgium), Rotterdam (Netherlands) and now Teesside (UK). These processing plants convert the petroleum, sometimes in two or more stages of refining, into base chemical products such as polymers, which are used in adhesives, building materials, paper, cloth, fibres, plastics, ceramics, concrete and house paint. The polymers are transported by rail to more specialised chemical plants that make them into emulsions. The emulsions are then sent by rail to the paint manufacturers. The paint is ultimately shipped by rail or truck to distributors, who package it in smaller units such as cans or drums. Large distributors have many distribution centres, which collect different types of products and sort them into outbound loads mixed with many different shipments for customers in a wide geographic range. The long and multi-tiered supply chain involved in paint manufacture means that there is a lot of inventory and about a third of it is in between processing locations at any point in time. Therefore, management of these inventories is like a moving target, and takes skill and collaboration to control so that the right product gets to the right place at the right time.

2 The bullwhip problem

Long supply chains dramatically increased the complexity of almost any firm involved in selling any product since 1980. International trade expanded, and starting with Wal-Mart on the consumer side and maintenance, repair and operating (MRO) supplies on the industrial side, most western companies began importing some raw materials or components from Asia during this period.

Without systems, processes and information to manage the long pipeline of product, retailers were doomed. With 40 days on the water and in customs, and 40 days in domestic distribution centres and trucks, consumer products companies and retailers needed to have a clear picture of which T-shirts and toys were going to be in demand about three months before they reached the shelves. They also had to know how much of what they already had in the stores would be sold at that point – a nearly impossible task.

Most retailers struggled to match supply with demand, and failed. The number of green size 8 T-shirts on the shelf never seemed to be right. Either there would be too many, and they would be heavily discounted or thrown away as obsolete; or there would be too few. The latter case would be the hardest to diagnose and to remedy, since it was usually impossible to tell how many would have been sold if they had been available on the shelf at the right time.

The period was expensive and painful. Retailers lost margin and threw away large amounts of unsold product. Consumers could not find what they wanted on the shelves, and frequently settled for something other than what they really wanted.

Retail stock-outs

The problem became most evident in the grocery industry and in fast-moving consumer goods (FMCG), which includes lower-value household items that are sold in consistently high volume such as toilet paper and toothpaste. One study[1] forecast that grocery chains could save 10% of their costs by implementing a system that replenished these goods based on actual consumption rather than on projected consumption. Retailers and the companies that supplied them, called consumer packaged goods (CPG) companies, established a movement around the effort to do this. It was called efficient consumer response (ECR). Fourteen major US retailers joined the effort.

Implementing ECR was a big challenge. Most companies only knew how to operate on a push system, whereby they would forecast consumption and replenish by assuming that a certain amount of the forecast had been consumed, even if it was not. An elaborate system of reorder points triggered replenishment; most often before the product was actually sold, in order to have it available in the store when the product really did sell.

A French grocery chain, Monoprix, was involved in one of the early efforts to implement ECR. Several major chains had achieved some success with this in the United States, and Monoprix and its hypermarket competitors were pioneering the technique in France in the early 1990s. Implemented in real-time to various degrees, all the chains were trying to record actual sales and then pull the exact amount sold all the way through the supply chain by transmitting readings from the retail store systems back to the source supplier.

Tesco also pioneered supply chain concepts during the 1980s and early 1990s. The company implemented lean processes and systems that were designed to help it synchronise its supply chain. For example, it implemented point-of-sale scanning and electronic data interchange (EDI). It also used cross-docks to consolidate multiple shipments on to a single vehicle so that its store deliveries could be more efficient. These advantages gave it an advantage when expanding internationally and competing against entrenched local stores.[2]

Even though the bulk of early effort was put into consumer goods and retailing, the principles applied to other industries as well. Much later, researchers quantified the opportunity. One study concluded that forecast errors at bulk chemical producers ranged from 10% to 24%, and had an average error rate of 26% and a median error rate of 11%.[3]

Academics' discovery of the bullwhip effect

Academics were the first to identify the root cause of retail stock-outs, which came to be called the bullwhip effect. Yanfeng Ouyang describes the concept in practical terms as "where a small perturbation at the handle (customers) causes huge movements at the tip (upstream suppliers)".[4] It is called the bullwhip effect because the phenomenon resembles the way a whip oscillates when flexed. A Procter & Gamble (P&G) executive used the term "bullwhip" in the early 1990s to describe the fact that although diaper (nappy) usage was relatively constant, P&G's order flow from retailers was cyclical and highly volatile.[5]

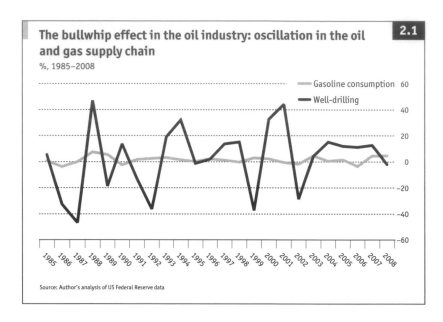

2.1

The bullwhip effect in the oil industry: oscillation in the oil and gas supply chain

%, 1985–2008

Gasoline consumption
Well-drilling

Source: Author's analysis of US Federal Reserve data

John Sterman, in Octavio Carranza Torres' book *The Bullwhip Effect in Supply Chains* explored this issue in detail as it applies to economies and industries.[6] He points out that the oil and gas industry provides a stark example of the bullwhip effect. While the volume of oil and gas consumed is remarkably constant, drilling owners and operators and oilfield service activity is highly cyclical. Perceived disturbances in demand and supply, transmitted through the price of crude, cause predictable upward and downward swings of up to nearly 50% in well-drilling activity, based on the 33-year trend shown in Figure 2.1.

In other industries, the impact is more subtle. The semiconductor industry showed signs of amplitude magnification – minor swings in industrial production led to wider and successively increasing fluctuations in semiconductor production – between its birth in the 1950s and the early 1990s (see Figure 2.2). In this case, the semiconductor production responds belatedly to industrial production and overcorrects for fluctuations therein. However, while the swings in industrial production are + or –10%, the resulting swings in semiconductor production are up to five times that amount. The bubble in the 1995–2001 period was a combination of bullwhip and the internet boom and bust.

A similar phenomenon can be observed in the machine tool industry, which responded belatedly and excessively to the peaks and valleys of the

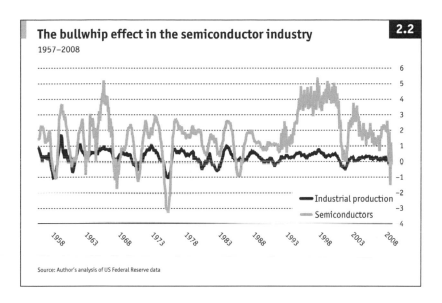

The bullwhip effect in the semiconductor industry   `2.2`
1957–2008

Industrial production
Semiconductors

Source: Author's analysis of US Federal Reserve data

automotive production cycle. While US automotive demand fluctuated by no more than 20% between 1970 and 2000, machine tool orders lagged behind auto production and then overcompensated, resulting in boom-and-bust cycles that damaged sales and share prices.

Longer supply chains magnify the impact of the bullwhip effect and increase the amount of inventory held across the system. Conversely, the fewer the layers in a supply chain, the less the resulting bullwhip effect. Hewlett-Packard measured the bullwhip effect by comparing the standard deviation of orders at the stores with the standard deviation of production at the upstream suppliers.[7]

The rules of ordering, such as the timing of order placement, the acceptance or refusal of back orders, order quantities and lot sizes, and cancellation rights and penalties, can have an enormous impact on the total system inventory and the bullwhip effect when, for example, there is a holiday demand surge.

The effect of ordering rules and exceptions can be chaotic in a large and interdependent system. Chaos theory, first outlined by a French scientist, Henri Poincaré, in 1890, tried to decode the spread of chaotic patterns. Edward Lorenz introduced the "butterfly effect" to point out the sensitivity of the ensuing pattern to tiny changes in the initial condition. Lorenz initially published his theory in 1963 at the New York Academy of Science, and in 1972 he gave a now famous presentation entitled "Predictability:

The butterfly effect 2.3

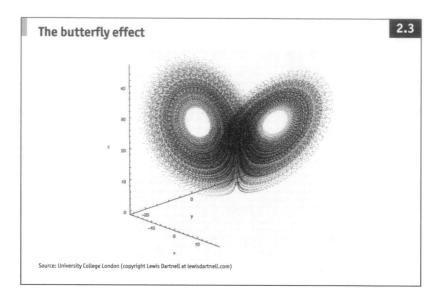

Source: University College London (copyright Lewis Dartnell at lewisdartnell.com)

Does the Flap of a Butterfly's Wings in Brazil Set Off a Tornado in Texas?" to the American Association for the Advancement of Science in Washington, DC.

The Lorenz attractor was one of the first mathematical systems that described chaos. Using three equations, Lorenz determined the evolution of a system (see Figure 2.3). Lewis Dartnell of University College London explains: "The Lorenz attractor never settles on a single point, nor ever repeats itself – it forever whirls round and round the double-lobes seen in the diagram." The system is deterministic, prescribed by three equations, and there is no way of predicting or calculating what value the system will take in the future without actually simulating it all the way and finding out. "It is like a fly that buzzes around inside a room, its direction of flight at any time is determined by equations depending on where it currently is relative to the bottom corner (i.e. its x,y,z co-ordinates inside the room)."

Complex transportation networks such as airlines and railways can sometimes be described as exhibiting chaotic operational patterns. After system delays and disruptions – for example, after severe storms – the schedules can be so out of alignment that the only way to get them back on schedule is to reset by starting afresh the next day or the next week.[8]

The bullwhip effect is evident in macroeconomics as well as supply chain management (SCM) because of the human propensity for delayed response and overreaction. Stockmarkets over extended periods of time show signs of bullwhip overcorrection, resulting in boom-and-bust cycles. Business cycles are generally viewed as the result of the bullwhip effect of inventory flowing through supply chains and causing alternating excess demand (growth spurts accompanied by inflation) and overstocks (recessions sometimes accompanied by falling prices).

Barilla Pasta, an Italian foodmaker, was quick to measure the bullwhip effect. Demand at its central distribution centre had a standard deviation nearly four times that of the demand at its regional distribution centre. The implication was that almost three-quarters of the fluctuation in demand from one level to the next was attributable to problems in the restocking process.[9]

Although some bullwhip effect is inevitable in any system with feedback loops and delays, Barilla's and other corporate and academic research identified aggravating but controllable factors, the effect of which becomes more severe as the number of layers in the supply chain increases. The factors are as follows:

1 **Overcorrection.** Buyers order before they are ready to consume, in order to keep a stock buffer "just in case", or by opportunistically profiting from market price fluctuations, or by hoarding in order to prevent or mitigate a shortage or possible shortage. Overcorrection is the worst aggravator of bullwhip. This tendency is aggravated by long order cycle times, which reduce buyers' sense of confidence and make them overorder. But when five players in succession each order 10% extra, the company farthest from the customer (usually the manufacturer) will end up ordering 61% extra (1.10^5).

2 **Promotions.** Sellers create incentives for buyers to buy when they would not have otherwise bought, thereby creating an initial disturbance that ripples through the supply chain. This is the case with quarter-end low pricing or clearances and many other promotions.

3 **Batching.** Buyers batch orders to get volume discounts and to lower their production set-up costs as determined by their reorder point formulas, their inventory costs as determined by economic order quantity (EOQ) formulas and their transportation costs as determined by their distribution resource planning (DRP) software.

4 **Tweaking.** Buyers update demand forecasts, creating changes to which their suppliers and their suppliers' suppliers react.

At first glance, it may seem that "buy now", "bulk up" and "tweaking" (factors 2–4) could be addressed by software and perfect information.

However, as the beer game (see page 9) can illustrate if played with a scoreboard visible to all, even experts make bad ordering decisions in the face of good information, because it is still necessary to guess ("forecast") retail demand (or trust the provider of that information) and to compute the requirements for the product through the whole supply chain, and to face impending shortages without ordering just a little extra. Moreover, supply chain software has to be extremely sophisticated to operate successfully across multiple tiers of a supply chain, and getting better information requires trading partner collaboration, which relies on trust between corporate entities that in many cases have had transactional, guarded relationships for years.

Why supply chain management became a buzz word

These four factors are clearly problematic, but if they were the only problems, SCM would remain the domain of a narrow band of logistics and supply professionals. SCM has gained currency and become mainstream, discussed and analysed in the press because of factors such as cost, security, compliance, safety and the environment.

Cost competition
Global cost competition
Competition and consolidation in the retail sector heightened awareness of the need for and benefits of SCM. Retail chains such as Macy's were purchased by holding companies such as Federated Department Stores. Grocery chains such as the Great Atlantic & Pacific Tea Company (A&P) lost money and their ownership changed hands. In Europe and South America, hypermarkets such as Carrefour eroded the margins of traditional centre-city grocers and merchants. In Japan, western firms such as 7-Eleven and McDonald's ate into the market share of small stores everywhere. All players – both the winning and the losing parties – looked to SCM to gain a competitive edge.

The problem was not confined to retail. Industrial companies also faced cost pressure and looked to SCM for help. Starting with automotive companies, which faced direct cost pressure from Japanese competitors, European companies turned to better management of their service (aftermarket) parts supply chains for help in reducing costs. American automakers did likewise. Companies in other industries, such as chemicals and mining, faced price erosion (see Figure 2.4), which stimulated them to search for cost reduction solutions, and SCM has been a large focus of that search.

More recently, service-sector companies have faced a similar need to

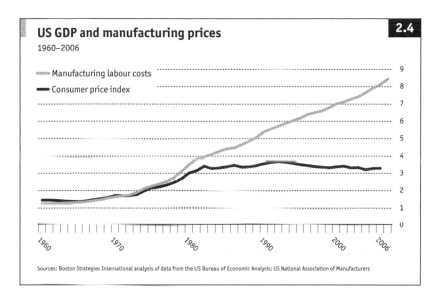

US GDP and manufacturing prices
1960–2006

2.4

Manufacturing labour costs
Consumer price index

Sources: Boston Strategies International analysis of data from the US Bureau of Economic Analysis; US National Association of Manufacturers

reduce their costs through operations improvement, and consultants have adapted SCM principles to help them become more competitive, under the name of service chain management.

Fuel and labour costs
Spikes in oil prices and consequently fuel costs heightened interest in SCM in 2007 and 2008. Oil prices increased by 380% between 1993 and 2008, and price volatility became the norm.

While some carriers, such as those in the parcel express business, implemented surcharges, others such as railways rebased their rates to embed fuel surcharges, effectively using increased fuel costs as a profit centre.

An east European discount airline, Wizzair, saved 8–9% simply by managing its fuelling strategies in 2006, according to its ground operations director, Tony Colliss. The advantage is important to Wizzair: since it competes on the margin with cars and trains, anything it can do to cut fuel costs can give it an edge. At one American airline 18 staff members are dedicated entirely to managing fuel contracts to achieve the lowest price. Outside the transportation industry, an American sound system retailer consolidated its distribution centres and held more inventory in order to reduce transportation expenses.

MTR Foods India

India-based MTR Foods is a pioneer in SCM efficiency, and sees it as essential to increasing its growth from the current 10% to a torrid 20–30% a year. While most of its business has been in India (it serves a traditional domestic market of grocers), the company is developing markets in the United States, the UK and Japan. It is currently wholesaling to companies such as multinational Carrefour to reach a new market of expatriate Indian IT professionals as well as people of other nationalities who would like to eat prepared Indian food in the workplace.

It is also targeting organisations that provide their employees with lunch, tea and dinner. MTR started its supply chain crusade on the demand side, rationalising unnecessary inventory and intermediaries. Now it is trying to establish itself in new geographies by using strategic supply relationships with large multinational customers.

MTR is using IT to manage inventories through seasonal peaks. It is the first major Indian food company to fully implement a major enterprise resource planning (ERP) system.

It swung from a loss to a Rs3m ($60,000) profit by aligning IT and business strategy to better manage inventory. It aims to make 80% of its sales through retail customers that are visible to it, and to plan its production using these customers' point-of-sale data.

Security

Since September 11th 2001, security issues have highlighted the importance of supply chains, and especially global supply chains that involve imports through less-than-perfect security procedures. For example, Tiffany & Co, a global jewellery and gift company, has beefed up its insurance, its vendor compliance guide and its efforts in US security programmes in response to terrorism. It has implemented a four-point programme around the precepts of "protect-detect-respond-recover" for its airfreighted cargo.[10] The US Customs and Border Protection Agency now has over 95% advance cargo screening through electronic manifests. China, one of the largest exporters to the United States, and other countries have enacted similar cargo screening methods, often in response to programmes initiated by the United States. This and similar programmes have resulted in the screening of 97% of containers at non-US ports prior to their importation into the United States.[11] The CT/PAT (Customs Trade Partnership

Against Terrorism) initiative, which pre-certifies companies with safe cargo handling practices, now covers companies that account for 86% of the cargo entering the United States. The next-generation trade-processing systems, Automated Commercial Environment (ACE) and International Trade Data System (ITDS), are scheduled for phase-in around 2010.

Compliance

The collapse of Enron and Worldcom and scandals such as those at Ahold in the 2002–05 period resulted in the institution of Sarbanes-Oxley (SOX) legislation and comparable legislation in Europe, the EU 8th Company Law Directive. SOX has raised the profile of SCM by exposing the ways in which it could be misinterpreted, or worse, used to deceive investors.

Three sections of SOX legislation address SCM:

- ◪ Section 404 governs internal process controls. SCM implications include control over inventory (such as write-offs), risks and exposure to price changes (up and down), and sloppy procedures regarding any type of supplier transaction that does not provide a clear and timely picture of the real situation to investors (such as inadequate information posted to transactions).
- ◪ Section 409 governs the timely reporting of material changes affecting supply chain transaction posting, which can be pervasive in some companies, especially if they are implementing a new information system.
- ◪ Section 401a governs off-balance-sheet obligations. SCM implications include lease obligations and contingent contractual obligations with suppliers (such as shared investment in tooling or shared risk of input price fluctuations).

Most companies complain about the additional obligations that SOX has placed on them. Companies in the electronics, IT and transportation industries say that SOX is making it harder for them to compete because of the added burden and decrease in flexibility that SOX imposes. This is particularly challenging for medium-sized companies, which need to be nimble in order to maintain their competitive advantage over their larger rivals.

Safety

Western companies adopted low-cost country sourcing nearly universally. Then, in 2008, Mattel recalled 21m Chinese-made toys that it thought might be tainted with lead paint and small parts that could cause children to choke. Consumers started clamouring for the type of oversight that the US Food and Drug Administration (FDA) and the UK's Medicines and Healthcare Products Regulatory Authority (MHRA, the FDA's equivalent) provides. Outsourcing became a safety concern in the public conscience.

Environmental concerns

The sharp increase in offshoring during the 1990s and early 2000s drew attention to its environmental cost. In 1988, imports of goods represented 17.6% of US manufacturing sector output. In 2008, the proportion of imports rose to 35.4%, doubling over the 20-year period.[12] Imports rose in the UK as well, from about 21% to 28% of GDP over the same period.[13] Moreover, while the country's North American free trade agreement resulted in a 55% increase in imports from its largest trading partner, Canada, a nearly equal increase came from China.[14] This spike in imports raised environmental concerns about the supply chain, including the lack of emissions controls in low-cost countries (that is why they are low-cost, in part), the pollution involved in shipping items halfway round the world, the costs versus benefits of recycling, and the total supply chain cost of renewable energy, which makes it less attractive than it may otherwise seem.

Environmental legislation is affecting supply chain management practices. First, the establishment of stricter environmental and social standards in developing economies is affecting low-cost country sourcing, and an acceleration of the trend could mean a reversal of global sourcing. Second, recycling and green treatment of returned and end-of-life items is increasingly important, given how much packaging is generated by modern supply chains. Toxic end-products (such as used toner cartridges) and end-of-life disposals (such as the disposal of plastic toys in landfills) are getting more attention. Third, renewable energy sources are an important element of the green car movement, which also includes fully recyclable cars that are gentle to the environment. However, renewable fuels such as hydrogen take so much energy to produce and distribute that the cost of production and distribution outweighs the consumption by the vehicles that use it, at least for now.

3 What supply chain management is and where it is going

The range of cost, security, compliance, safety and environmental issues that catalysed the rise in popularity of SCM brought a broad expansion of its scope far beyond the original problems of the bullwhip effect. Consequently, practitioners and academics have struggled to clearly define it. The profession, if it is indeed a profession, has evolved from a multitude of functions, and as John Dischinger of IBM[1] points out:

> A more formalized characterization of the SCM profession is obviously needed. Continued progress requires a more broadly accepted definition of SCM.

A fashionable buzz word for logistics?

The difficulty in defining SCM is that, while each of the functional areas under its umbrella used to be defined by a central dilemma (its raison d'être), SCM has so far had no clear overarching central dilemma that defines its purpose. Transportation used to be about minimising the cost of routing and scheduling; logistics used to be about finding the least-cost network design; purchasing used to be about minimising purchased costs; manufacturing used to be about scheduling production to achieve the greatest fill rates at the least cost; and customer service used to be about minimising customer complaints. Although each function has evolved to be more complex in purpose, they each retain a strong historical legacy of their original purpose. So while it is clear that individual functions may have optimised their own performance at the expense of the end-to-end system, to date there has not been a simple explanation of the core problem that SCM solves.

Despite the absence of a clear scope – or in some cases perhaps because its ambiguity attracted a broader audience – many professional groups affiliated with SCM. Many professional magazines covering logistics, procurement, etc, have rebranded themselves as supply chain magazines with little change in their content. For example, *eProcure* was renamed *Supply and Demand Chain Executive* and *Global Sites and Logistics* was renamed *Global Logistics and Supply Chain Strategies*. CHAINa, the largest association for supply chain professionals in China, says it attracts "a highly targeted group of supply chain, procurement and logistics executives",[2] implying that the supply chain is a separate but equal function like procurement and logistics. There is even disagreement about whether SCM is a profession. Michael Quayle of the Welsh Development Agency says:[3]

> *Supply chain management is not a profession, and it should not seek to become one. However, supply chain managers should certainly be professional.*

Supply chain management in enterprise resource planning systems

A major enterprise resource planning (ERP) provider offers a set of solutions, including SCM, customer relationship management (CRM), supplier relationship management (SRM) and product life-cycle management (PLM).

The scope of its SCM solution is largely based on the boundaries of the logistics function. It includes strategic planning and network design and advanced demand planning. Demand planning, which is focused on execution, includes manufacturing (making), warehousing (storing) and transportation (moving). Although SCM includes collaboration with external parties (customers for on-demand ordering, contract manufacturers for supply, product development for new product launches and suppliers for advance shipping notices), it is distinct from the capabilities of its sister modules like CRM (focused on buying), ERP (finance and accounting) and PLM (manufacturing).

Its executive dashboard regroups the data from these modules into industry-specific key performance indicators. For example, it measures plant utilisation (which is critical for asset-intensive industries like oil and gas), inventory management and cash-to-cash cycle times (which are critical for fast-moving consumer goods, or FMCG, industries like retail and consumer packaged goods, or CPG).

Is supply chain management just a perspective?

The ambiguity caused by the emergence of global manufacturing and distribution was difficult to sort out. David Simchi-Levi, a professor of engineering systems at MIT who has done extensive work in logistics, says:[4]

> *Supply chain management is a very broad area and it would*
> *be impossible for a single book to cover all the relevant areas in*
> *depth. Indeed, there is considerable disagreement in academia*
> *and in industry about what those relevant areas are.*

APICS, trying to shed its high reputation as a manufacturing association, branded itself as the Educational Society for Resource Management, and when few people could figure out exactly what that meant, it changed its name again.[5] In teaching lean manufacturing, many manufacturing experts insist that "lean" needs to be experienced; that studying a body of knowledge cannot teach the essence of it. Some have even claimed that lean manufacturing is a cult or a religion that can be best learned experientially and must permeate parts of one's personal and professional life in order for it to sink in.

SCM is not a cult, a religion or a philosophy.[6] Companies like APL (see below) have come far in developing integrated thoughts that have improved operations in a variety of situations.

APL's multiple custom supply chains

A supply chain design should be based on the manufacturing situation, the customer situation and the value of the product, according to David Noe, vice-president of sales and marketing for APL Logistics. For a high-end fashion retailer, transit time is the most critical since retail sales are heavily dependent on availability and changes in styles. However, bulk and heavy industries should have supply chains that are designed around cost management rather than demand flexibility. There is a lot of commonality within industries, he states. Electronics, fashion and retail should each have a different supply chain set-up. Noe says:[7]

> *In the past, supply chains were managed around cutting costs. Today, it's*
> *the exact opposite. You need to customize the supply chain in line with the*
> *customers' needs. Retailers need multiple supply chains to address different*
> *situations. A mid-market apparel retailer might have three different supply*
> *chains.*

The first supply chain design is for the initial load that delivers the summer, winter and autumn set-up. In this supply chain, APL loads containers with different products in Asia and bypasses distribution centres where possible to deliver boxes direct to the retail stores four times a year. For example, a Christmas tree supplier loads trees for delivery to a major home improvement retailer once a year. It packs the containers in Asia and APL ships the trees direct to the retailer's stores. The key success factors for this supply chain design are capacity, visibility and flexibility. Since the APL group owns the ships that handle the ocean leg of the journey, it can guarantee the capacity at the right time. Since it has good information capability, it can provide the visibility that allows the retailer to know when the order is coming. And since it has agreements for shipment consolidation and deconsolidation at the ports, it can offer the flexibility to change the store of delivery while en route.

The second supply chain design is for consistent replenishment once the initial seasonal load has been delivered. This supply chain design must provide reliability and consistency of service. To achieve the former, APL Logistics has negotiated capacity with the railways and it uses a proprietary computer program that calculates a metric representing buffer capacity to ensure that it does not have any service failures. The program considers lifts, empty lifts and time in port, and spits out a contingency figure. A figure of 91% means there is a 9% buffer. The contingency model helps APL manage a consistent service as conditions around it change, for example through storms, port delays and surges in volume.

The third type of supply chain design is for rapid replenishment. It replenishes the items that are selling faster than the others during the first ten days of store operation. It focuses on rapid response to get production and deliveries up to the levels dictated by the initial demand within a 90-day timeframe. This type of supply chain requires flexibility at the manufacturing level, for instance the ability to change production quickly (within 90–120 days). APL has had to extend its organisation in order to provide this level of responsiveness, since ocean carriers have traditionally been in the business of operating heavy assets on a fixed and infrequent time schedule. It set up combined air and sea freight links from India to Dubai and from Dubai to New York and Chicago. These links are a joint service operated with a trucking company, Con Way. The service is a date-definite guaranteed service, in which the customer's container is the first one unloaded from the ship, flowing straight into the domestic trucking network.

Balancing demand with supply amid uncertainty

The central dilemma that SCM addresses is that supply and demand are imbalanced because they are separated by time, distance and a host of uncertainties between the source and the point of consumption. Since the variables change over time, any approach to balancing supply and demand in the supply chain must address risk and uncertainty.

Transactions over short timeframes and distances involve little risk and uncertainty, and represent the more operational dimension of SCM. In contrast, global supply lines and strategic agreements over long time-frames involve substantial risk and uncertainty, and represent a more complex and challenging dimension.

So the central, defining issue in SCM is how to balance demand with supply, with the least risk and cost of over- or under-fulfilment. The same is true of how to eliminate bullwhip.

Why software alone cannot solve the problem

Many of the variables in the supply–demand matching are known, and many of them have now been codified in software. The essential elements of any modern SCM system include the following software modules:

- Materials requirements planning (MRP) systems, invented in the 1970s,[8] take independent order streams and, using a bill of materials, generate detailed order requirements for every component and sub-component needed to make it. They also time the order placement to account for typical delivery times.
- Warehouse management systems (or WMS) calculate how much inventory companies need to hold in order to meet expected demand, and in some cases deal with the unreliability of incoming supplies of raw materials and components. They also tell where to place inventory of each stock-keeping unit (SKU) in warehouses to minimise the time required to gather orders.
- Transportation management systems (or TMS) figure out the set of carriers and/or routes that minimises the total miles travelled, and sometimes the total cost incurred, by a fleet of delivery vehicles.
- Advanced planning and scheduling (APS) systems calculate the production schedules that can meet demand with the highest fill rates and the lowest cost, given finite capacity that usually needs to be allocated across multiple products and conflicting due dates.

The fact that such automation has already occurred to a large extent leaves the possible misperception that SCM has been addressed and can now be delegated to the IT department for any follow-up. If all the information were known, planners would just need to push the button and the software would produce all the answers.

Unfortunately, SCM is not as easy as running supply chain execution software, and it is crucial to understand why important challenges have not been addressed through software applications. Donald Rumsfeld, a former US Secretary of Defence, said about military intelligence:[9]

> *There are known knowns; there are things we know we know. We also know there are known unknowns; that is to say we know there are some things we do not know. But there are also unknown unknowns – the ones we don't know we don't know.*

"What we know" generally constitutes a small subset of the spectrum of operating decisions that managers make. It includes, for example, firm orders (which are usually a small set of total orders) and production capacity.

"What we know that we don't know" includes a certain number of operational uncertainties that can often be forecast based on past history. Historical data or quotes from supply chain partners can help to estimate some important variables, as follows:

- The amount of raw material and components that are needed can change in the time between when these materials are ordered and when they are received at the factory. For example, if a manufacturer is building television sets and screen displays take four weeks for delivery, the number of displays needed is likely to vary in the four weeks lead time, especially preceding a seasonal peak like Christmas.
- The order lead time for incoming raw materials and components can vary substantially, aggravating the problem above, especially if deliveries are made to order or if they are being delivered via ocean and rail transport. Furthermore, the lead time can fluctuate as backlogs expand and contract.
- The demand may fluctuate during the delivery cycle time from the factory to the customer. To extend the example above of a television manufacturer, if the delivery lead time varies between three and five weeks, the manufacturer's ability to match supply with demand at week three may be different from the manufacturer's ability to meet lead times at week five.
- The transportation delivery time to the customer can vary substantially, especially if deliveries are made via ocean or rail transport.

The cost of bad forecasts is usually unsold product or services. The cost is especially high in industries with perishable capacity. For example, unsold hotel rooms and unsold airline seats cannot be resold later. Once the flight takes off, the airline pays directly for all seats on the flight, whether they have been sold or not. To complicate matters, the number and class of hotel rooms or airline seats changes until the cut-off time, or if there is no cut-off time, until the moment of consumption. Meanwhile, the airline has to decide how many aircraft to operate, and how many seats to offer in first class, business class or economy class.

"What we don't know that we don't know" includes factors that are very difficult to forecast because they have no history. These can cause the biggest headaches in balancing supply with demand. These include factors such as the sales volume of new products and promotions and the configuration of products or services that would delight the customer. Most customers want more tailored products or services than mass-production or even mass-customisation methods have produced, but the supplier and often the customer cannot articulate exactly the attributes of those ideal products or services.

Few software applications exist to respond to the strategic and marketing dimensions of SCM involving variables that have no historical data series. Some advanced software suites with embedded forecasting and risk management modules can provide best solutions for making operational decisions under conditions of operational uncertainty. However, these have achieved limited penetration and managers still usually trust risk-based decisions and their own judgment rather than let a black-box system make decisions for them.

Moreover, implementing a solution in one company is hard enough; implementing it across multiple companies in a global supply chain has generally been found to be extraordinarily difficult.

Essential definitions

Because of the broad bodies of thought that have influenced SCM and the wide range of interpretations of what it is, a taxonomy and some definitions are helpful (see Figure 3.1 overleaf). The glossary in Appendix 4 provides more definitions. Note that all definitions in this book are deliberately simplified in order to clarify interrelationships between subjects that are often confused, and to focus on how to generate value through SCM. For more complete definitions, the reader may wish to consult the APICS Dictionary or the CSCMP Glossary.

Operations management

Operations management (OM) is the process of adjusting demand and

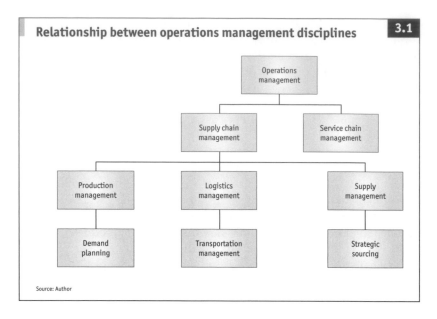

Relationship between operations management disciplines 3.1

Source: Author

capacity at work centres throughout a constrained system to generate output that satisfies customer goals such as cost, quality and speed.

OM is broader than SCM. It applies to both product and service flows, whereas the latter applies primarily to physical flows. It also encompasses qualitative topics such as manufacturing strategy, quality and project management, which are essential to successful execution but are not normally covered in operations research.

Supply chain

A supply chain is the set of activities involved in moving a product (such as a machine tool) and its ancillary services (such as installation, maintenance or repair) from the ultimate supplier to the ultimate customer.

The contemporary literature offers slight variations on this definition. Some consider the supply chain to be a supply network, meaning that it is non-linear and the actors interact among each other. For example, Dan Reid says in his book (with Nada R. Sanders) *Operations Management: An Integrated Approach*:[10] "A supply chain is the network of activities that deliver a finished product or service to the customer."

Some include products and services, whereas others include just products. Some include manufacturing in the scope, for instance Poirier, who referred to "those core business processes that create and deliver a product or service, from concept through development and manufacturing or conversion, into a market for consumption".[11] Others consider the term "supply chain" to include just the movement or flow through the chain, and not the actual manufacture.

For our purposes, the supply chain includes services only in so far as they relate to product flows. Otherwise, the chain would be a service chain, as described below.

Supply chain management

SCM is the co-ordination of the set of activities involved in moving a product (such as a machine tool) and its ancillary services (such as installation, maintenance or repair) from the ultimate supplier to the ultimate customer so as to maximise economic value added (EVA).

SCM includes manufacturing value added as it accrues along the chain, but excludes the initial manufacturing or conversion activity, so an initial basic activity such as extraction or farming would be considered a manufacturing activity (a node), not an SCM activity.

Service chain management and supply chain management

Service chain management is the engineering and management of a flow of services and funds in order to maximise customer loyalty. No goods are involved. The underlying concepts and principles are the same as in OM. They apply to SCM and to services management, for example in claims management processes in insurance, loan approvals in banking and the closing process in real-estate (property) transactions.

Supply management and supply chain management

Supply management is the process of getting goods and services from the supplier to the point of production on time and within budget in order to minimise the total life-cycle cost to the organisation. Supply management is a subset of SCM when it addresses the sourcing of products, but it is also a subset of service chain management when it addresses the procurement of services.

Logistics and supply chain management

Logistics is the co-ordination of flows of goods, information and funds from a supplier to a customer to maximise availability while minimising operating costs. Logistics includes transportation, warehousing and inventory management, and the transactional activities of customer service, forecasting, assembly and production control. Unlike SCM, logistics does not address the entire span from the ultimate supplier to the ultimate customer, nor does it address the interfaces between transport, marketing, product development, sales, maintenance, production, quality, engineering, R&D, new product development and procurement.

Demand management

Demand management (also called yield pricing) is the process of adjusting pricing to influence demand and thereby increase sales and margins. See Chapter 8 for more details.

Demand chain management or supply chain management

Demand chain management is an alternative form of the phrase "supply chain management" that emphasises the importance of customer requirements in triggering replenishment. Demand chain effectiveness is a goal of many of the techniques within the synchronisation and customisation strategies discussed in this book. All the concepts and tools of demand chain management are the same as for SCM. "Demand chain" is a more appropriate expression since it connotes the primacy of customer requirements, while SCM implies that the process starts with suppliers. This book uses the term "supply chain management", since that is more commonly understood.

The four principles of supply chain management

From the customer's point of view, benefits result from increased efficiency, reliability, flexibility and innovation, and these are the underlying principles of SCM.

Many authors and practitioners include collaboration as a guiding principle. Actually, collaboration in itself delivers no value to the end-customer – it is necessary but not sufficient. Collaboration and its pal, visibility, are both needed to achieve the end-goal, since sharing forecast information between trading partners is of prime importance in reducing the bullwhip effect. Collaborative planning, forecasting and replenishment are covered in Chapter 8.

Efficiency

Lean, no-waste, supply chains are not only less costly. Driving out waste also enforces clear-headed thinking that improves other processes as well. Kate Vitasek[12] analysed lean supply chains and identified waste and cost reduction as one of six core competencies. Eli Schragenheim extends the list of waste reduction and lean concepts to include the drum-buffer-rope concept in Carol Ptak's compilation *ERP Tools for Integrating the Supply Chain.*[13] Popularised by Eliyahu Goldratt,[14] the drum represents a production rhythm; the buffer represents the time between units of production; and the rope represents the pulling of production through the system. If all are synchronised, then there is no inventory. In order for this system to work, experts usually prescribe just-in-time (JIT), total productive maintenance (TPM), an extremely rapid production changeover called single-minute exchange of die (SMED), standardised work, mistake proofing, a visual workplace, standard container sizes and collaborative supplier agreements.

Reliability
Most companies achieve consistency of quality in the product and services by engaging in process improvement programmes to synchronise demand and supply at every link in the supply chain. Like efficiency, reliability has associated benefits: improvements in service usually bring process simplicity, lower costs and higher levels of customer satisfaction.

Flexibility
Flexibility, or agility as it sometimes called, means not only having the ability to ramp up production volume, but also having adaptable supply relationships, customisable transactions processes, and streamlined and rapid data flow.

Sometimes becoming efficient and reliable also provides flexibility, especially if the improvement is generated by eliminating waste. For example, rapid replenishment and postponement, whereby finishing touches are put on products or services close to the customer and often only after orders are received, in order to keep inventories low, are not only less costly but also permit change to be absorbed into the system more quickly than in a fixed supply chain.

However, organisations often generate efficiency and reliability by establishing rigid parameters and rules, which presents a problem when customers' requirements change or when both demand and supply fluctuate at the same time.

A clear definition of customers' needs and standardised processes for fulfilling them, as well as industry standards, are crucial for ensuring the ability to flex.

Innovation

Efficiency, reliability and flexibility will go stale over time, as more creative competitors overtake. Therefore, supply chain processes, including product and service introduction and development, need to be innovative and self-regenerating to be truly capable of creating sustainable advantage for the company.

The four supply chain strategies

The principles of efficiency, reliability, flexibility and innovation serve as important pillars for defining supply chain strategies (see Figure 3.2). The myriad methods, techniques and methods under the umbrella of SCM can be regrouped into four corresponding supply chain strategies: rationalisation, synchronisation, customisation and innovation. Rationalisation is aimed at containing operating costs. Synchronisation is aimed at balancing supply with demand. Customisation aims to enhance the customer interface. And innovation is focused on achieving rapid new product development and introduction. These strategies flow from the principles above, which explains why the linkage between supply chain and business strategies such as cost, quality, service and innovation has been identified previously, notably by Shoshanah Cohen and Joseph Roussel.[15]

Importantly, the strategies operate in an environment of shared

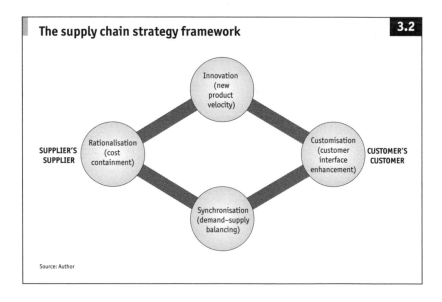

The supply chain strategy framework 3.2

Innovation (new product velocity)

SUPPLIER'S SUPPLIER

Rationalisation (cost containment)

Customisation (customer interface enhancement)

CUSTOMER'S CUSTOMER

Synchronisation (demand–supply balancing)

Source: Author

infrastructure. Infrastructure is often assumed to be adequate to support all four strategies, but this is not always the case, as public investment sometimes trails growth.

Five SCM techniques are essential to making all four strategies work:

1 **Supply chain network design** that allows rapid response and low cost. This includes the site location and order terms and conditions.
2 **Capacity planning** that makes enough capacity available at the right time, including long-range decision modelling.
3 **Risk management** that balances risk and reward to achieve high performance without undesirable risk.
4 **Organisational change management** that sets the pace of human change to align with corporate supply chain objectives.
5 **Performance monitoring and measurement** that focus on the important metrics needed to track performance against the strategy.

Project management, training and an understanding of organisational dynamics are essential to any SCM initiative. Project management is critical to all SCM approaches, since most initiatives need to be implemented in the form of a project. Training is imperative since the field is evolving, so even seasoned professionals in any of the functions need to stay abreast of current thinking.

Beneath the framework as a whole lies inter-organisational psychology and game theory. Inter-organisational psychology, organisational development (OD) and related fields of organisational behaviour will set the pace at which the field can advance. Game theory explains why organisations choose to co-operate or behave defensively and independently, which in turn determines how much of the collective benefit can be attained.

In each strategy there are SCM techniques and traditional functional processes (see Table 3.1 overleaf). The distinction is important; while the literature has usually considered both to be SCM, this framework distinguishes between what has always been the domain of the function, and what is uniquely SCM. The litmus test of whether an activity is a value-adding SCM activity is whether it can consistently be used to generate quantifiable success in one of the following four strategies:

■ Rationalisation includes basic processes that have always occurred under procurement, such as: auctions/events, collections, contracting, sourcing (including global sourcing, negotiation, purchase order processing, requests for quotation, supplier

Table 3.1 **Value-adding supply chain activities compared with traditional functional responsibilities**

CUSTOMERS

SUPPLIERS

Supply chain strategy	Rationalisation	Synchronisation	Customisation	Innovation
Overall value-adding supply chain management techniques	Supply chain network design Capacity planning/shaping Risk management approach and tolerance Organisational behaviour/change management Performance monitoring and measurement			
Strategy-specific value-adding supply chain management techniques	Strategic sourcing Outsourcing Lean (waste reduction) Standardisation and simplification of specifications Transportation optimisation Tier-skipping Supplier *kaizen* Consignment and vendor-managed inventory Design for manufacturability Electronic data interchange and paperless work flow	Constraints management and throughput analysis "Pull-based" demand trigger Just-in-time Perfect order Make-to-order Optimal inventory placement Sales & operations planning (S&OP) Collaborative inventory management Everyday low price Anchor tenant ensures stability Shifting demand and capacity Better forecasting, less emotional reaction Risk mitigation	Control of customer relationship Value analysis Customer knowledge management Linking customer data to all interactions Customer profitability management Mass customisation Available to promise Personal interactions On-demand availability Design for configurability Lifetime services	Continuous market feedback Concurrent product development Rapid and early prototyping Product life-cycle management Early supplier involvement Early customer involvement Forward branding Design for supply chain

CUSTOMERS

Supply chain strategy	Rationalisation	Synchronisation	Customisation	Innovation
Traditional function-specific activities	Auctions/events BOM maintenance Collections Contracting EDI Global sourcing Negotiation Purchase order processing RFx Supplier performance management Supplier selection Supplier conferences Outsourcing TCO and delivered cost	APS Fixed cost accounting DRF Enterprise asset management Inventory and order status Order fulfilment Returns, repairs, recycling Maintenance Routing and scheduling MRP S&CP Sales forecasts and customer orders	Customer analytics Customer segmentation Data mining NPI Pricing Trade finance	New product introduction
Traditional departments	Procurement	Assembly Inventory management Maintenance Materials management Operations Production Production control Quality	Customer service Forecasting Marketing Product development Sales Transportation	Engineering R&D NPD
Traditional cross-functional activities		Project management Change management Training Inter-organisational psychology and game theory		

SUPPLIERS

Source: Author

performance management, supplier selection, supplier conferences, sourcing and vendor management), production (including manufacturing planning, lot sizes, production and production control, and quality) and facilities management. But it also includes important SCM activities such as SKU rationalisation, value engineering and supplier *kaizen* (continuous improvement). (Table 3.1 provides a complete list.)

◪ Synchronisation includes basic processes that have always occurred under assembly, inventory management, maintenance, materials management, operations, production, production control, and quality such as APS, fixed-cost accounting, enterprise asset management, inventory and order status, order fulfilment, returns, repairs, recycling, maintenance, routing and scheduling, demand planning (including sales and operations planning or S&OP, sales forecasts and customer order handling) and distribution centre management (including warehouse design, receiving, inspection, materials management, stocking policies, rack specifications, facilities maintenance, picking, packing and packaging). But it also includes important SCM activities such as constraints management, cross-docking, lean distribution, product life-cycle management (PLM), postponement, Six Sigma (a form of statistical process control designed to ensure the ability of a process to repeatedly deliver output within a prescribed range of tolerance), design for assembly/modularisation, standardisation and collaborative inventory management. (Table 3.1 provides a complete list.)

◪ Customisation includes basic processes that have always occurred under customer service, forecasting, marketing, product development, sales, customer analytics, customer segmentation, data mining, distribution resource planning (DRP), new product introduction (NPI), pricing and trade finance. But it also includes important SCM activities such as channel design, pull (ECR, JIT, etc), yield pricing, value analysis, and design for maintainability and operability. (Table 3.1 provides a complete list.)

◪ Innovation includes traditional processes in engineering, R&D, and new product development that facilitate change, such as bill of materials (BOM) maintenance and new product introduction new product introduction (NPI). It extends to important SCM activities such as early involvement from suppliers, gain sharing for innovative ideas, make-or-buy/outsourcing, partnering, risk management, supplier consolidation, supplier pre-packaging, consignment and vendor-managed inventory (VMI), and design for prototypeability, manufacturability and the supply chain. (Table 3.1 provides a complete list.)

Financial processes, including trade finance, which have been considered in the traditional definition of logistics since the mid-1990s, are not part of SCM per se. Billing, collections, claims processing, auditing and trade finance are operational in nature and do not make any of the supply chain strategies more successful. These types of financial considerations sometimes affect the design of the supply chain, but in themselves they offer no supply chain benefit like the four core supply chain strategies do. For example, a tax strategy might suggest producing in China rather than South Korea, but that difference provides no supply chain benefit, just tax benefit, and can even make the supply chain more complex and costly than it would otherwise be.

4 Why CEOs need supply chain management today

A competitive necessity to stay in business

For many companies that have become caught in a profit squeeze, especially manufacturing firms that are threatened by low-cost competition, SCM has become a competitive necessity. And as many competitors have implemented SCM solutions and programmes and realised cost savings, the pressure has been on to understand and implement the concept.

Dell faced the same competitive environment that all PC-makers faced in 1985. Its success stems from its decision to compete on SCM, and specifically the skipping of levels in the supply chain through direct to customer sales, the co-location of suppliers for just-in-time (JIT) delivery, and the deliberate up-selling and cross-selling through a highly trained inside sales force that handled customers who entered the website and then had questions.

Meanwhile, thousands of smaller private companies in industries such as plastic injection moulding, steel, industrial distribution and wholesale consumer goods that were late to pick up on the SCM signals have been crushed as their competitors sourced from China and established anchor distributorships that were able to efficiently import product in bulk and ship it to national retailers such as Wal-Mart. For small distributors such as Boston Warehouse Trading Company, a US distributor of household goods, and Carolina Biological, a US educational products wholesaler, supply chain management is a key to survival. Explains Peter Jenkins, CEO of Boston Warehouse Trading Company:[1]

> If you disappoint a key customer like Target, your business will halt immediately with them, and there are fewer and fewer retailers to sell to.

Shorter product life-cycles

Many factors have led to the increasing importance of SCM in recent years, such as the following:

◨ Shorter product cycles are increasing the risk of stock-outs and obsolescence. With short product life-cycles, late deliveries result in stock-outs and overstocking results in obsolescence.

◨ Fiercer competition is increasing the importance of low costs and product availability which can both be addressed by better inventory management practices.

◨ Technologies such as e-commerce, e-procurement, auctions, automated requests for quotation and compliance solutions are "flattening the world"[2] and enabling global supply chains. As a result, new technological platforms will carry SCM into the next generation. As Claus Heinrich and David Simchi-Levi reported in *Supply Chain Management Review* in 2005:[3]

> *Companies that support their demand planning modules with a corresponding software module (such as a demand planning module) shorten their order fulfilment lead time by 47% and cut their cash-to-cash cycle by almost half ... supporting the demand planning process with IT systems reduces inventory days of supply by about 40%.*

These improvements will be implemented by tools[4] in areas such as:

◨ returns, repairs, recycling and maintenance;
◨ product management, design and engineering;
◨ radio frequency identification (RFID);
◨ manufacturing;
◨ supply chain software and technology;
◨ collaboration between supplier and customer;
◨ marketing, sales and customer service;
◨ inventory and materials management;
◨ forecasting, planning and scheduling;
◨ logistics, transportation and warehousing;
◨ purchasing, procurement and sourcing.

To keep up, manufacturers need to combine value-added services, technology and a focus on premium quality. The "mutually reinforcing cycle of technical and commercial advances ... bring full circle the link between the economy's services-intensity and its information-intensity, creating a huge, growing market for the most advanced information technologies that the economy's goods-producing industries can deliver."[5]

SCM will play a critical role in helping manufacturers build a strong revenue base in ancillary services. In the light of a global trend towards service economies, manufacturers achieve growth by leveraging the service–technology–premium cycle to achieve sustainable high margins.[6]

This cycle integrates value-added services, technology and a focus on premium quality. Value-added services extend the life of manufactured products and increase the value of the products to the buyer. Technology, when embedded in the products' design, makes them difficult to copy or reverse engineer. And premium quality differentiates the products in the marketplace and pre-empts comparison with low-cost competition. SCM can help the transition to services since it provides the basis for better goods and ancillary services management.

Advanced SCM is critical to executing this services–technology–premium cycle. Customer knowledge management together with cost and pricing, elements of the customisation strategy, can help to reliably deliver the value-added services and ensure premium positioning. Rapid and repeatable new product introduction (NPI), part of the innovation strategy, can secure the technology edge.

Large impact on financial results

For an individual company, the benefits of SCM translate to improvements in revenue, cost and assets. Since economic value added (EVA) captures all of these in one metric, it can be said that the primary benefit of SCM is an improvement in EVA. Figure 4.1 shows the relationship between the underlying levers affected by supply chain management initiatives and EVA. Revenue increases the top line. Cost savings improve profits and/or profit margins. And inventory and capital asset utilisation reduce assets and thereby improve EVA.

Effective SCM offers at least a 30% potential improvement in EVA. Rationalisation strategies can contribute 4–6%. Synchronisation strategies can generate 5–7%. Customisation can add up to 6–10%, and innovation benefits can exceed 15% (Figure 4.2).

These estimates are based on actual results achieved by companies worldwide over 20 years, as well as statistical compilations of companies that practise each strategy compared with their peer groups. SCM has demonstrated cost leverage opportunities. Boston Strategies International, a consulting firm that has conducted an annual benchmarking study since 2004, tracks the savings from 13 SCM techniques. According to its 2008 study, low-cost country sourcing saves companies 4–7% of expenditure on their largest spend category, net of all costs. Although the saving

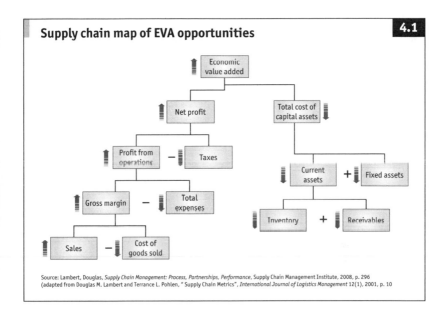

Supply chain map of EVA opportunities 4.1

Source: Lambert, Douglas, *Supply Chain Management: Process, Partnerships, Performance*, Supply Chain Management Institute, 2008, p. 296
(adapted from Douglas M. Lambert and Terrance L. Pohlen, " Supply Chain Metrics", *International Journal of Logistics Management* 12(1), 2001, p. 10

is down from previous years (some of the ripe fruit has already been picked), such sourcing still has a substantial effect on the bottom line. Request for quotes saves 4–6%. Long-term agreements, group purchasing and auctions all save companies around 3–5%. Value engineering saves 4–5%.[7]

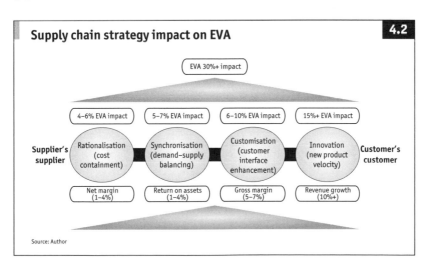

Supply chain strategy impact on EVA 4.2

Source: Author

Rationalisation allows a 12–13% cost decrease to yield the same profit impact as a 19% sales increase because of the leverage of cost reduction (there is a detailed example of this in Chapter 8). Moreover, supply chain management can increase revenues. A 2006 study[8] showed that 29% of respondents said that SCM increased their companies' revenues by more than 5%. Out of the total, 3% said it increased by more than 20% and 9% said it increased by 10–20%. Successful implementations with large categories of goods at large companies have reduced inventory by 25–30%; the average cycle time by 30–40%; and total costs by 15–30%; and have increased sales by 8–15% and availability by 10–20%.

The savings multiply when considering extended supply chains composed of multiple layers. Funda Sahin, an associate professor at the University of Tennessee, estimates:[9]

> *The potential savings from co-ordination in the supply chain and avoidance of the bullwhip effect could reach 35% of total system costs ... Comparing the research findings across the studies indicates that information sharing and co-ordinated decision-making may reduce supply chain costs anywhere from 0% to 35% depending on the specific supply chain structure and problem assumptions.*

In addition, the application of the principles of SCM to anticipate and smooth patterns of capital investment in the economy at large could dampen the destructive impact of business cycles, since they are primarily caused by reverberations of overcorrection in investment and inventory caused by the same bullwhip phenomena that create inventory imbalances in supply chains. While most people use SCM to reduce inventory fluctuations resulting from moving boxes across space, others will apply the underlying principles to reduce price inflation and capital investment peaks and valleys over time. Michael Hugos, in the conclusion to his book *Essentials of Supply Chain Management*, says:[10]

> *Adaptive supply chain networks using real-time information and negative feedback can effectively dampen excessive market swings. This ability alone will have a wealth creation effect that is even more powerful than what was created by the effect of the steam engine.*

A geopolitical weapon for countries

At a higher level, SCM practices can improve national competitiveness. Robert Metcalfe's law[11] states that the value of a telecommunications network is proportional to the square of the number of nodes in the system. SCM connects the nodes in a trading system, adding synergistic value. Conversely, insufficient nodes lead to the system underperforming. Boston Strategies International's analysis of worldwide transportation infrastructure[12] showed that countries with poor infrastructure spend more on logistics as a percentage of their national economies than countries with well-developed arteries and high transportation and logistics productivity. For example, France, which has a radial hub-and-spoke road network and builds roads to last a long time, has relatively low logistics costs as a percentage of its GDP. In contrast, China, which has a less developed infrastructure compared with its land mass, has high logistics costs as a percentage of its GDP.

South-East Asia is growing more rapidly than any area of the world, in part because of the links and connections that are being established and catalysing trade in Asia and between the region and other areas of the world. Efficient supply chains bring cost advantages, which enhance export competitiveness, and the supply chain effect – the interaction between infrastructure and exports – grows interactively and exponentially.

Vietnam

Vietnam's transport costs are as low as 1% of its GDP, but its supply chain costs are high on the same basis, especially for international water-borne commerce. Vessels face major delays in port because of inefficient practices. In a country where container traffic is growing at 20–25% per year, inefficiency is inhibiting the country's fast growth path.

Investors are addressing the capacity shortage. They plan to pour more than $4.5 billion into port infrastructure from 2009 till the end of 2013.[13] To mitigate the congestion that is accompanying the port build-up, and thereby keep its supply chains flowing smoothly, the country needs to build more paved roads, continue to aggressively privatise ("equitise", as it is called in Vietnamese) its manufacturing sector, and stabilise foreign investors' concerns by establishing clearer judicial, legislative and financial frameworks and safeguards.

The country's ultimate supply chain advantage may be linkages to other countries in the region, especially to southern China through the north and to Thailand via Cambodia and Laos. The Asian Development Bank (ADB) has agreed to lend $60m to restore a 100-year-old rail link between

Hanoi and the Chinese border,[14] and an ambitious east–west corridor may one day connect Danang (Vietnam) to near Rangoon (Myanmar).[15] However, for both domestic growth and connections to China, it must first build major north–south infrastructure; three-quarters of the cargo traffic activity is in Ho Chi Minh (in the south) and it can take up to 30 hours to make the 272km trip from Ho Chi Minh to Hanoi in the north.[16]

Thailand

Exports from ASEAN countries (Brunei, Cambodia, Indonesia, Laos, Malaysia, Myanmar, Philippines, Singapore, Thailand, Vietnam) grew fivefold between 1988 and 2008[17] because US and European companies greatly increased their sourcing in Asia between 2004 and 2007.

The development of Laem Chabang port, a deepwater alternative to Bangkok port with an expected volume of 11m TEU (20-ft equivalent units), with the prospect of a rail link connecting Thailand to China through Laos, are major supply chain advantages that will reinforce Thailand's export growth. However, in its role as a hub, it both collaborates and competes with Singapore, which absorbs its exports but also limits its internal growth. In the longer term, integration within Asia and connectivity to Europe will greatly contribute to Asia's export competitiveness, similar to the way in which hub-and-spoke networks allowed airlines to greatly increase passenger air-miles in the 1980s and 1990s at little incremental cost. After deregulation, larger airlines almost all switched to hub-and-spoke networks to benefit from greater traffic density, and "in 1985, the marginal cost of carrying an extra passenger in a high-density network was 13–25% below the cost in a medium- or low-density network, giving the high-density carrier a distinct competitive advantage. This advantage may help explain the failure of those smaller carriers that, despite rapid growth, could not achieve adequate density levels."[18]

The Trans-Asia railway project covers over 80,000km in South-East Asia (Cambodia, Indonesia, Laos, Malaysia, Myanmar, Singapore, Thailand, Vietnam), North and North-East Asia (China, South and North Korea, Mongolia and Russia), Central Asia and Caucasus (Armenia, Azerbaijan, Georgia, Kazakhstan, Kyrgyzstan, Tajikistan, Turkmenistan and Uzbekistan), and South Asia (Bangladesh, India, Nepal, Pakistan and Sri Lanka), Iran and Turkey. The Trans-Asia highway projects are connecting Singapore north into Thailand, Laos and China, and west into Myanmar and through to Bangladesh and India.

China

China has the second-highest logistics costs in the world, according to a recent study for the US Chamber of Commerce.[19] All-in logistics costs, including inventory and personal transport, are about 22%, compared with a world average of 13%.

The reasons for this high figure are, for a start, that transportation takes up a higher percentage of GDP than other countries its size. China's road system is inadequate. Inventory levels are higher than in other countries because transit time variability is high, and labour is relatively immobile, partly because personal transport expenditure is high.

China's high supply chain costs are limiting its growth. While its export and import capabilities are limited by port throughput, its internal demand for chemicals and other products that are not manufactured in sufficient quantity inside China is choked by the high cost of inbound logistics.

As in other fast-growing world areas like South-East Asia and the Middle East, China's government is investing massively in infrastructure. In its 11th Five-Year Plan, the Chinese government laid out a broad-scale and ambitious programme to improve supply chain performance by creating third-party logistics (3PL) enterprises and deregulating certain transportation areas (especially in response to joining the World Trade Organisation); promoting the establishment of logistics networks throughout the country; and building 30 modern logistics parks that will serve as distribution centres throughout the country.

5 Setting the right supply chain strategy

Companies that focus on a specific supply chain strategy are more likely to build shareholder value than those that do not. Wal-Mart has used its supply chain to become a low-cost leader. Dell uses its supply chain to deliver reliably and just-in-time (JIT). Nokia lets its customers customise and even personalise its mobile phones. And Apple has refined its product development process to be able to innovate repeatedly and rapidly.

Similarly, deploying the wrong supply chain strategy can create problems. Nypro, a US plastic injection moulding company, attempted to produce low quantities of custom orders in a job shop model in the 1980s. This flopped because the model did not provide a sufficient volume to justify the investment required in the moulding machines. To correct this, the company dropped more than 400 of its 500 customers to get to the high volumes that made sense. The result was a very profitable make-to-order (MTO) production operation that generated an average 34% annual revenue growth from 1996 to 2006.

While it can be tempting to try to implement every supply chain improvement programme that is covered by the popular press, companies that try to apply all the supply chain strategies are less effective at achieving any of the desired results. Focused companies have these advantages over companies with dispersed supply chain strategies, according to the author's consulting experience:

- between three and four times the return on capital employed;
- between two and three times the return on assets (ROA);
- two-thirds less time to increase output by 20%;
- one-third less variation in sourcing and production order cycles.

The difference between supply chain management and supply chain strategy

SCM has become a widely used cliché for anything touching the movement of goods from one place to another. Few people question the word "management", but they should. Whether the supply chain is used strategically, tactically, or both at once determines the value that it provides. So, SCM is dealing with today's actual situation to generate improvement through process excellence. Supply chain strategy is forming the unique positioning that is intended to result in a future competitive advantage.

Strong SCM can deliver a competitive advantage in the long run, but if it is not guided by a supply chain strategy it usually delivers only incremental improvement. Strong supply chain strategy can define a unique end-state that has the potential to change the competitive landscape, but if not followed by reliable execution, it usually delivers no value.

Thus both supply chain strategy and supply chain execution are needed to deliver competitive advantage.

Manufacturing strategy

Historically, the closest analogy to supply chain strategy was manufacturing strategy. The business strategy should directly determine the manufacturing strategy, but the business strategy is not always clearly articulated, documented and available to those needing to set the supply chain strategy. A business strategy built on low cost requires a more standardised process than one built on premium quality or differentiation. Similarly, a business in which the average order size is very large requires a different production process from one where there are many small orders.

Robert Hayes and Steven Wheelwright developed a diagonally sloped

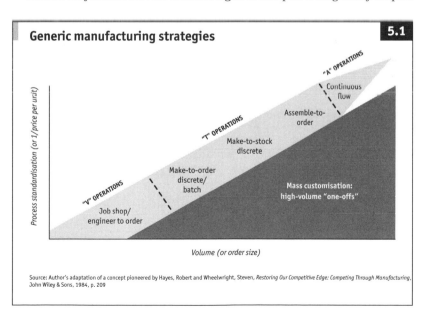

Generic manufacturing strategies — 5.1

Process standardisation (or 1/price per unit)

"A" OPERATIONS

Continuous flow

Assemble-to-order

"T" OPERATIONS

Make-to-stock discrete

Make-to-order discrete/batch

"V" OPERATIONS

Job shop/ engineer to order

Mass customisation: high-volume "one-offs"

Volume (or order size)

Source: Author's adaptation of a concept pioneered by Hayes, Robert and Wheelwright, Steven, *Restoring Our Competitive Edge: Competing Through Manufacturing,* John Wiley & Sons, 1984, p. 209

volume-variety mix chart that compared process standardisation and the volume of production (see an adaptation of this concept in Figure 5.1 on the previous page).

At one end, job-shop production (like auto body work where every job is different and usually small) and engineer-to-order production (like ship-building, where most jobs are different and require unique processes) are the lowest-volume production models, and no two jobs are ever exactly the same. Make-to-order (MTO) work uses a consistent type of product that does not need to be engineered each time and is made in either a discrete (one at a time, as in expensive furniture) or a batch (many at a time, as in printing) process. Make-to-stock (MTS) production results in deliberate inventory. For example, shoes that are sold in retail stores are manufactured on production lines and inventory is held in multiple locations. Assemble-to-order (ATO) production starts with prefabricated components and joins them together when the order is received, which results in a short production cycle but requires inventory at intermediary stages. Continuous production is especially used in making liquid and bulk products such as float glass or chemicals, where the plant is too costly to stop and restart, so it produces constantly.

The different types of operations can be simplified into three basic types: V, T and A, each representing the shape of the flow of materials that results in the final product. Job-shop and MTO (including batch) operations are "V" operations, since production orders start with few or no standard items and end with many or even infinite products (visualise starting at the bottom of the V and fanning out to the top). MTS items, ATO and configure-to-order (CTO) operations are "T" operations since production orders start with a finite number of inputs and result in a large number of possible outputs (visualise starting at the bottom of the T and reaching a point at which the options proliferate sideways in both directions). MTS and continuous flow are usually "A" operations since production orders start with a wide number of inputs and result in one or just a few outputs (visualise starting at the bottom of the A and converging on the point at the top).

Industries often apply multiple manufacturing strategies, depending on the type of product. Historically, consumer packaged goods (CPG) have been MTS, and chemicals and pharmaceuticals have been predominantly so. Shipbuilding and aircraft manufacture have typically been MTO, while computers have become CTO.

Supply chain strategy

For years, many companies' supply chain strategies focused on reliability, basically eliminating blatant mistakes, and simple aphorisms such as "the right product at the right place at the right time" or more recently "the perfect order" were sufficient to capture the essence of the initiatives. Today, the basics of SCM are in place at most companies, so reliability is necessary but not sufficient to gain or even maintain competitive advantage.

Some of the supply chain strategy is given, based on the physical assets and industry in which companies operate. For example, retailers would find it easier to execute a customisation strategy than mining companies since they are closer to the end-customer. The part of the supply chain strategy that is given is dictated by the business's place in the value chain. Upstream companies (those that are closer to the ultimate supplier) tend to focus more on asset and cost strategies. Mid-stream companies tend to focus more on synchronisation and innovation. Downstream companies (those that are closer to the ultimate customer) focus more on customisation.

The rest of the supply chain strategy should flow from the business strategy. A mining company typically focuses on asset utilisation and economies of scale, which are rationalisation strategies, due to the continuous nature of its production. However, if it pursued a customisation strategy, it could crush and blend unique grades for each customer, and arrange delivery in dump trucks rather than in barges, as each customer wishes.

Table 5.1 **Correlation between the value chain role and supply chain strategy**

Type of business	Rationalisation	Synchronisation	Customisation	Innovation
Extraction	Positive	Negative	Negative	Negative
Process manufacturing	Positive	Negative	Negative	Negative
Design-to-order manufacturing	Negative	Positive	Negative	Negative
Discrete manufacturing	Negative	Positive	Positive	Positive
Distribution	Negative	Negative	Positive	Positive
Reselling	Negative	Negative	Negative	Positive

Source: Boston Strategies International survey, 2008

Michael Porter defined three generic business strategies in his hallmark book *Competitive Strategy*.[1] According to surveys conducted by Boston Strategies International, over 50% of companies pursue a low-cost business strategy, 28% opt to focus on a specific market, and 18% try to differentiate their product or service and still pursue a broad market.

Empirical evidence shows that business strategies are correlated with supply chain strategies (see Table 5.2):

- ◪ A low-cost strategy implies a supply chain strategy that cuts costs, and indeed, companies that follow this strategy typically favour rationalisation and synchronisation strategies over innovation and customisation, according to a survey of 500 companies worldwide.[2]
- ◪ A focus strategy implies a supply chain strategy that helps to make the product or service more special in the eyes of the customer. Survey respondents who said their companies followed a focus strategy favour customer-oriented strategies such as customisation or innovation over low-cost strategies.
- ◪ A differentiation business strategy means a supply chain strategy that achieves the ability to serve a mass market yet be different from other companies on one or more dimensions. Indeed, companies that try to differentiate tend to follow an innovation strategy more than companies that do not try to differentiate.

Table 5.2 **Correlation between business strategies and supply chain strategies**

Business strategy	Rationalisation	Synchronisation	Customisation	Innovation
Differentiation	Negative	Negative	Positive	Positive
Focus/specialisation	Negative	Negative	Positive	Negative
Low cost	Positive	Positive	Negative	Negative

Source: Boston Strategies International survey, 2008

A fourth supply chain strategy that does not correspond to any of Porter's original three generic business strategies is innovation, since this is an extension of more recent management movements such as time-based management and disruptive technologies. It more closely

resembles Michael Treacy and Fred Wiersema's concept of product leadership, which they also dubbed "innovation".[3]

Defining the four generic supply chain strategies

There are four strategies for gaining competitive advantage through SCM:
rationalisation, synchronisation, customisation and innovation (RaSCI)
(see Figure 5.2):

◪ Rationalisation is excellence in managing the operating costs
  through SCM so as to achieve cost leadership and greater
  profitability than competitors. It focuses on operating expense
  management rather than asset management (which is part of a
  synchronisation strategy), because many companies are driven by
  earnings targets rather than balance-sheet optimisation.

◪ Synchronisation is achieving reliable and flawless supply chain
  execution (the right product at the right place at the right time)
  so as to be able to produce the same volume of output with less
  fixed assets (production capacity) and working capital (inventory)
  than competitors. Asset productivity is part of the synchronisation
  strategy rather than the rationalisation strategy because some

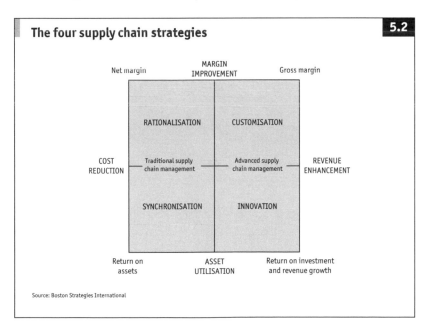

The four supply chain strategies   5.2

Source: Boston Strategies International

companies' business and financial strategies, and hence executive compensation and performance, are driven by balance-sheet performance.

▰ Customisation is excellence in building a unique capability in using the supply chain to enhance customer relationships, which leads to higher gross margins. Customisation embeds both responsiveness ("the velocity at which a supply chain provides products to the customer") and flexibility ("the agility of a supply chain in responding to marketplace changes to gain or maintain competitive advantage").[4]

▰ Innovation is using supply chain activities to enable rapid, frequent and effective new product introductions that enhance the presence of the brand in the mind of the customer (mindshare), thus leading to an acceleration of revenue that otherwise would occur over a longer timeframe.

Across all industries, about a third of companies choose to follow an integrated strategy. Among companies that choose to focus on a specific

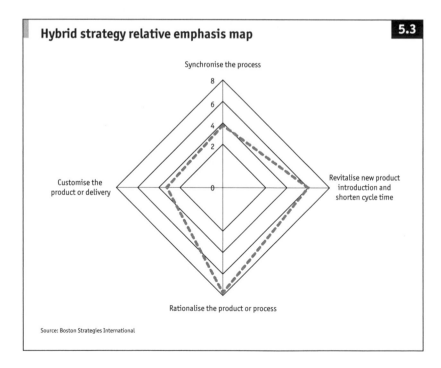

Hybrid strategy relative emphasis map   5.3

Synchronise the process

Customise the product or delivery

Revitalise new product introduction and shorten cycle time

Rationalise the product or process

Source: Boston Strategies International

supply chain strategy, about equal proportions follow rationalisation and synchronisation strategies (a third each) than any other strategy. Customisation and innovation are practised by 15–21% of companies.

The choice of which strategies to pursue and how much effort to put into each is a multi-faceted one. With limited management bandwidth, most companies have to select which strategies to emphasise, and from that, select which tools can help them be most successful at those strategies. Chapters 7–10 outline the tools that are most effective in achieving each of the generic supply chain strategies. Figure 5.3 shows a "spider diagram" that can be used to plan the emphasis on each strategy.

The integrated supply chain strategy

The benefits from SCM are so compelling that nearly 40% of companies try to execute an integrated strategy to get the benefits from all the four strategies combined.

Doing it all at once can yield few results if resources are too thin to execute multiple strategies concurrently.

However, the benefit of an integrated strategy is that there is strong synergy between the strategies if they are sequenced properly (see Figure 5.4). By channelling cost savings into price reductions, pricing more aggressively, personalising the product at customer touch-points, and launching new products rapidly and systematically, companies such as Wal-Mart,

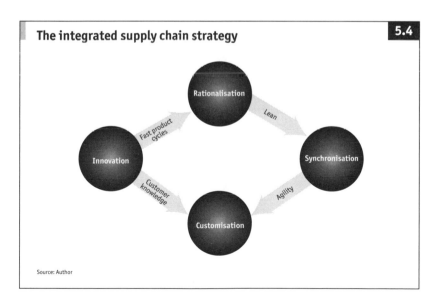

The integrated supply chain strategy · 5.4

Source: Author

Dell and Amazon are increasing demand and loyalty, and reaching customers farther away. In short, they are competing on a basis of world-class performance in SCM.

From cost-cutting to rationalisation

Cost-cutting can be done in such a way that it yields higher quality and increased sales, and this approach to cost-cutting is the first step of an integrated supply chain strategy.

Cost-saving in the retail industry has enabled supermarkets to increase sales volume by lowering costs and prices. Wal-Mart, Dell and Costco have adeptly used high-volume purchasing and logistics operations to facilitate deep price discounting. Through its Chinese import-based low cost and its everyday low price (EDLP) approach, Wal-Mart climbed to 20% market share in the United States (and 10% of the world's retailing dollars) in 1999, nearly four times more than any other retailer in the world.[5]

Lean distribution helps to earn more revenue by serving customers farther away. These companies generally compete within a geographic territory, and can serve a larger market area when they reduce costs. With lower supply chain costs (distribution, transport, ordering, and so on), they can transport farther for the same delivered price. For example, a global minerals company extended its market reach of heavy products such as calcium carbonate by consolidating its transportation arrangements among fewer carriers and negotiating lower transport rates based on the increased volume. It increased its geographic reach by switching modes from truck, which economically hauls bulk material up to about 1,000km (600 miles), to rail, which economically hauls heavy material 1,600km or more at least in the United States, and also by lowering the rate paid per tonne-km on each mode in order to be able to afford a long haul for the same amount of money.

From rationalisation to synchronisation

Rationalisation is an excellent platform for synchronisation since it exposes waste that results in misalignments and bottlenecks, both of which cause inconsistencies in performance levels. Rationalisation efforts reduce or eliminate waste, and a leaner organisation is easier to synchronise since there are fewer inventory buffers and each resource exists to serve a specific order stream.

Most of the lean tools that are concerned with waste reduction (the "seven types of waste", the 5s approach to workplace organisation, total quality management or TQM, total productive maintenance or TPM, cellular manufacturing and diagnostic tools – see pages 82–7), as well as standardisation, SKU rationalisation, and so on, all support synchronisation, since it is much easier to synchronise a lean process than a wasteful process.

From synchronisation to customisation

Synchronisation, particularly through its ambitious one-piece flow system, enables the agility that is needed to deliver customised or personalised output. Non-synchronised supply chains are slow to adjust to change since they are characterised by misalignments of expectations and of physical flows between parties in the chain. When change occurs, non-synchronised supply chains cannot adjust quickly. In contrast, directly linked supply chains with a one-to-one relationship between the parties involved can react instantaneously.

While synchronisation conjures up images of efficiency and industrial engineering, synchronous engineered operations can become agile delivery systems that flex up and down on demand, even on a per-customer basis. The engineering approach that is typically used in a high-volume, low-mix operation can be applied to finely sub-segment customer types and deliver a unique supply chain to each one.

From customisation to innovation

Customisation enables innovation by providing an understanding of customers' needs and wants. When these are clear, innovations have a far better chance of succeeding.

Effective SCM facilitates faster product introduction by using the extensive customer knowledge that it gathers, through its customisation efforts, to fuel an innovation engine. This brings three benefits: first, more profits accrue because the product is in the market longer before it reaches the decline stage of its product life-cycle; second, the product commands higher margins for being in the market earlier than its competitors; and third, the firm gets a reputation for being a market leader, which in turn may command even greater market share and higher margins. Operations decision-makers can enable faster product launches through concurrent design and rapid prototyping.

A company that exemplifies innovation is Apple, which used the customer knowledge that it gained through the launch of the iPod, the Mac and other popular consumer devices to nearly double its product range between 2002 amd 2009. Research in Motion (RIM) achieved new heights of customisability, even personalisation, with the BlackBerry.

Users can configure it for their own tastes, not only in the user interface but also in the content that they load on it.

From innovation to rationalisation again

Innovation inevitably leads to the need to clean up. Many new products have fast product life-cycles that expire, leaving obsolete or at least heavily discounted product on the shelves. End-of-life SKU management becomes important so as to prevent the erosion of profitability through excessive inventory costs.

The first end-of-life decision is when to remove the products from the shelves. The decreasing chances of incremental sales must be balanced by the (sometimes increasing) cost of maintaining inventory and production at lower volumes. Here, the cost of holding inventory extends far beyond the financial carrying cost, which is usually low (around 5%). The real cost is the cost of obsolescence (throwing the unsold product away) and the administrative overhead cost of managing more unimportant and ageing SKUs. In a world of rapid SKU turnover, not having a process for withdrawing end-of-life SKUs is asking for trouble.

The pruning and fitness that comes with a fully integrated supply chain strategy leaves every organisation more lean, agile and responsive.

Honda and Delphi: examples of integrated strategy

R. David Nelson developed and implemented many of what are considered today to be leading practices in procurement. After spending 30 years at TRW and ten years as a corporate officer of Honda of America Manufacturing, he ran Delphi Automotive's global supply management task team.

Nelson demonstrated the integrated strategy approach at Delphi. He pursued best-in-world cost ("rationalisation") by eliminating waste rationally and logically. Then he started to improve on his record by collaboration, in order to achieve new and even lower levels of cost. As part of this, he has been adamant about the necessity to share savings in order to improve the margins of both his company and its suppliers.

He brought collaborative planning to suppliers ("synchronisation"), helping to reduce the total production cycle time for raw material inventory by 35–45% at Delphi's European and North American suppliers. At Delphi, he also improved operational availability by 12–40% and productivity as measured in pieces per labour hour by 33–80%.

Lastly, Nelson has developed people, suppliers, commodity teams and enhanced relationships to ensure not only efficiency but also flexibility to produce what is needed when it is needed ("customisation"). His work at Honda and Delphi also stimulated innovation through early involvement with suppliers, early sourcing, and timely and error-free product launches ("innovation").

Supply chain strategies for economic growth

SCM is typically considered to be a corporate issue. However, strategic SCM is also a matter of economic policy when it comes to transportation infrastructure. Just like companies, national and regional economies progress through four stages of infrastructure development: rationalisation (for example, building roads that reduce average unit travel costs), synchronisation (for example, building industrial parks that help minimise inventory), customisation (for example, building information networks that allow data to be accessed individually) and innovation (for example, building universities and learning institutions that spur creative new ideas) – see Figure 5.5.

Capacity needs to be planned far in advance to avoid bottlenecks and to facilitate long lead-time investments such as ports and highways. Governments need to decide how much capacity to buy or build, and how much investment to seek from the private sector.

Links and connectors need to be added to strengthen and increase the reliability of the traffic network, and the supply chain network should be designed for efficient system-wide flows. Since most European import

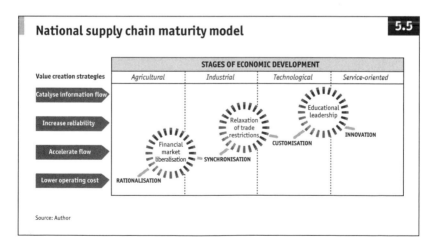

National supply chain maturity model 5.5

Source: Author

container traffic enters via northern European ports such as Hamburg and is hauled to inland European destinations before returning as empty containers, APM Terminals envisages the construction of a multi-modal north–south link that would carry a surplus of empty containers after they are unloaded in northern Europe to southern European ports such as Marseille-Fos (France) or Gioia Tauro (Italy), where they can be loaded on to eastbound vessels that would take them back to Asia, where most of them originated.

Backbone information technology infrastructure is needed to facilitate strong communication links. The French government's dissemination of the Minitel in 1984 accelerated that country's adoption of the internet. In contrast, the United Arab Emirates' current telecommunications duopoly (between the companies "du" and Etisalat), while stimulating the penetration of mobile phones, prohibits the use of voice over internet protocol (VOIP) add-ons.

Many countries enter into the rationalisation mode at an early stage in their development. For example, Vietnam is building roads where there were only weeds. The move towards synchronisation is catalysed by a liberalisation of financial markets, which brings industrial parks and logistics infrastructure, as has happened in emerging economies such as China. The move towards customisation is catalysed by the relaxation of trade restrictions, which allows technology investments in logistics information networks, as happened in South Africa. The move towards innovation is catalysed by the development of leading educational institutions, which happened in European countries such as Germany and France.

6 Rationalisation: competing on low cost

Low cost is a basic requirement of doing business in the 2000s. Whether measured in landed cost (the delivered cost including freight and duties), total cost (the cost over the life of the product or service) or "should-cost" (what the cost would be if all the cost elements were set to the lowest cost level), cost and therefore price must be competitive or customers will take their business elsewhere. No surprise then, that executives such as Barbara Kux, member of the Group Management Committee at Philips Electronics, espouse the importance of making things "better, faster, and cheaper". Moreover, the traditional emphasis on cost has been accentuated in recent years by global competition and the extraordinary rise of low-cost country sourcing (LCCS). In numerous Economist Intelligence Unit studies from 2004 to 2007, senior executives ranked cost as a prerequisite for staying in business, especially in the retail sector.[1]

It is not surprising, then, that the main goal of about a third of companies in embarking on supply chain management (SCM) initiatives is to lower costs. SCM is particularly well-adapted to lowering costs because of its historical association with industrial engineering, lean manufacturing and quality initiatives, which have all focused on stabilising and reducing costs.

Companies that focus on cost management have better profitability than those that do not. Companies that actively manage cost achieve a 2.6% higher net margin than those that do not.[2]

While actual performance will vary substantially across companies, Table 6.1 overleaf provides a reference point for the performance of companies following rationalisation supply chain strategies in a wide range of product and service industries.

The cost leverage factor

When companies reduce operating costs, they increase profit more than if they had increased sales volume by an equal amount, because sales are typically accompanied by expenses. Take, for example, a company that sells sunscreen. It sells 200 units at $5 per unit, and earns $1,000. If its costs are $3 per unit, it has a fixed cost of $600. Add to that labour of $100 and overhead of $100. That makes for a total cost of goods sold of $800 and leaves a profit of $200 (see Table 6.2 on page 65).

Table 6.1 **Benchmark net margins of rationalisation-focused companies**

Industry	Benchmark net margin of companies with a rationalisation focus, %
Software & services	18.2
Diversified financials	18.1
Energy	16.7
Utilities	12.3
Household & personal products	10.4
Materials	10.2
Banks	9.8
Insurance	8.5
Transportation	6.8
Food & drug retailing	6.3
Capital goods	6.3
Technology hardware & equipment	5.5
Telecommunications services	5.0
Average	9.8

Source: Boston Strategies International, based on an analysis of data from Thomson Reuters and Boston Strategies International's 2008 supply chain performance benchmark study

If the company is able to reduce its variable cost from $3 per unit to $2.50 per unit (a 17% cost decrease), its cost of goods sold decreases from $600 to $500, and its profit increases from $200 to $300, which is a 50% increase. So in this simple case (which assumes labour is fixed), a 17% reduction in direct costs results in an increase in profit of 50%.

But if the company sold $100 more in revenue at the same cost per unit, it would realise only a 20% increase in profits because of the corresponding rise in direct costs. So in this case, a decrease in costs yields two and a half times the amount that would result from an identical percentage increase in revenue.

Across a variety of supply chain areas, improvement programmes can often result in savings equal to about 5% of revenue. Savings from rationalisation can broadly be characterised as a percentage of revenue, with savings from direct spend at about 2%, savings from sales at 1–2%,

Table 6.2 **The leverage impact of cost reduction on corporate profit**

	Before improvement	With $100 cost reduction	With $100 revenue increase
Sales price ($)	5.00	5.00	5.00
Units sold	200	200	220
Revenue ($)	1,000	1,000	1,100
Direct cost ($)	600	500	660
Labour ($)	100	100	100
Overheads ($)	100	100	100
Total cost of goods sold ($)	800	700	860
Profit ($)	200	300	240
Profit increase (%)		50%	20%

Source: Author

savings from logistics at 0.5–1% and savings from R&D expenses 0–1% of revenue.

Most companies measure cost savings as a percentage of the acquisition cost. Acquisition (or "first") cost is the cost to get something at its place of use, including the supplier's cost, the supplier's value-added, the supplier's profit, and the cost of delivery and installation, including inbound freight and duties. For example, the acquisition cost of an office printer is the cost to purchase it, plus the cost of delivery and installation. Acquisition cost is widely used as a measure of cost, but it can be misleading. For example, increasing the number of suppliers can increase competition and reduce first costs, but the savings may be offset by the added costs of repairing inferior quality machines, managing multiple suppliers and maintaining non-standard equipment. Supply chain cost takes these factors into consideration by including the cost of designing, planning and moving a part, item, material or service from its point of ultimate sourcing to its point of ultimate consumption and on to retirement.[3] Although very few companies quantify supply chain cost, many use it as a conceptual framework for identifying improvement opportunities.

Supply chain cost starts with the cost of design and launch. (As noted in Chapter 3, SCM excludes the initial manufacturing or conversion activity. An initial basic activity such as extraction or farming would not be considered an SCM activity.) The total supply chain cost includes the following:[4]

- Planning costs, which include the cost of demand/supply planning, including the software applications used for advanced planning and scheduling and inventory management.
- Order processing costs, which include the cost of taking, creating and maintaining customer orders, contract administration, channel management (maintaining relations with channel and trading partners), order fulfilment (distribution), and billing and collections.
- Sourcing costs, which include the cost of product engineering, the cost of strategic sourcing (see opposite), the cost of source quality management, the cost of receiving and materials storage, document control and inspection of supplier deliveries.
- Inventory management costs (raw materials, WIP and finished goods throughout the extended supply chain), which include warehouse operating costs, inventory carrying cost, shrinkage, insurance and taxes, obsolescence, and inventory reconfiguration costs such as kitting.

Supply chain costs also include the cost of externally purchased materials, components and services (which are part of supply chain costs but not part of supply chain *management* costs), value-added assembly or production and end-of-life costs such as the cost of returns, remanufacturing and recycling.

Then there is the cost of SCM failures, for example:

- Excess purchases and inventory management costs due to failure to see and mitigate the bullwhip effect from one end of the supply chain to the other.
- Excess capacity investments due to failure to see and mitigate the bullwhip effect as reflected in cyclical supplier pricing.
- Excessive prices paid to suppliers due to failure to adequately plan capacity or contract for secure and stable supply at a reasonable long-term price.
- Lost orders due to inability to increase production capacity rapidly enough.
- Internal and supplier quality failures, including the four dimensions of the cost of quality (internal failure, external failure, prevention and appraisal).

End-of-life costs include the cost of returns, remanufacturing and recycling.

Another related measure of cost is the total cost of ownership (TCO). TCO is the supply chain cost, plus the value of the materials, components and services purchased from other firms, minus the cost of SCM failures. TCO is sometimes referred to as life-cycle cost. There is a wide variance in the use of TCO; roughly 30% of companies use it moderately.[5]

Elements of rationalisation strategy

For typical multinational companies, some of the better methods of reducing costs – and thus rationalising – through SCM techniques are as follows, in rough order of effectiveness:

- Strategic sourcing and outsourcing using integration, scale and value engineering techniques
- Lean manufacturing, in so far as it is focused on waste reduction and quality management
- Standardisation and simplification of specifications
- Transport optimisation, including mode selection, cross-docking and direct-to-store or "DC bypass"
- Tier-skipping, whereby companies analyse and make decisions based on the extended supply chain
- Supplier *kaizen*, in which lean principles are extended to suppliers
- Consignment and vendor-managed inventory
- Design for manufacturability
- Electronic data interchange (EDI) and paperless work flow

This set of initiatives delivers particularly high savings compared with other approaches: a benchmarking study of over 100 companies worldwide[6] found that centralised purchasing, supplier partnering and long-term agreements offer three of the top five opportunities for supply chain savings. They help to create economies of scale and scope, reduce excess supplier margins through competitive pressure and ensure that the product specifications deliver just the amount of functionality desired by the customer.

Strategic sourcing and outsourcing
Strategic sourcing
Supplier management is an effective way of reducing TCO. The cost of purchased materials and services typically accounts for 40–80% of

companies' cost structures, depending on the industry. In the early days of strategic sourcing, well-known companies realised up to 20% cost savings from purchasing, for example 3% in one year at Ford Motor, 20% over five years at AMR (the parent of American Airlines), 17% over four years at Honda and 4% over one year at Chrysler.[7] Today strategic sourcing often reduces acquisition costs by 8–12% on large companies' largest-spend categories.

A well-conceived strategic sourcing programme starts with a breakdown of the total spend in the company. This analysis identifies the sourceable spend as distinct from other expenses (such as taxes, depreciation and interest) for which the strategies cannot effectively be applied. The top-down analysis should also divide the total spend into waves, and the waves into categories. For example, Bristol Myers Squibb separated its purchases into three sourcing waves. Each wave consisted of approximately 25 categories, which were determined by commonality of suppliers or commonality of users. The categories included direct (raw materials and packaging, for example) and indirect (facilities, software, office supplies, and so on).[8]

The resulting external expenditure (spend) can be divided into four categories with distinct characteristics and therefore also distinct sourcing strategies:

- Low-spend, easy-to-source categories such as office supplies. These are "non-critical". They usually account for a small percentage of the total spend, and there are plenty of suppliers who would want to bid for the business on a competitive basis.
- Low-spend, hard-to-source categories such as cafeteria services. These are considered "bottleneck" and are not usually given much attention in strategic sourcing programmes because they often take more time and resources to address than the savings that come from the effort.
- High-spend, easy-to-source categories. These are usually materials used directly in the product such as plastic housings for television sets, are called "leverage" categories because they can often result in a quick savings opportunity if the company is going through strategic sourcing for the first time.
- High-spend, hard-to-source strategic categories. These are usually in the core competency of the company as, for example, steel stampings would be to a carmaker.

Sourcing and supply chain strategies

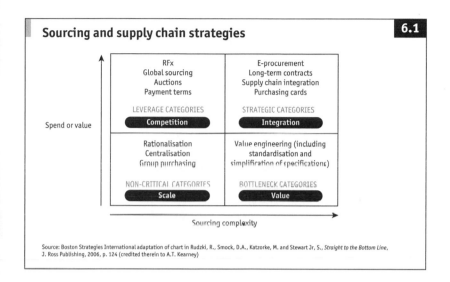

6.1

Source: Boston Strategies International adaptation of chart in Rudzki, R., Smock, D.A., Katzorke, M. and Stewart Jr, S., *Straight to the Bottom Line*, J. Ross Publishing, 2006, p. 124 (credited therein to A.T. Kearney)

Four specific sourcing strategies – competition, scale, value and integration, as illustrated in Figure 6.1 – address each of these categories of spend. Competition works best for leverage categories; integration for strategic categories; scale and volume aggregation for non-critical categories; and value strategies for bottleneck categories.

Competition-based strategic sourcing techniques are addressed in Appendix 2 because they are based primarily on reducing immediate suppliers' margins rather than creating win-win value in the end-to-end supply chain.

Value engineering is covered in this chapter since it applies to the supply chain more broadly than just to strategic sourcing. Note that for bottleneck items, the most effective solutions are value engineering, standardisation and simplifying specifications. Reducing the number of products and suppliers can help to simplify the cost structure and make the products more appealing to a broader array of suppliers. Simplifying specifications reduces the number of permutations that are subject to bullwhip, thereby reducing the overall effect of bullwhip on the supply chain.

Integration, most often accomplished through technology, plays a critical role in reducing the per-unit transaction costs of low-value items and services that are bought in large quantities. E-procurement is the use of information systems to identify and manage suppliers in a way that eliminates paperwork, delays and cost. Electronic data interchange (EDI), now common, saves data input time and eliminates errors. Electronic billing saves costs and makes it easier for buyers to audit historical payments made to suppliers. Billing by assumed usage based on an easier-to-collect variable, such as billing for machine hours based on electricity consumption, since electricity consumption can be more easily tracked than machine hours (this practice is called back-flushing) saves labour and, if done correctly, sacrifices very little accuracy. In addition, technology is used to automate and improve many of the traditional manual processes, such as requests for quotations (RFQs), reverse auctions, spend visibility and contract compliance. Electronic RFQs are embedded in enterprise resource planning (ERP) systems, saving both buyers and suppliers overhead cost.

For strategic categories the most effective solution is usually tighter integration with suppliers to reduce their operating costs. This includes partnering to increase the role of the suppliers, as well as approaches that minimise the cost of transactions between the buyer and the supplier, such as long-term agreements and supply chain integration. Long-term contracting reduces transactions costs by allowing suppliers to reduce their sales costs, and consequently their prices, with fewer customers.

For non-critical items, the best solutions are ones that use economies of scale to reduce unit costs and simultaneously reduce complexities in purchasing, thereby mitigating the bullwhip effect. These solutions include consolidating suppliers, centralising the procurement function and long-term contracting.

Reducing the number of suppliers helps the chosen few realise economies of scale and thereby reduce their costs and their prices. Many companies have consolidated the number of suppliers, making reductions of 50–80%. Here are some examples of the more aggressive consolidations seen in participants in the study carried out by Boston Strategies International:

- A Dutch retail chain consolidated its supply base for interior decoration products by 62%, for a 28% savings.
- Two US medical device manufacturers reduced the number of their suppliers by half in two years.
- A regional utility in the United States typically awards its largest supplier 40% of the business, compared with 5% in 2000, in order to get better reliability and responsiveness.
- A US switch and connector manufacturer is single sourcing to reduce administrative costs, provide an easy and simple product pricing structure and achieve economies of scale. The company is

collaborating increasingly with its suppliers in demand forecasting, shipment visibility and sharing proprietary information.

◼ A manufacturer of coated paper halved the number of equipment suppliers that it had between eight and ten years ago, and cut the number of indirect suppliers by 50% between 1993 and 1995.

Group purchasing can also achieve the economies of scale that are needed to negotiate better prices with suppliers. For instance, many companies belong to shippers' associations in order to get better transportation rates. Even large companies benefit from group purchasing: FedEx and General Mills have participated in a group purchasing initiative for indirect products and services. Independent of that group, General Mills organised 11 companies to make a transportation consortium using a solutions provider called Nistevo. The companies included Fort Howard Packaging, Land O'Lakes, Morrell, Nestlé and Pillsbury.[9] Service industries also use group purchasing organisations (GPOS): Dana-Farber Cancer Institute participates in a consortium buying group called Novation as a mechanism through which it sources surgical supplies and pharmaceuticals.

Outsourcing

Outsourcing and offshoring are often confused. Outsourcing, the contracting of a third party to manufacture or deliver a service, can be offshored but does not have to be. Offshoring, sourcing from overseas, is often outsourced, but does not have to be.

Cost reduction is often the driving force behind a management's decision to outsource, so it is an important element of rationalisation strategy. There is an important financial advantage in the transfer of assets to third-party logistics (3PL). Offloading tangible assets such as warehouse facilities and vehicles and intangible assets such as information systems increases ROA, making companies more attractive to lenders and shareholders. If the value of an outsourcing deal is significant, it can result in a rise in the share price.

Just as important, however, outsourcing can help improve supply chain effectiveness by better serving customers. Outsourced providers often provide serious advantages over doing the job in-house, such as the following:

◼ If it is a more global network than the company purchasing the services, it will allow that company enhanced access to foreign markets.

◪ Heavy investment in IT platforms provides measurably higher service levels and service reliability compared with in-house systems. For example, best-of-breed transportation management systems (TMS) and warehouse management systems (WMS) offered by 3PL providers frequently can handle complex pick/pack operations more readily than in-house solutions.

◪ Value-added services which would be challenging for a company that is not a logistics specialist to provide. For example, while most production operations can handle basic boxing, 3PL providers often excel at custom packaging operations involving plastic ("bubble" or "clamshell") packaging, security (hermetically sealed) packaging, kitting, customised packaging by customer, or personalised packaging by consumer (for example, through individualised insertions).

Outsourcing has gone from being almost non-existent in 1985 to being prevalent, even predominant, today. Activities targeted for outsourcing include contract manufacturing[10] and various logistics including, in order of frequency of outsourcing: transport (67%), customs brokerage (58%), freight payment services (54%), freight forwarding (46%), warehouse management (46%) and shipment consolidation (42%). The value of offshore arrangements has increased steadily. The cumulative value of deals in place has increased. Between 1950 and 2005, US manufacturers moved huge amounts of work abroad, as manufacturing's percentage of US GDP was more than cut in half. Most of that was as a result of offshore contracts.

Three aspects of an outsourcing decision should be considered as part of a complete analysis:

◪ Which activities to outsource and which to keep in-house – core competencies should never be outsourced.

◪ When to vertically integrate – for example, whether to purchase a dedicated supplier.

◪ How many services to buy as part of complex product purchases – for example, when buying complex equipment, sellers often offer to provide maintenance and repair services for the life of the product.

Sydney airport[11]

Airports have become more profit-driven in recent years, as governments worldwide have moved to privatise transport infrastructure and operations. European and Middle Eastern governments have regulated airport ground handling services to ensure adequate competition and hence lower costs.

Australia's Sydney International Airport outsourced a particularly wide range of services in the early 2000s in conjunction with its privatisation. It handles 27m passengers per year and employs 62,000 people.

The airport used a set of criteria to decide which activities to outsource. Not surprisingly, cost advantage was the first criterion. However, this was balanced with other considerations, such as the operational and contractual risk involved in the activities, confidence in the outside providers' level of skill and expertise, and security.

After screening and consideration, its outsourcing initiative has been extensive, covering many activities such as:

- civil infrastructure and ground maintenance;
- fixed plant and equipment maintenance;
- baggage handling systems at the domestic terminal;
- support services, including fleet management and call centre;
- service contracts, including cleaning, trolley retrieval and waste disposal.

Based on the responses to its initial requests for proposals, the airport targeted a 10% savings in Phase 1 and a 15% savings in Phase 2. The quotation process allowed the airport to identify potential savings of 40% on street sweeping and 10% on paving. Encouraged by the results, it divided the outsourcing initiative into two phases: phase 1, which involved a consolidation of maintenance areas into one group for baggage, airfield, terminal, services, utilities and asset planning; and outsourced ground maintenance (airfield line marking, mowing and sweeping); and phase 2, which involved a comprehensive facilities maintenance contract. Phase 1 achieved the targeted 10% cost reduction and phase 2 saved the additional targeted 5%.

The outsourced providers' contracts were structured in a gain-sharing fashion. The contractors received a fixed management fee and reimbursement for direct expenses, the total of which needed to be below the previous year's budget. The contract also called for continuous cost reduction over time, and measurement according to a balanced scorecard with predefined key results areas (KRAs), which were measured quarterly. The KRAs had a minimum score of 50, an expected score of 75 and a maximum score of 100. If the supplier fell below the minimum score, the airport notified it that it was in default and put it on notice of potential dismissal. Above-expected performance on KRAs led to a bonus payment.

Sydney's actual experience with the outsourced maintenance provider got off to a shaky start. The provider had a slow start-up, delaying the transition, and had trouble taking over responsibilities from previous contractors on schedule. There were also communication gaps between the airport staff and the contractor team, and some turnover problems, perhaps related to the supplier's inexperience in airport operations. In addition, it was discovered that the supplier did not fully understand the KRA compensation scheme. However, the minimum savings of 5% sought by the airport were achieved. The contractor also scored satisfactorily on quality and safety. Over time the contractor's performance has significantly improved and is still working at the airport.

Despite the challenges of implementing the outsourced contracts, the airport's financial results have been impressive. The savings achieved by the outsourcing initiative helped the airport realise earnings before interest and tax (EBIT) of 57% and earnings before interest, tax, depreciation and amortisation (EBITDA) of 80% in 2004–05.

Lean manufacturing's focus on waste reduction

Lean manufacturing concepts have broad applicability to the supply chain. Lean is often described as a philosophy or even a religion. One lean consultant described it as a set of principles that includes putting the customer first, having an end-to-end total value stream perspective, focusing on consistent flow and eliminating waste.[12] There are innumerable ways to characterise and define lean, and experts work with many process tools that may be classified as part of lean thought. The breadth of scope of lean makes it both important (the reason why it has had such a profound impact on business) and challenging (it seems to defy definition and boundaries).

Lean applies to SCM in two ways. First, its focus on eliminating waste fits squarely with the rationalisation supply chain strategy. Second, its toolkit for inventory reduction directly supports the synchronisation strategy (see Chapter 7).

The purpose of this section is not to provide a comprehensive list, or even to claim a direct linkage between these tools and lean, but rather to outline methods that relate to lean and are especially effective at reducing cost and executing a rationalisation supply chain strategy. The following tools have yielded exceptional results in waste elimination programmes:

- the seven types of waste;
- the 5S approach to workplace organisation;
- total quality management (TQM);
- total productive maintenance (TPM);
- cellular manufacturing;
- diagnostic tools such as the 5 Whys, the plan-do-check-act (PDCA) cycle, value stream mapping, work sampling, root cause analysis and throughput analysis.

Seven types of waste

Lean theory has identified seven types of wasteful activity. While the concepts were originally formulated to apply to manufacturing environments, a broader interpretation is entirely applicable to service industries. Below are the seven types of waste and an interpretation of each type of waste's applicability to SCM across a variety of industries.

1 **Overproduction and overprocessing.** Overproduction means anything more than is required by customer orders. Overprocessing and the related concept of overengineering refer to any extra work steps than are required to satisfy customer demand.
2 **Unnecessary inventory (see Chapter 7).** In pure lean theory, all inventory is ultimately bad since the ideal state is a one-piece flow through the entire production system. In reality, small amounts of buffer inventory are required because of the differences in capacity from operation to operation.
3 **Transport and motion.** Transportation is wasteful since it adds cost that could be avoided if the product was made or service provided at the point of consumption.
4 **Wasted steps or efforts in the production process.** Anything or any service that takes two steps but could be made with one step is wasteful. This type of waste can often be readily identified in day-to-day office or plant activities.
5 **Defects and rejects.** Defects represent wasted effort that must either be discounted or thrown away. Rejects are worse since they also incur customers' wrath and discontent and are a possible adverse influence on buying behaviour.
6 **Waiting.** Time, as a resource like labour or materials, can be wasted by waiting. Queue time often comprises up to 90% of the production cycle time, so waiting can be a prime target for waste reduction efforts.
7 **Unnecessary motion.** Excess motion, such as back-and-forth movement

that could be accomplished in a single well-designed motion, or excess keystrokes that could be accomplished with a shortcut key, is similarly wasteful since it consumes energy and cost. Motion at the activity level is analogous to transportation at the supply chain level.

Other wastes have been added to this list since the original seven were developed by Taiichi Ohno, vice-president of manufacturing, and Shigeo Shingo, head of industrial engineering and factory improvement training at Toyota in the 1950s. For instance, reprioritisation or replanning, especially if it involves changes to the plan, wastes management time and production effort. The ideal state is a stable plan that has a minimum of change and reprioritisation. And wasting human talent can exacerbate all the other wastes since it is required to avoid and eliminate waste in the first place.

5S

Another lean tool for waste reduction is "5S", which stands for sort, sequence, shine, standardise and sustain. Simple in concept, but challenging to execute, 5S can have a dramatic impact on organisations if applied in depth to all aspects of the work process.

Sorting at a simple level just means organising things, but at a detailed level it means thinking about and understanding the best way to organise every aspect of every step of the work, which is an engineering process and arguably a science in its own right. To illustrate the range of complexity, consider these two examples. First, simple: a secretary organises incoming mail by addressee; and second, more complex: FedEx organised its jet engine maintenance to handle routine maintenance as a separate work stream from repairs, thereby more efficiently organising work to lower cost and improve reliability.

Sequencing at a simple level means putting work activities in the optimal order. But in the context of a supply chain, sequencing is fundamental. A US company imports minerals from China, then screens, crushes and dries them. It also takes precipitated calcium carbonate (PCC) from its paper operations and de-waters it to produce bagged ground calcium carbonate, then trucks it to market so it can go into diverse products such as floor tiles and chewing gum. If it screened, crushed and dried the stone before importing, its operations and its cost would be very different. Also, if it trucked the bulk PCC to market and bagged it in the local market, its cost and network would be very different. The sequence of operations is a key determinant of its supply chain cost.

Shining means keeping things clean, but if it is applied methodically, can have dramatic impact on companies' long-term costs. Again, this can be practised at many levels. For example, a plant manager insists on keeping the floor clean for safety; and UPS is able to maintain a high degree of uptime in its fleet of 100,000 ground vehicles because of its careful attention to maintenance and individual drivers' pride in their vehicles.

Standardising is easy to conceptualise but hard to implement. Take, for example, Southwest Airlines' standardisation of its aircraft fleet (see page 81). A large decision like that one is difficult, especially if the current fleet is highly non-standardised and the cost of standardising is high. Yet the benefits have proved to be high as well.

Sustaining is a way of saying that, to be effective, the improvements from 5S initiatives changes need to stick.

Total quality management

Quality management, a theory of work evolved by W. Edwards Deming, an American author, professor and consultant who is best known for his early contributions to Japanese quality systems (see also page 88), and Walter Shewhart, a physicist, engineer and statistician famous for his pioneering work in statistical process control, laid the groundwork for the elimination of gaps between the product or service and the customer's perceived needs. TQM is the engagement of the workforce in ensuring processes that continuously eradicate quality problems. Although not classically considered to be part of lean, TQM and other quality management programmes can play a major role in reducing costs. When implemented in a culture of *kaizen* (the Japanese term for continuous improvement), tools such as the cost of quality, *poka-yoke* and Six Sigma can reduce total cost significantly:

1 **The cost of quality.** This concept, pioneered by Joseph Juran, who worked at Western Electric's Hawthorne (Illinois) plant and helped Japanese companies improve quality, as Deming did, attributes the cost of managing poor quality to direct (internal failure and external failure) and indirect (prevention and appraisal) causes. A proper accounting of the costs of quality often yields a shockingly large value, and this motivates an organisation to deploy resources to eliminate quality problems.
2 **Poka-yoke**, the Japanese term for foolproof, is a process by which things are designed to prevent misuse (for example, an item numbering system would randomise digits to prevent inadvertent inversions). *Poka-yoke* saves cost by preventing costly failures before they occur.

3 **Six Sigma** originated at Motorola in 1986. It is a process improvement methodology designed to ensure that a process will reliably deliver output within a prescribed range of tolerance. Sigma (σ) is the mathematical symbol for standard deviation, which is a measure of the spread of a distribution. When output of a process is normally distributed, 99.73% of the output will lie at ±3 standard deviations of the distribution's mean. Traditionally, a process was considered to be capable of meeting customer specifications if those specifications were at least 3 standard deviations from the process mean. The idea of Six Sigma quality is to have the variation of the process so narrow that the customers' specifications are at ±6 standard deviations. When the output of the process is so tightly distributed within the customers' requirements, a defect will rarely occur. But processes have a tendency to shift from their target mean. Some studies have demonstrated that a shift of 1.5 standard deviations is not uncommon. Six Sigma capable processes produce only 3.4 defects per million opportunities even if the process has shifted away from its mean by 1.5 standard deviations.

Although the criteria for process capability at six sigma sound strict, operations that run at high volumes need to be capable at this level. The compounding of errors in a multi-stage production process amounts to a far greater chance of error than any one individual operation. For example, if a television set requires 500 parts and each part has an industry-leading six sigma defect rate of 3.4 parts per million, the process will still generate up to 1,700 faulty television sets for each 1m that are produced (assuming that each part has an independent chance of being faulty and that there is only one defective part per unit). In mission-critical operations such as surgery, airline flights and military supply lines, process reliability can be a matter of life and death.

Six Sigma is about teamwork and problem-solving, using lean diagnostic tools such the PDCA cycle (see page 80), the DMAIC cycle (define, measure, analyse, improve and control), a systematic quality process improvement process that includes a variety of tools including Pareto charts, root cause and statistical process control.

A well-known camera-maker implemented statistical process control quality in its manufacturing plant in the mid-1980s to root out the causes of quality problems in production. It gathered data on the process and the defects by production area. Through statistical process control, it was able to determine relatively quickly that the errors stemmed from two causes. However, the process of measuring quality feedback and working towards process consistency shed light on much larger issues, such as how the organisation perceived quality (customers found certain aspects of the packaging unacceptable, but quality control staff did not include those aspects in their scope of work), how much value quality control inspectors actually added compared with what the line operators could have done, and the behavioural tendency for the staff to drive numbers to where they wanted them.

General Electric and FedEx, to name just two, have had extensive Six Sigma programmes, and have sponsored and developed hundreds of individuals who have earned the title of "black belt" in Six Sigma. One company has involved tens of thousands of employees in Six Sigma projects in the last several years.

4 **Zero defects** is a concept related to Six Sigma, but much simpler. The idea is that the ultimate goal of Six Sigma and related quality improvement programmes should be an absolute intolerance of any error.

5 **Total productive maintenance (TPM)** combines the principles of preventive maintenance with the concepts of TQM and *kaizen* to achieve continuously improving reliability.

6 **Jidoka**, the process of making mistakes immediately apparent, is a Japanese concept that empowers anybody working in a process the right and the responsibility to stop the process immediately upon sign of a defect. It is an ingrained part of the Toyota production system, but western automakers found it difficult to change their plant cultures to accept *jidoka*.

7 **Cellular manufacturing**, the efficient layout of production operations whereby workers are located near each other in a U-shaped production area, was originally designed to eliminate wasted motion in production environments. Today it applies to service environments as well, for example the layout of production activities in the kitchen of a restaurant.

Process analysis tools
Several process analysis tools that have roots in operations management (OM) are routinely applied and are effective problem-solving tools in SCM. The relevant tools include the "5 whys", the PDCA cycle, value stream mapping, work sampling, root cause analysis and throughput analysis.

1 **Root cause analysis:** the "5 whys" and fishbone diagrams. To identify the root cause of waste and make rationalisation measures stick, managers often ask "why" the problem exists. A "fishbone" diagram

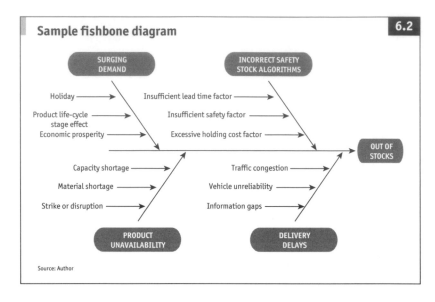

Sample fishbone diagram 6.2

Source: Author

(also called the Ishikawa diagram after Kaoru Ishikawa who invented it) can identify both the apparent cause (the symptom) and the root causes. For example, in Figure 6.2 stock-outs can be traced back to product unavailability, which in turn can be traced back to a capacity shortage. This represents two "whys". Completing the "5 whys" involves a similar investigation, using a fishbone diagram or not, and going three more levels back. For example, "why is capacity short?" If the answer is that a machine is down, then "why is the machine down?" And if the answer is that a critical spare part was not in stock, then the answer that will prevent the problem from recurring would be to make sure the critical spare part is always in stock or available.

2 **The PDCA cycle** (also called the Deming cycle or Shewhart cycle after the theorists who invented it) puts in place a systematic process for identifying and acting upon potentially faulty processes that would lead to quality problems in the final product or service. The cycle uses brainstorming and analysis frameworks ("plan"), logic flow diagrams ("do"), charts, checklists and prioritisation graphs ("check"), and problem-solving tools ("act") to avert and mitigate the effects of quality problems.

3 **Value stream mapping.** Process mapping, or value stream mapping, is a way of documenting current process flows and identifying

opportunities for improvement. Improvement opportunities are typically measured in reduced cost, reduced cycle time or improved quality.

A world-renowned luxury automaker conducted a process improvement programme, in which it used value stream mapping to document processes such as new product development and order fulfilment. Cross-functional teams mapped processes and noted the lead times, frequencies, volumes and the parties responsible for all the steps in each process. The improvement initiative led to a 35% reduction in order fulfilment lead time.

4 **Work sampling.** Observation, coupled with industrial engineering methods such as work sampling or time study, is another way of identifying opportunities, especially efficiency opportunities.

Work sampling is a quick way of determining how time is spent. If enough observations are taken, the data can be statistically significant, but often it is useful to make fewer observations and spend more time asking questions based on the sample.

Time study and elemental time study are ways to set standards. Both are useful techniques for making quick assessments of operational efficiency in the supply chain. For example, when operations consultants tour distribution centres, they often observe the number of trucks that load and unload in a shift (this would be a form of work sampling). And when Iron Mountain, a US-based records management company, sends people to ride with its couriers, it uses time study methods to ensure that each courier has an appropriate number of delivery stops.

Standardisation and simplification of specifications

Standardisation of items and services, the reduction of the number of items, can increase the purchased unit volume per item, thereby lowering the average purchase price. For example, Southwest Airlines is often credited with standardising its aircraft fleet on the Boeing 737. Not only does this reduce the average purchase cost of the aircraft, but it also reduces the life-cycle cost of spare parts, maintenance, repair and training.

Three methods help to standardise and simply specifications: stock-keeping units (SKU) rationalisation, simplification of specifications and value engineering.

SKU rationalisation

Gillette used SKU simplification as the core link in its 2004 supply chain turnaround. Aimed at reversing a major inability to fulfil orders reliably, it embarked on four improvement initiatives: minimising complexity, improving demand–supply planning processes, improving supply planning processes and establishing optimal support systems. SKU rationalisation was central to the first objective, minimising complexity.

SKUs had been allowed to proliferate wildly, explains Mike Duffy, vice-president of North American Value Chain at Gillette. "For example, there were too many customer-specific SKUs", constituting what Duffy called "a disaster waiting to happen". Gillette launched a programme to eliminate thousands of SKUs. That involved using its enterprise resource planning (ERP) system to flag SKUs with usage patterns that would classify them as redundant and eliminate them. As a result Gillette eliminated about 30% of its SKUs, a good deal of that through harmonisation of SKUs for sale in different countries.

The results at Gillette were astonishing. Customer service levels rose by 10%. Inventories decreased by 25%. Overall costs decreased by 3%. Demand planning was simpler, less resource-intensive and more accurate. Production processes became more flexible because there were fewer constraints. Inventory turns increased through the elimination of redundant, slow-moving and sometimes dead SKUs.[13]

Mitsubishi Heavy Industries also rationalised its SKUs, but on much more complex products: steam turbines used in power plants. It standardised its replacement parts so that the rotating and stationary blades fitted within the existing cylinders of many different types of steam turbines. By standardising along an advanced design for stationary components and sealing technologies, Mitsubishi was able to improve efficiency, increase electrical output, lower fuel costs and keep emissions constant with no change in operating steam flows. This amounted to a retrofit and upgrade at the same time, thanks to standardisation.

Simplification of specifications
Simplification of specifications – reduction in the complexity of items – is akin to value engineering, but relates specifically to items with many components. For example, Saudi Aramco, an international petroleum company, buys custom-designed gas compressors to keep its oil rigs functioning reliably. Through discussions with its suppliers, it found that it could reduce the lead time as well as the cost of installation maintenance and repair by simplifying its specifications.

Value engineering

Value engineering, the reduction of design specifications to conform to the value needed, saves money by eliminating wasteful extra, and helps to simplify planning and forecasting, thereby making forecasts more accurate. A US electric and gas utility reduced the specifications on its underground polyethylene pipe when it discovered that its pipe specifications were designed such that the pipe would last more than twice the average maintenance interval at which the ground would be dug up and the pipe exposed.

Optimising transportation

Transportation routing and scheduling can be a way to reduce operating costs, especially if routing is currently done manually or in several different ways within the same geographic area. Examples of variations on the routing opportunities include the following:

- Mode selection, in which expedited (often air) shipments are shifted to another mode that optimises cost and service (often ground).
- Cross-docking, in which shipments are unloaded and reloaded at an intermediary point without being stored, as part of a rapid-delivery hub-and-spoke network.
- Distribution centre (DC) bypass, in which freight moves direct to store, or if not retail, directly to its end destination without being stored at a distribution or even a mixing centre.
- Equipment pooling, in which fleets' assets are shared or borrowed among users, as happens frequently with railcars and intermodal chassis.

Mode selection

Shifting from a more costly mode such as air to a less costly mode such as rail can be one way to save money. SinaWest, a Chinese metals company, shifted from truck to barge and saved money. James Joyce, general manager, explains:

> Our company needed to ship many hundreds of tons of steel from China to Europe. Trucking to port was taking too much time and becoming cost prohibitive. Our manufacturer was situated near a river, so we employed local barges to carry our steel down river to port. This saved more time and money than

we originally estimated. As a result we were able to pass those savings on to our customers. This resulted in some very happy, loyal clients and additional business.

A salesman has to call on customers in disparate locations, and needs to decide the most efficient way to sequence the stops so as to avoid backtracking and to minimise the total mileage. This is the travelling salesman problem. Routing and scheduling can save companies 20–40% on the cost of fleet operations. This is especially true if previous methods had been manual, as was the case at Iron Mountain. The company's rapid growth through acquisitions left it with many competing routing methods and overlapping routes within the same region. To optimise the routes, it implemented an advanced routing and scheduling software system on its fleet of 2,900 vehicles across North America. By using the vehicle routing and scheduling software, Iron Mountain found it could reduce route miles and resources by 34% and improve its on-time delivery rate from 96% to 99%.

Although switches like that may sound easy, they involve complications. For example, the order quantities, delivery lead times and variability of arrival times change depending on the mode, which changes safety stock requirements.

Cross-docking and DC bypass

Cross-docking, the relaying of products directly across a warehouse floor to an outbound vehicle instead of stocking it and retrieving it, and flow-through warehouses where goods are passed from vehicle to vehicle without being put into stock, can save warehouse put-away and pick-pack time by transferring goods directly from one truck to another.

Instead of operating point-to-point traffic flows from everywhere to everywhere else, a US trucking company, Yellow-Roadway, set up nine regional hubs that form a hub-and-spoke network through which it can serve both long-haul and short-haul freight, reducing its average transit time to under three days, thereby allowing it to compete with regional trucking companies.[14] The hubs also allow the carrier to reduce costs and therefore be more price-competitive.

A US paper products company, Georgia Pacific, operates multiple cross-docks across its network of distribution centres. To identify which SKUs were candidates for cross-docking, it commissioned the development of a software application that identified inbound shipments that were scheduled to arrive within 24 hours of customer requirements, and assigned them to an outbound truck so they could be cross-docked instead of put away in the warehouse. The pilot program clearly identified about half of the SKUS studied as candidates for cross-docking.

Even better than cross-docking is never touching the distribution centre at all. Historically, wholesalers operated distribution centres, and so did retailers, resulting in at least two stocking points between the source and the retail outlet. This made for redundant stock in each location, and a time-consuming journey, both of which lowered inventory turns.

UPS operates a service (called Trade Direct) for major retailers like Wal-Mart where the product is transferred at the port of entry in the destination country to small-package trucks that deliver it directly to stores. The product never touches a distribution centre (DC) in the destination country. Note that the ideal way to run this type of DC bypass operation is to pre-sort and pre-package the product for final delivery before the product leaves the manufacturing plant in the source country, or at least before it is loaded on to the ship. This means that more advanced planning is needed, which can work well for seasonal goods and promotions.

Equipment pooling

When transportation equipment is expensive, pooling can provide economical access to it. The cost savings from pooling are particularly attractive when peak demand varies by carrier or location (different lanes peak at different times), and shared equipment can be deployed more in each period than individually owned equipment would be.

A European ground support equipment pooling company provides a clear example.[15] Airport ground handling is often performed by only one provider, so airports like to, and in some cases are required to, introduce a second company to compete against the first. However, each company's investment in equipment is costly, especially for the more expensive equipment needed to service large aircraft. For example, a push-back tractor for wide-body aircraft or freighters costs about $250,000. While the incumbent ground handling company with the majority share of the volume can keep its equipment busy, a new provider cannot gain enough additional business to justify the capital investment required to buy a second push-back tractor.

With pooling, and by charging marginal costs for a piece of equipment whose costs are already covered by the incumbent handler, the airport can lower its equipment costs for both the incumbent and the new provider. The incumbent's costs drop from $63,000 to $49,000 per year, and the new provider's costs drop from $63,000 to $35,000 per year, says the company's CEO.

Tier-skipping

An extension of the DC bypass is bypassing the middleman altogether. In complex supply chains there can be many middlemen, and each one can add significant value to the product or service. Nonetheless, the more links there are in the value chain, the longer it takes material to move from one end to the other, and the more it costs. That is why companies such as Wal-Mart, IBM and Delphi Automotive sometimes skip levels in designing their worldwide end-to-end supply chains.

Western retailers generally prefer to deal with their Chinese sources rather than agents, brokers or wholesalers because that eliminates those parties' mark-ups and the overhead cost of dealing through them. IBM views its customer as its customer's customer, and conversely, its supplier is its supplier's supplier. It wants its suppliers to see their customers as the end-customer, not IBM. "[Tier-skipping] completely changes how you put the supply chain together and the reward system," says Ian Crawford, vice-president of Global Procurement Sourcing.

Ghana Nuts, a global trader in soya, groundnuts, cashew, sheanuts and sesame, and a producer of soya oil and meal for Ghana, Burkina Faso and Côte d'Ivoire, set up an out-grower programme whereby it buys directly from soybean farmers rather than purchase through multi-layered distribution channels. The more direct relationship ensured a consistent and reliable source of supply at prices at lower prices than were previously found on the market.

Such a mentality requires much more transparency – even open books between trading partners. That is why Delphi Automotive shares the gains of improvement programmes with its suppliers. If they find ways to save money, the two companies share the savings.

Supplier *kaizen*

Kaizen, a Japanese term for continuous improvement, uses management involvement, self-directed employee work groups and failure analysis tools to achieve steady and incremental improvements that cumulatively make big improvements in productivity and flexibility.

Herman Miller, a US furniture manufacturer, has had extraordinary success making its suppliers' operations lean. The company measures its cycle time in flow-days, which is the cumulative cycle time from supplier to the customer. It took 60 days to get from metal fabrications at the supplier to chairs at the customer. The material was handled 80 times and underwent only five hours of actual work during the 60 days. "The customer is not willing to pay for that," says Drew Schramm, vice-president of supply chain at Herman Miller. "We need to bring the cycle from 60 to 30 days." To do that, the company is bringing lean concepts to its suppliers. It is also grading its suppliers and classifying them. The company's classifications include new product development partner and preferred supplier. If the supplier does not fit into either of these classifications, it falls backwards, so to speak, to become a transactional supplier.

Consignment and vendor-managed inventory

Consignment programmes, whereby the supplier owns the inventory until it is consumed by the customer, can be an effective way to push inventory cost back on to the supplier. Under these programmes, the customer does not pay the supplier until the inventory is used, even if it sits on-site at the customer's warehouse. Consignment is common practice among retailers. For example, Monoprix, a French retailer, has suppliers replenish the display stock of their cosmetic items at their own cost until the items are sold.

In vendor-managed inventory (vmi), the supplier determines the right level of inventory to be held at the customer's location and replenishes the inventory without instructions from the customer. For example, W.W. Grainger, a US hardware supplier, replenishes nuts, bolts and small spare parts for its customers as they are consumed. vmi can lower inventory costs (both labour and inventory carrying costs) while increasing item availability when the supplier has more sophisticated logistics processes and information systems than the buyer.

Design for manufacturability

Design for manufacturability is about conceiving new products not for beauty but for ease and cost-effectiveness of manufacture. When he started his business in 1945, Marcel Bich did not invent a beautiful pen – he invented a pen that could be manufactured at low cost. The bic pens took the market by storm and set the design for ballpoint pens for nearly 50 years. More complex products such as automobiles and high-value electronics are harder to design for manufacturability because of their many parts, but General Motors created a breakthrough in 2000 when it launched the Celta, a $5,000 car, in Brazil.[16]

Electronic data interchange and paperless work flow

One way to rationalise cost is to cut overhead, and paper-based transactions certainly create overhead. Many purchasing transactions are handled today via UN/EDIFACT (Electronic Data Interchange for Administration, Commerce and Transport) or by ANSI (American National Standards Institute) ASC X12 transaction sets, which eliminate redundant data entry and improve accuracy. In small companies, the move to electronic transactions can be a hassle, but in large companies it often eliminates entire clerical departments, so is an important efficiency gain.

Air transport authorities, for one, are standardising data transfer formats to streamline interfaces between organisations and increase interoperability.

David Brennan, assistant director, special cargo standards at the International Air Transport Association (IATA), is involved in making revisions to the International Civil Aviation Organisation (ICAO)'s Technical Instructions and the UN Model Regulations to permit the use of electronic data transmission in lieu of paper documentation. Associated with this work is a review of the regulatory requirements to harmonise the different modal regulations to remove specific requirements, or at least have mutual recognition between the modes to facilitate multi-modal transport. The work at the UN and the ICAO supports the IATA e-Freight programme, which is aimed at helping the airfreight industry eliminate the need to generate paper documents for air cargo shipments. One aspect of e-Freight is aimed at converting 13 standard shipping forms[17] from faxed documents to electronic data interchange (EDI) formats.

Christophe Eggers, head of international network and transport at La Poste, the French postal service, experimented with a no-paper waybill on a shipment in Canada, as a test of the ability of the system. Often, the problems with paperless transactions are in the details.[18]

Members of IATA's container committee highlighted the type of missing information that stymies the progress of paperless document exchange: missing fields of data on forms, such as unknown contact person at the final delivery location, missing ID codes, wrong quantities or using numbers already used for previous orders, no stickering/marking layout, and no information about changes in corporate identity or logos. In fact, the top ten messaging errors are mundane, such as missing or erroneous account information.[19, 20]

Savi Networks, an information services company, is helping the Chinese and Thai governments to implement technology that will save time in customs and increase cargo screening accuracy.[21] It gathers, merges and assesses data from multiple document sources to develop a more accurate profile of risk. The papers include purchase order/advanced shipment notice, booking confirmation and routing, terminal receipt and drayage detail, vessel load plan, conveyance and container location and intermodal interchange status, truck status and proof of delivery. The programme results in both improved efficiency and increased security. The efficiency benefits include reductions in inventory carrying costs, out-of-stocks, lead time variance, theft and lost containers, and administrative costs and fees. The security benefits include advanced trade data for risk targeting, end-to-end location and status information, and electronic seals to better track international shipments.

Tension Envelope, a US manufacturer of speciality envelopes, implemented electronic payments and summary billing to simplify its internal processes (that is, reduce paperwork and overall transactions where it was not necessary).

7 Synchronisation: competing on reliability

FedEx set the standard for reliability in 1973 with its bold new air express delivery model and its claim that the packages it handles would "absolutely, positively" be delivered on time. SNCF, the French national rail company, defined reliability in the 1980s: if a train was scheduled for 13:00:00 and you arrived at 13:00:15, you'd know you'd need to run and jump to catch the train. Toyota and Honda raised the bar on the reliability of automobiles throughout the 1990s.

Reliability is a crucial aspect of customer service, and high service levels can command customer loyalty and support premium prices. The perception of reliability may be more important than reliability itself, since the price that buyers are willing to pay is usually tied mostly to perception. Yet the fact remains that reliability is not a given today. These companies became famous because it is hard to be reliable and not many companies are. Hence many companies look to supply chain management (SCM) tools and techniques to back up their strategy (or their claims) of reliability.

Success factors

To compete on reliability, the bullwhip effect must be reduced or eliminated. This means addressing its root causes: seasonal peaks, promotions, cyclical peaks and order batching. This is where SCM gets tricky. Influencing seasonal peaks or promotions, as in retail promotions, involves close collaboration with marketing and sales. Predicting the timing of or mitigating the effects of cyclical peaks, as in the oil industry, is almost as hard as predicting the stockmarket. And reducing order batching is hard because it often goes against the natural incentive for buyers, which is to place large orders to get volume price discounts.

If the four aggravators of bullwhip were visible to all the parties in the supply chain, theoretically they would have the information needed to avoid or counteract it, which is why there has been a lot of investment in visibility solutions and event management – detailed recording and posting of order information for customers (and sometimes suppliers) to see. Even if there were full visibility, however, companies need to develop the information systems to compute the optimal order, and people need to be willing to share data and limit counter-productive behaviour such as maintaining extra buffer stock and hoarding.

Performance advantages

Companies that achieve synchronous supply chains outperform those that do not. Eliminating or reducing the bullwhip effect allows companies to function effectively with less inventory and less fixed assets, which produces a higher return on capital.

A synchronous flow requires less inventory, which means less working capital. The average stock being held is substantial, so the gains if you reduce it can be too. In the US in 2008, the average days held were 47 days for electrical equipment, 63 days for motor vehicle and parts dealers, and 54 days for clothing and clothing accessory stores.[1] In contrast, Tesco,

Table 7.1 **Benchmark asset turnover rate of synchronisation-focused companies**

Industry	Benchmark asset turnover rate of companies with synchronisation focus
Hotels, restaurants & leisure	2.75
Technology, hardware & equipment	1.63
Household & personal products	1.63
Capital goods	1.60
Energy	1.54
Transportation	1.42
Software & services	1.35
Materials	1.31
Telecommunications services	0.95
Utilities	0.77
Diversified financials	0.58
Insurance	0.44
Banks	0.10
Average	**1.38**

Source: Boston Strategies International, based on an analysis of data from Thomson Reuters and Boston Strategies International's 2008 supply chain performance benchmark study

a large UK retailer, which is often heralded for its supply chain efficiency, held only 18 days of inventory in 2007, over a third less than US grocery stores such as Safeway and Kroger, and only slightly below that of convenience stores.[2]

For more asset-intensive companies, less bullwhip effect means less plant assets needed to handle peak requirements, which translates to less fixed assets.

Both inventory and fixed assets are reflected in return on capital employed (ROCE, net income divided by fixed assets plus working capital), and for capital-intensive companies fixed asset turnover can be used as a proxy. Companies that follow a synchronisation supply chain strategy earn 2.6% higher fixed asset turnover than those that follow other supply chain strategies (16.5% for those that focus on strategies to reduce inventory and working capital compared with 13.9% for those that do not), according to a 2008 survey by the author of 29 companies. In addition, companies that have managed to synchronise their supply chains have better ratios of cash flow to sales than those that do not. That puts companies that work on making their supply chains lean – such as McDonald's, Ahold, Blyth, PepsiCo, The Limited, Wal-Mart, Famous Footwear, Galeries Lafayette and Marks & Spencer – ahead of their competition. Table 7.1 (on the previous page) shows asset turnover performance benchmarks for synchronisation-focused companies.

Table 7.2 shows benchmark cash-flow performance levels for synchronisation-focused companies in a range of industries.

UPS follows a careful synchronisation strategy. By applying industrial engineering principles to improve the efficiency and reliability of every aspect of the company's operations (for example, by conducting time studies of its couriers and developing standard procedures that every depot must follow), UPS earned a return on equity of 23% in 2002–06. In contrast, US freight trains cannot compete effectively with trucks even at much lower prices, because of their unreliability compared with trucks.[3]

Superior financial performance is related to better operational performance, as follows:

◼ Higher first-pass yield (the percentage of good output generated through the production process the first time – not including rework): 78.2% compared with 75.8% for companies not oriented to synchronisation.
◼ Lower variance (standard deviation) of production cycle time (production cycle time is the time between start of production and

Table 7.2 **Benchmark cash flow:sales ratios of synchronisation-focused companies**

Industry	Benchmark cashflow:sales ratios of companies with synchronisation focus, %
Telecommunications services	24.2
Energy	22.5
Utilities	19.4
Diversified financials	18.6
Software & services	18.5
Materials	16.8
Insurance	15.7
Household & personal products	13.5
Transportation	13.4
Hotels, restaurants & leisure	12.3
Technology, hardware & equipment	11.1
Capital goods	8.6
Banks	8.4
Food & drug retailing	3.5
Average	**14.8**

Source: Boston Strategies International, based on an analysis of data from Thomson Reuters and Boston Strategies International's 2008 supply chain performance benchmark study

delivery to the department interfacing with the customer): 86.8% compared with 91.1%.

- Lower percentage of incorrect orders: 1.1% compared with 2.4%
- Less inventory: 20.9 days, compared with 35.4 days for non-lean companies.[4]
- Better performance on operational metrics such as defects per 100 units, space required, operator time, materials consumed, cycle time, equipment used, rework/rejects/scrap, set-up time, waiting time, downtime and distance travelled by a part,[5] in addition to the metrics above.

Note that the companies that performed well on synchronisation did not necessarily have higher margins like the companies that focused on rationalisation. Lean manufacturing and lean distribution reduce operating cost, but a well-executed rationalisation strategy can do better at that. These results support the concept of sequencing rationalisation, synchronisation, customisation and innovation initiatives. If resources are limited, it may make sense to choose a strategy and orient resources to it rather than trying to be excellent at everything.

Toyota production system

If Henry Ford's assembly line was the original example of a synchronised supply chain (most activities were literally synchronised with the next ones in the production line), then the Toyota production system (TPS) is the modern equivalent. The TPS embodies many synchronous concepts, and has for that reason been applied by many firms both inside and outside the auto industry since its development in the 1960s. It is a set of norms, philosophies and tools, interrelated as a system, that form the mental mindset of teamwork at the company. As there are numerous books on the subject, this brief overview is intended only to describe how the various elements in this chapter form a consistent system.

The TPS operates on a number of high-level principles, each complementing the other. Four principles underpin it:

1 Continuous improvement (*kaizen*). The system is geared to provide a learning environment where each mistake turns into an opportunity for improvement, so that eventually no error should be repeated twice.
2 The systematic elimination of waste (*muda* in Japanese) and the related drive to ensure that every action and every effort drives towards adding value for the end-customer.
3 People-centredness. The TPS only works if people believe in it and execute it; it cannot be mandated and it cannot be managed virtually through information technology. People must internalise the norms and the values, and bring them to bear on the myriad problems that they encounter each day.
4 Simplicity, which means fewer breakdowns than in a complex system, and reliability: these are central to the TPS.

Six norms guide execution within the TPS:

1 The whole system works to a rhythm (*takt* time), so that when everybody follows the same rhythm, it is harmonious and easier to control.
2 Control, stability, reliability and predictability: these are critical to the success

of continuous improvement initiatives since a process that is in control can be adjusted much more easily and quickly than a process that is out of control.

3 Workplace organisation and cleanliness: these are prerequisites for control and stability, since dirt and clutter introduce randomness that causes unstable processes and results.

4 A one-piece flow: this is the best way to validate that there is no waste in the system. A wasteful process never produces a one-piece flow.

5 Repeatable processes: these ensure continuity and consistency of purpose and practice over time.

6 Worker empowerment: ensures the longevity and durability of the system, since top-down and autocratic systems are less effective at handling the wide range of problems that may occur.

The TPS is responsible for the creation of many of the tools that are associated with lean management, as follows:

- The pull-based demand trigger eliminates waste by focusing all effort on satisfying customer needs rather than a forecast, which is inevitably erroneous.
- Just-in-time (JIT) production minimises the waste that may occur when customer demands change, by eliminating buffer inventories throughout the pipeline.
- *Jidoka* prevents problems before they occur, thereby improving system stability and reducing the need for problem diagnosis and remediation.
- Visual controls, including *kanban* cards (physical cards that are placed at the end of a batch of inventoried items; the card itself triggers replenishment rather than an information system), ensure universal, real-time and easy-to-update access to information about the pace of production (*takt* time) and the status of errors and remediation efforts.
- Capacity balancing and level loading ensure small lot sizes and hence minimum waste from changes in demand.
- Root cause problem-solving, including diagnostic tools such as plan-do-check-act (PDCA) and the Ishikawa fishbone diagram (see Figure 6.2 on page 80), enables the working team to diagnose and resolve errors and restore normal operation following disruptions.

Elements of synchronisation strategy

Synchronisation strategy includes the following elements:

◪ Constraints management and throughput analysis
◪ Pull-based demand trigger
◪ Just-in-time (JIT)
◪ Perfect order fulfilment
◪ Make-to-order (MTO)
◪ Optimal inventory placement
◪ Sales and operations planning (S&OP)
◪ Collaborative inventory management
◪ Everyday low price
◪ An anchor player that ensures stability
◪ Shifting demand and capacity
◪ Better forecasting, less emotion
◪ Risk mitigation

Constraints management and throughput analysis

To synchronise throughput in the supply chain, capacity must be aligned at each step in the process, or bottlenecks will constrain the output. For example, for a computer manufacturer that makes laptops in six steps – production, assembly, configuration, testing, labelling and packaging – the throughput will be constrained by the operation with the least capacity. As shown in Figure 7.1, testing is the bottleneck operation that constrains the system throughput.

Aligning capacity across the partners in a supply chain requires collaboration and advance planning. Many countries have capacity limitations

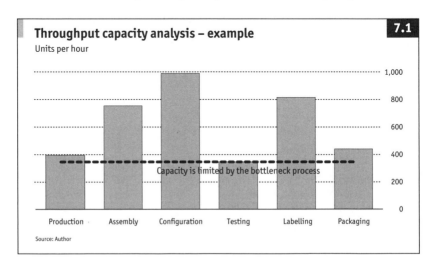

Throughput capacity analysis – example   `7.1`

Units per hour

Capacity is limited by the bottleneck process

Production · Assembly · Configuration · Testing · Labelling · Packaging

Source: Author

in their port and rail networks, which constrain the volume of imports and exports that can flow. The ports are creating incentives for off-hours pickup, upgrading to equipment with higher throughput and changing labour rules. The railways are transferring to inland transfer stations to alleviate congestion at the ports, and changing the way they load containers onto intermodal trains in order to speed up loading operations. However, some of these investments can take years (delivery of new cranes and locomotives, for example), so the ports and the railways need to collaborate or else they risk having misaligned capacity.

Theory of constraints
The theory of constraints addresses bottlenecks in operations and offers a systematic process for alleviating them. The concept is based on the premise that every process has one binding constraint (based on the throughput analysis above), and that throughput can be increased by eliminating that constraint. The process involves clarifying the mission of the organisation, identifying the binding constraint, eliminating it, aligning other processes to the new throughput levels and then pursuing the next constraint.

The theory of constraints is a hallmark in manufacturing thinking because it highlights the extent to which manufacturing has historically been driven by management's desire to lower average standard unit costs by increasing the volume of production so as to amortise fixed costs over a larger number of units, and management's behaviour in increasing plant capacity utilisation, both of which historically resulted in overproduction and excess inventory. It highlights the accounting mirages that have been at the root of decades of overproduction.

BNSF Railroad in the United States underwent a detailed study of bottlenecks in its end-to-end supply chain, using the principles of the theory of constraints, when the tide of Asian imports streaming into the country brought the transportation system to its limits. To enable the free flow of cargo from the West Coast to population centres, which were mostly in the east, it identified the port of Los Angeles/Long Beach and its Chicago gateway and hub as bottlenecks, and took actions to eliminate the constraints. The actions included, for example, increasing the percentage of railcars that it loaded on-dock, requiring terminal operators at the ports to release full trainloads instead of partial trainloads, and differentiating between northern and southern trains by specifying that they must consist of cars destined for either northern (Kansas City, Chicago or the north-east) or southern (St Louis, Texas, Memphis, the south-east and Florida) stations. After eliminating the bottleneck in Los Angeles, it turned to the congestion at Chicago and the possibility of making joint public–private investments to alleviate that bottleneck.

Bottleneck elimination can occur at a macro level as well. When raw materials such as ore and minerals are in short supply, downstream companies consider acquiring the source in order to ensure supply. Nampak, a South African packaging company, acquired a paper mill in order to eliminate a bottleneck in its supply chain.

Spares management

Companies that operate in capital-intensive businesses like transportation and oil and gas need to place expensive spare equipment in the right place to minimise the risk of downtime at the least cost. Optimisation of the number and placement of highly capital-intensive spares is a branch of throughput analysis that requires special tools. Statistical analysis of failure is required to know how many spares are required and where they should be placed to maximise the chance of their availability. Logistics plans are needed to ensure their movement to the points of need. For example, aircraft engines are needed in repair centres around the world, but given their high capital cost there is a limited number that can be available at any time. FedEx conducted detailed modelling that permitted it to more precisely forecast the number of spare engines needed, so that it would be sure to have enough to keep planes flying at the Christmas peak. It discovered that it had more than it needed and was able to eliminate spare engines.

Pull-based demand trigger

Inventory management techniques and technologies frequently reduce inventory by 20–30% in major companies, which often equates to 1–3% of sales. Single and multi-echelon inventory management software applications determine the optimal amount and type of inventory to hold at each location. A regional utility reduced its inventory by 28% by implementing a software model to set the optimal reorder points.

The overarching shift that has driven dramatic inventory decreases is a move from push to pull demand triggers. In the old push-based system, the product was pushed forward towards the point of sale, based on forecasts. Since the forecasts were inevitably wrong, there was excess inventory in the field.

Pull-based demand triggers used not to be feasible, but today they are the principal mode of replenishment, largely because of the improved ability of information systems to transmit production, sales and inventory data throughout the supply chain. The retail and automotive (see next section) sectors offer two examples of how pull has changed SCM for ever. In the retail industry, the real-time availability of point-of-sale data and the ability to reconcile consumption with inventory levels have made pull-based replenishment the only way to run a modern retailing operation. Wal-Mart has been able to reduce its in-store inventory from 10–12 weeks to 3–4 weeks by transmitting actual stock counts via wireless handheld devices to the distribution centres, and replenishing weekly. The improved accuracy has also enabled more direct-to-store shipments (facilitating the DC bypass component of rationalisation strategy) by reducing the need for a safety stock buffer.[6]

Just-in-time

JIT is a logical extension of lean thinking, since having material in advance of when it is needed is wasteful. It is addressed here rather than in Chapter 6 because it results in savings in working capital rather than in the cost of goods sold.

JIT, when properly implemented, significantly reduces or even eliminates inventory requirements, which explains why the concept has been so widely implemented. Of the three principal types of inventory – cycle, seasonal and safety – JIT primarily reduces safety stock, which is the buffer that protects the business from the effects of variability in demand and supply. Cycle stock is meant to satisfy consumption while orders are being processed and are en route (technically, that would be in-transit stock), so if the JIT supplier is moved to a nearby or adjacent facility, JIT can also reduce these stocks. Seasonal stock is meant to push stock to market in anticipation of seasonal sales.

In the automotive industry, component suppliers co-locate next to assembly plants in order to offer JIT capabilities:

- ◪ General Motors set up a large supplier park next to its assembly operations in Brazil to ensure tight communication and JIT replenishment.[7] Fiat and other automakers have followed the same principle.
- ◪ The "Smart Car" was another auto industry experiment with lean production and distribution. The company (Micro-Compact Car, or MCC), which was originally a joint venture between Mercedes-Benz and Swiss Watchmakers and was eventually taken over by Daimler Benz, attempted to build cars in 7.5 hours. The trick was

modular assemblies and postponement. The chassis, power train, doors and roof, electronics and cockpit were modules that could be rapidly assembled.[8]

▪ InterSwitch in Nigeria implemented a JIT approach to its electronic funds transfer (EFT) solutions across about 20 banks in 2004/05. Seyi Oluwehinmi, team lead for SCM, explains:

> We employed a JIT approach. We made sure that equipment and supplies were delivered just at the time they were needed, hence eliminating high inventory costs and mitigating the risks of tied-up capital.

One-piece flow concept

JIT is fundamental to the concept of the one-piece flow. One-piece flow is an ideal state based on a philosophy of production that replenishes upon use and in the smallest quantities possible, with an ideal order quantity of one unit. The ability to place more, smaller, orders more frequently addresses the source and the magnitude of the bullwhip effect related to order-batching.

Kanban and reliable replenishment

Kanban, the use of a visual signal to trigger replenishment, has helped to convert forecast-driven managers to JIT by making them go back to the basics. Workers have a kanban card, which has all the necessary information listed on it. In a repetitive production operation, workers learn the information on the card by heart.

Rapid replenishment eliminates the need for buyers to hold safety stock for the demand during the lead time of the order cycle. Companies can also enable inventory reduction by increasing the reliability of the timing of delivery, especially on products for which the transit time is long. In a continuation of a trend that started in the retail environment, companies are increasingly dictating delivery time windows to their suppliers and the time windows are getting shorter: 15 minutes is typical in retail trades in the United States.

Making the delivery straight to the point of consumption removes all delivery uncertainty from the buyer's inventory calculations. Automotive parts suppliers often co-locate next to the automaker's plant in order to remove delivery time uncertainty, and in the Japanese model they are responsible for delivery not to the dock door but directly to the worker on the line who is doing the assembly. To minimise handling, companies carefully study direct delivery options that bypass distribution centres. Third-party logistics (3PL) companies set up services that collect product at its source, package it in the sequence in which it will be unloaded when it arrives, consolidate it and ship it direct to the store using multiple modes of transportation. Direct delivery service involves careful planning and meticulous execution, especially for complex global and multi-modal services.

Takt time
Takt time is the rate at which the production operation produces output (for example, four cars per hour). But it has a much deeper connotation than the word "rate" conveys. Takt time is the rhythm or heartbeat of the operation, and the musical and visceral connotations are deliberate. It is the pace at which everybody in the process works in order to keep capacity aligned, at the pace of the bottleneck process. Without takt time, there would be inventory in between work stations and shortages of material (or services) between others.

Level loading
Level loading is the practice of scheduling work so that a little bit of every product is made every period, rather than in large batches of one product at a time. Applying it in an office environment might involve taking a day-of-the week schedule with five activities (one performed each day of the week) and scheduling that work so that one-fifth of each activity gets done each day. This requires more changeovers, which forces quick set-ups (see single-minute exchange of die, below). However, level loading allows the quicker identification of errors and defects, ensures the balanced use of resources and mitigates the impact of unforeseen circumstances. For example, if one person handles a given task once per week and he or she is off sick that day, the task will not get done until the following week, but with level loading every problem and irregularity is corrected within one day.

Set-up time reduction and single-minute exchange of die
To attain level loading, companies must frequently change over from one product or service to another. When companies move from infrequent changeovers to frequent changeovers, they often realise that their current pace of changeover will never work with the frequency of changeover that is required for level loading. Therefore, they need to learn how to change over quickly. The concept of single-minute exchange of die (SMED)

stems from the automotive industry (Toyota, specifically, which uses dies in stamping presses to produce stamped parts like hoods), in which changeovers were reduced to a minuscule period of time in order to facilitate flexible manufacturing.

Despite its automotive legacy, the concept of SMED applies to all industries. Even in pure service industries like banking and consulting, lean theory prefers flexibility and responsiveness to efficiency, on the basis that there should always be as tight a linkage as possible between demand and the pace of production, and if possible, a one-piece flow.

Postponement

Retailers with global supply chains often find that when goods arrive in stores demand for them is significantly different from what they had predicted when the store's order was placed, which is often eight or more weeks beforehand. To mitigate the difference, most leading retailers establish an interim level of product build-up (variations of assembly or packaging) that can be finished off late in the supply chain according to current demand patterns. This strategy is particularly useful in fashion industries. For example, apparel importers can dye shirts upon entry into the country rather than at their point of manufacture, thereby eliminating this industry's largest element of variability (colour) that causes inventory shortages and excesses.

Using real-time feedback loops between the stores and its production facilities, Italian clothing-maker Benetton can distribute the styles and colours that sell the most to the stores, while avoiding excess and obsolete inventory of pre-dyed styles that are not popular with shoppers. Sources at the company say it saves money through the avoidance of clearances and the lower inventory carrying cost involved with stocking undyed garments (the material has less book-keeping value than finished goods, and it needs to hold fewer units in stock to satisfy the same demand because demand for the undyed garments is less variable than demand for specific styles and sizes).[9]

A well-known fine writing-instrument-maker imports pens in bulk and creates multipacks of pens in the United States. This is an example of postponement that saves on inventory costs and allows the company to have a high fill rate by being more responsive to the market. Sherwin-Williams, a maker of paint, mixes paint at the point of purchase rather than at the point of production to reduce the variations of inventory that would have to be kept in stock. CEVA Logistics, formerly TNT Logistics, ships laptops from China to its German distribution centre, where it configures them for sale in European markets, to reduce the number of finished goods SKUS that its customers need to keep there, and to reduce theft.[10]

The opportunity for postponement is such that UPS established a special service that includes the option for the shipper to postpone the decision about where the packages should go. For customers using the service, UPS packages products for delivery to specific stores at factories in Asia, then reassigns some of those packages to different stores about two weeks later when they arrive in the United States, based on the customers' updated store sales information. The result is the best of both worlds: no need for deconsolidation and warehousing in the United States (by shipping direct to the stores) and elimination of overshipments (by using real-time sales and restocking information).

In addition, postponement can help maximise sales value for commodities and regional goods whose prices vary geographically and over time. The price of steel scrap, for example, varies regionally, so one carmaker has a team monitoring its prices in different regions and diverting railcars of scrap to the most lucrative sales outlet while the railcars are en route. Technology such as track/trace, radio frequency identification (RFID) and GPS will make this process more efficient and more flexible.

Design for assembly, modularisation and kitting

Design for assembly is engineering products so they can be efficiently produced. This often involves the use of modules and assemblies. Modularisation can allow production to be partially or mostly completed before orders are received, allowing postponement of the finishing operation or operations. This way, the order fulfilment cycle can be very short since all that needs to be done to fill the order is to assemble pre-prepared modules. Modularisation can also be used throughout the production process to compress the fulfilment cycle at multiple points along the way. The end result can be a nearly instantaneous response to orders. FedEx creates kits of parts for each jet engine type so when they come in for repair, the mechanics can quickly bolt on an assembly of "quick engine change" (QEC) and get the engine onto the wing of the aircraft with minimum delay. During periods of peak demand, such as the Christmas rush to get packages to consumers' doors, it is the only way that the company can deliver all the packages. Kitting, the process of preparing assemblies to be used in a production operation, can be useful when it allows the main production process to be quicker or more flexible.

Perfect order fulfilment

Errors and returns cause confusion and noise in order data, contributing to overordering and inventory imbalances. The concept of the perfect order sets a standard for logistics similar to zero defects (see page 79) in quality management. Perfect orders are orders in which the right product arrives with the right quantity from the right source at the right destination in the right condition at the right time with the right documentation at the right cost.

More than 99% of Australia's Futuris Automotive's orders meet the qualifications of perfect order fulfilment. Futuris Automotive is a provider of car interior products, such as interior trim, controls and DVD rear seat entertainment, for leading brands including GM Holden, Chery Automobile, Daimler, Ford, Toyota and Mitsubishi. In addition, Futuris maintains less than 0.08% obsolete inventory and 0.05% back orders as a result of its flexible manufacturing methods.

Make to order

Companies have moved towards make-to-order (MTO) models for the same reasons as lean management emphasises one-piece flow. MTO is more responsive to changes in demand and less likely to result in unused inventory.

Five demand mechanisms can trigger replenishment:

1 **Make to plan (MTP)**, in which a fixed production plan is established and there are no demand triggers. This is often the case in continuous production operations like float glass. Production and product or service availability are often continuous.
2 **Make to stock (MTS)**, in which demand is triggered by reorder points. Availability is constant as long as there is inventory.
3 **Engineer to order (ETO)**, in which demand is triggered by individual orders and each order requires custom design. No materials, components or finished products are available, until demanded by individual orders.
4 **Make to order (MTO)**, in which demand is triggered by individual orders and there is no pre-staging. Raw materials are available at all times, but neither components nor finished products are available except when demanded by individual orders.
5 **Assemble to order (ATO)**, in which demand is triggered by individual orders and material is pre-staged for quick assembly. Components are available at all times, but finished products are only available on demand.

Typology of operating environments   7.2

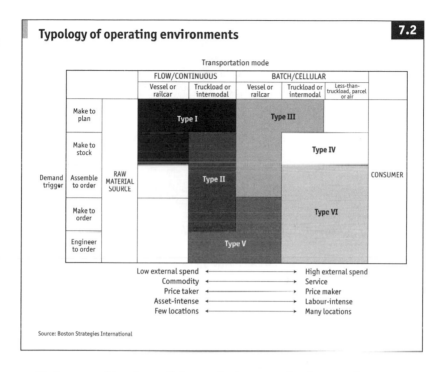

Source: Boston Strategies International

Various combinations of demand trigger mechanisms and transportation modes define six operating environments in which companies are moving towards smaller unit sizes over time (see Figure 7.2):

1 **Type I** companies like Bunge, Cargill and Mosaic have supply chains that involve extraction of some product from the earth. They generally have relatively few sites, use heavy equipment and operate in commodity businesses.

2 **Type II** companies like BASF, Cabot and DuPont have supply chains centred on process manufacturing. They generally use specialised equipment and operate continuous or large batch production facilities.

3 **Type III** companies like Coca-Cola, GE Lighting and Georgia Pacific Building Products have MTS manufacturing-oriented supply chains. They generally have many sites, have a lot of in-and-out product flows, and use as much labour as machinery and equipment.

4 **Type IV** companies like W.W. Grainger and UPS have distribution-focused supply chains. They generally have many small nodes, have

lots of in-and-out product flows each in small quantities and use a lot of vehicles.

5 **Type V** companies like Boeing, Northrop Grumman, Bechtel, Raytheon and many other commercial manufacturers have MTO and ETO supply chains. They generally have limited in-and-out product flows, are technologically advanced and make small numbers of high-value products.

6 **Type VI** companies like Ahold (Stop & Shop), Wal-Mart, Tesco and Lands' End (Sears) focus on reselling. They generally have a lot of ship-to points and in-and-out product flows in small quantities.

Beyond just increasing agility, MTO production (including ETO, MTO and ATO) can reposition companies into higher-margin operating environments with entirely different competitors. In order to make a strategic supply chain shift, companies must change not only the demand trigger mechanism, but also the transportation mode (making it quicker does not help if transportation still takes a long time). MTP companies often ship in large bulk vessels or railcars, and MTS companies often ship in full truckload. MTS companies ship in smaller quantities and more frequently, often on less-than-truckload or small-package carriers.

Automotive manufacturers have tried to move to an MTO approach. Only 25% of all showroom visitors get the car they want, and when they decide what they want, they want it within a week, according to studies.[11] Unfortunately, explains Martin Christopher, they generally have to wait a long time to get a car with exactly the specifications they desire. In response to the gap, Rover introduced the concept of personal production in 1993 to provide customers with vehicles built to their specifications within 14 days. Using the most advanced supply chain thinking of the time, it tried to eliminate delays by establishing a common data system across all manufacturing plants and dealers. It used postponement by building unpainted bodies and finishing them off only when it had firm orders. And it dealt with demand peaks by making its teams cross-functional, instituting flexible working hours and layering orders so that the predictable orders from fleet customers constituted the base load, while less predictable orders from customers were handled as needed. Finally, it adjusted its monthly sales targets to mitigate or avoid the bullwhip effect.

Examples of companies that have successfully made such shifts include the following:

- ◪ KGHM, a Polish copper mine, moved from MTP mining (Type I) into wire rod extrusion (Type II).

- Englehard, originally a German mining and minerals company specialising in catalysts (Type II), developed the catalytic converter for cars, as well as radiators and other automotive components (Type III companies).
- UPS, a distributor of packages (Type IV), bought Mailboxes Etc. and renamed it The UPS Store in order to have a retail presence (Type VI).
- A US customise-to-order maker of fine writing instruments (Type V) opened retail outlets (Type VI) to take advantage of its strong brand name.

HP introduced the idea of using tools such as real options to make the decision whether or not to invest in making the transition from MTS to MTO. If there is a tight linkage between the price that the products can be sold for in the market and the cost of producing them – the kind of linkage that would naturally occur under circumstances of a lean supply chain – deciding whether or not to make to order is essentially like buying a call option on the spread between the price it could sell for and the cost of producing it. Similar to the valuation of a stock option, investing in MTO is an investment and a gamble, but one whose pay-off increases as the uncertainties of a wasteful supply chain are eliminated.[12]

Optimal inventory placement

Better inventory management consistently helps companies decrease working capital and improve ROA. Opportunities may fall into two categories: centralisation and stratification.

Risk pooling by centralising stock can significantly reduce inventory requirements. TruServ Corporation turned a $13.9m loss into a $4.6m profit by consolidating its distribution centres and adjusting staffing levels.[13] Safety stock is a function of the square root of the standard deviation of the forecast errors over the supply lead time, and since having more warehouses increases forecast error and sometimes supply lead time, many companies have consolidated their networks to reduce inventory. The trick is to figure out which SKUs should be centralised and which should be kept locally. The logic gets more challenging in multi-echelon networks, and requires a good network modelling tool.

Fulham, a US manufacturer of ballasts for lighting products, has some customers that need its products immediately and others that can wait. It positions some inventory close to the customers (it calls this outposting inventory). "Service pays off, even though it's more expensive to maintain," says Brian Wald, president. The trick, of course, is knowing which inventory is worth the gamble of being positioned closer to which customer. To maintain balance, Fulham keeps other customers' inventory centrally located to take advantage of risk pooling, and juggles the two stocks to satisfy clients' needs as they change.

Inventory stratification helps manage the SKUs that are the most costly to hold. Usually, companies have so many SKUs that they are challenged to devote enough management time to address the proper stock levels for everything. ABC stratification can help focus on the items that generate the most inventory carrying cost. In a traditional ABC analysis, A items represent the first 80% of sales, B items the next 16% and C items the last 4%. If there is a large number of items, or if there are categories of inactive items, four tiers of stratification with a tighter definition of A items may help to sort out the important items. Here is an example of how one company's ABC analysis helped it focus on the items that drove its inventory cost:

- A items represented 70% of revenue (which could correspond to expenditure for an ABC analysis of purchased items) but only about 10% of the items. It checked these the most frequently, and tended to have them at most stocking locations because of their frequent use.
- B items represented 20% of revenue and about 20% of items. It monitored these items less frequently than it did the A items.
- C items represented 10% of the revenue and about 50% of items.
- Other, or "D" items represented slow-moving parts and obsolete items that constituted 20% of the items but had no activity during the period.

Cycle counting, the practice of reconciling physical counts with information system counts, calls for counting the A items more frequently than the B, C, or D items.

Sales and operations planning

Alignment on a common plan is a challenge when multiple functional departments each have their own visions, opinions and forecasts of demand, inventory and production. This is often the case in large organisations that the departmental figures do not reconcile. The problem with such divergence is that it eventually leads to too much stock or service failures, or both, and the larger the divergence, the larger and more sustained is the problem.

Sales and operations planning (S&OP) is a cross-functional process designed to eliminate divergences by structuring interdepartmental communication on a monthly basis. It aims to align sales, production and logistics on one common plan. Through a progressive reconciliation of plans and forecasts, the organisation forms a consensus plan that is used as the trigger for more production. This frequently results in the elimination of overproduction by bringing to the surface the underlying reasons for divergence. These often include, for example, the sales function's tendency to pad the plan in order to have enough inventory available for sale; the production function's tendency to overproduce to make asset utilisation look good; and those in charge of inventory's incentive to reduce stock levels to meet financial targets.

Tecom, a rapidly growing Turkish air compressor manufacturer, set up an S&OP process to keep cash flow under control. Prior to setting up S&OP, each function did its own planning. While the company's entrepreneurial culture encouraged a great deal of autonomy, it also meant that financial incentives were department-specific, and communication across functions was limited. The company set up an S&OP process involving the chairman, the production department, sales, purchasing and technical/engineering/R&D.

Collaborative inventory management

Visibility and collaboration can eliminate the part of the bullwhip effect that comes from not being able to see the whole chain. The potential savings from co-ordination in the supply chain and avoidance of the bullwhip effect could reach 35% of total system costs, according to Funda Sahin and John Mentzer.[14]

Visibility is most easily achieved through sharing demand forecasts, production plans and inventory positions with trading partners, and it needs to be combined with forecasting and keeping sufficiently high inventories to cope with any spikes in demand. Felipe Moran,[15] in quantifying the effect of bullwhip in alternative supply chain configurations, determined that advanced forecasting and co-ordination performed better than five other supply chain control methods.[16]

A 1992 efficient consumer response (ECR) working group consisted of members[17] from Coca-Cola, Crown/BBK, Kraft General Foods, Kroger, Nabisco Foods Group, Oscar Mayer Foods, Procter & Gamble, Ralston Purina, Safeway, Sales Force Companies, Scrivner, Shaw's Supermarkets, Super Valu Stores and Vons Companies.

ECR has evolved into a cross-industry initiative called collaborative planning forecasting and replenishment, and the Voluntary Inter-Industry Commerce Standards (VICS) organisation has defined a nine-step process for implementing it. The process involves agreeing on rules for working together, forming a joint business plan, sharing replenishment plans and identifying opportunities to reduce inventory imbalances. The most common forms of collaborative behaviour are cross-functional teams, frequent and regular meetings, process integration and synchronisation, joint goal development, and common performance assessment and monitoring mechanisms. Today, the Global Data Synchronisation Network (GDSN, formerly the Uniform Code Council) aims to reduce the bullwhip effect by sharing trading partner data.

Everyday low price

Since erratic buying and pricing behaviour (and both combined) are some of the fundamental causes of the bullwhip effect, stable prices will reduce it. Wal-Mart's "everyday low price" (sometimes abbreviated to EDLP) is not only a marketing strategy; it is also a supply chain strategy. Wal-Mart can predict its demand better than most retailers because its everyday low pricing invites less demand volatility. The same principle applies to business-to-business environments, where sellers can eliminate time-based discounts such as quarterly incentives to reduce batch buying.

How the anchor player ensures stability

One of the challenges in synchronising the behaviour of parties in a supply chain is providing the right incentives for collaboration. Influence over the supply chain can help improve brand recognition and negotiate leverage over margins. However, if all the players in a multi-tier supply chain have equal influence, none may exert enough leverage over the others to motivate data sharing. Therefore, some imbalance of power actually helps to establish the leader quickly and easily. Charles Poirier calls this leader a "nucleus company"; Douglas Lambert calls it an "anchor player".

Collaboration often fails because of a lack of trust. Large buyers frequently invite suppliers to partnering initiatives, only to put the squeeze on their prices. One in four participants in a Brigham Young survey said explicitly that real trust in supply chain partnerships is rare. They said that "the word trust is overused, misused, and frequently abused". Trust requires information sharing, risk sharing and strong personal relationships, says Stanley Fawcett.[18] Collaboration requires not only trust but also a dominant enough player to make the critical decisions, such as Wal-Mart's decision to enforce its suppliers to cross-dock or to use RFID.

The prisoner's dilemma

		Criminal B	
		Confess	Deny
Criminal A	Confess	A: 1 year in jail B: 1 year in jail	A: free B: 2 years in jail
	Deny	A: 2 years in jail B: free	COLLABORATION A: 1 year in jail B: 1 year in jail

Source: Author

Supply chain collaboration is not unlike the prisoner's dilemma, which is a game of trust in which two parties need to decide explicitly to co-operate in order to achieve an optimal result. In the prisoner's dilemma, two criminals (criminal A and criminal B) have been apprehended by the authorities for a jointly committed robbery. Prohibited from co-operating, both criminals need to make their own decisions about whether to confess their crime or not without knowing the other's decision. If one criminal confesses the crime to the authorities and the other does not, the criminal that confesses can go free as a reward, but the one who does not will be sentenced to two years in prison. If both criminals confess to the crime, they will both receive reduced (one-year) sentences. If both criminals deny their crime, they will both be held in the prison as suspects for six months. So independently, without communication, each criminal will confess his crime, thereby minimising his expected jail time to one year. However, if they could conspire to both deny their crime, they would be able to reduce both of their prison sentences to just six months. Unfortunately, the conspiracy is unstable since by knowing the other party's decision (to deny the crime), one criminal always has an incentive to free himself by double-crossing the other and confessing their crime. This is illustrated in Figure 7.3.

Similarly, in supply chain collaboration, trading partners can reduce inventory more through collaboration than they could on their own.

However, if each party makes their own production and inventory decisions, they will forgo the chance to dampen the bullwhip effect. Theoretically, the ideal solution would be to assign an omnipotent player to gather and optimise information from all the players in the supply chain, and instruct all parties on how much to order and when to order it. This party would be in a position to ensure that optimal decisions were made, while the parties would not have to share their information directly with each other.

Theoretically, the ideal solution would be to assign an omnipotent player to gather and optimise information from all the players in the supply chain, and instruct all parties on how much to order and when to order it. This party would be in a position to ensure that optimal decisions were made, while the parties would not have to share their information directly with each other.

Lack of trust and failure to share the investment, risks and benefits of integrated SCM are significant risks for its otherwise bright future. Game theory can address and resolve some of the most difficult challenges in behavioural dynamics. Future applications of game theory should include:

- dynamic games (in which player behaviour adapts to the decisions that other players make over time);
- co-operative games (in which players pool risk to improve returns for all players) and how signalling (which gives players information about the intentions of others) affects supply chain efficiency;
- screening (one player moves first without information);
- bargaining.

In the interim, supply chain relationships favour the partnership model. The transition from transaction supply chain partner to strategic supply chain partner progresses through three basic stages: first, transactional, where most interactions are data-driven; second, alliance, where the companies are engaged in one or more joint projects; and third, strategic partner, in which there is a documented mutuality of corporate goals and objectives.

Companies and individuals that excel at relationship management will exert more influence over the extended supply chain and move from transactional relationships to strategic partnerships. Because of the increasing focus on dealing with external partners, facilitation skills will be essential. Leaders should establish a governance model; establish mechanisms to communicate each others' goals and objectives; establish joint goals, objectives and metrics; share information, management talent and tools; and initiate joint *kaizen* (continuous improvement) projects.

Shifting demand and capacity

Demand is unpredictable in every industry, and demand that is unsatisfied at moments of high demand sacrifices sales. Capacity management techniques address these problems.

When building or buying capacity, companies may: first, ensure there is enough capacity to handle the peak demand; second, build capacity for average demand and shrink or stretch when needed; third, build capacity for low demand and supplement frequently. In periods of shifting demand, companies choose between chasing (building capacity ahead of demand), levelling (building capacity ahead of current demand but below expected future demand) and following (building capacity after demand has been demonstrated).

Thoresen, a Thai shipping line, doubled the number of ships in its fleet by buying ahead of the demand – and won. Given the cost of vessels (a second-hand Handymax vessel cost around $20m in 2005 before the rise in steel prices), buying ships is a major asset management decision. The management team decided to increase the fleet significantly as various signs pointed to a strong rise in its business, thus providing the company with adequate capacity to cement its market leadership on the Asia–Middle East trade route. As the price of steel soared after it purchased the ships, Thoresen was in a much stronger business position than most of its competitors, who expanded their fleets at higher price points.

However, building capacity beyond or ahead of demand is expensive and risky. So how can companies assure adequate capacity at a reasonable price when demand is fluctuating? Assuming that building capacity beyond or ahead of peak demand is an unrealistically expensive option and cutting capacity is not a problem, there are three ways to provide additional capacity during periods of peak demand: shift demand with peak period pricing; add resources during peak demand; and reduce cycle time to increase throughput.

Peak period pricing can shift demand away from the peak period by discouraging demand then. Time-based differential pricing encourages demand during a period when capacity is available and discourages it when it is not. For example, to solve daytime congestion of trucks picking up containers, the port of Los Angeles has instituted a programme called

113

PierPass that charges lower access fees at night. Shippers through the port have been doing more night and weekend deliveries as a result of the programme. Airlines also shift demand with yield pricing, but since this is commonly used in conjunction with stratifying customers into different classes, it is covered in Chapter 9. So-called yield pricing is not always easy to determine since it usually involves pricing at marginal cost for a given facility, time period or customer and many companies do not know their true marginal costs.

Augmenting capacity during peak demand is a second way to make capacity flexible while deploying a minimum level of capacity. Both FedEx and UPS do this at their Memphis and Louisville hubs, respectively. They hire students who work part-time but can extend their hours during peak periods, which are often school vacation periods for them. They ensure the students' commitment to work during the peak periods by hiring them when they enter school and sponsoring their tuition.

Reducing the cycle time that it takes for customers or orders to get through the process can also increase effective capacity. In cyclical upswings, suppliers to the oil and gas industry encounter extending lead times due to intense demand, often driven by rising oil prices. They frequently engineer their processes to reduce the order cycle time in order to increase throughput. One American power equipment supplier does this on multiple components that its customers consider critical in their supply chains – such as motors, compressors and turbines – in order to create a competitive advantage based on superior end-to-end supply chain performance.

No matter what capacity strategy is chosen, to be successful capacity management needs to be done in close collaboration with suppliers. FMC Technologies' Kongsberg Subsea division in Norway makes production systems for the oil and gas industry. Faced with a huge increase in orders following the big rise in the price of oil in 2007 and 2008, it needed to ensure capacity from its suppliers, which had all been tapped out of capacity for the foreseeable future because of the strong demand for oil-drilling equipment. It established frame agreements with key suppliers which secured capacity and quality in exchange for a share of the relevant equipment that FMC Technologies bought.

Better forecasting, less emotion

Emotion plays a considerable role in inventory ordering decisions. Nobody wants to get caught short of product or services to sell when the demand is hot, so the natural tendency is to overorder when demand appears to be increasing. However, if five supply chain partners in succession each order 10% extra, the company farthest from the customer (usually the manufacturer) ends up with 61% extra (1.10^5).

Thus reducing the emotional bias in ordering can generate substantial efficiencies. The greater the historical accuracy of the forecasting system, the more confidence inventory planners will place in it, and therefore the less emotion and bias they are likely to inject into inventory planning decisions.

Numbers-driven forecasting methods fall into three basic categories:

- ◘ Time series methods are the simplest forecasting method, but are the least accurate. This is why investment funds consistently advise their clients that past performance of a stock does not determine its future price. Such behaviour leads to extended runs in the market and consequent overcorrection to get to the right valuations – the same problem as the bullwhip effect in the supply chain.[19]
- ◘ Causal methods are more accurate. Econometric models relate parameters such as leading indicators and underlying variables to each other with coefficients that are carefully studied and include iterative feedback loops.
- ◘ Market intelligence methods can add granular company-specific (bottom-up) information to demand, supply and inventory models. These methods are particularly useful in rapidly changing markets where day-to-day news and information may affect the market as much as the underlying fundamentals.

Risk mitigation

The bullwhip effect is when small perturbations at one end of the whip cause larger ones at the other end, so avoiding the perturbations in the first place is of paramount importance. Therefore, reducing the risk of supply disruptions is crucial if synchronisation supply chain strategy is to be successful.

To achieve effective supply chain risk management processes, it is necessary to take all or whichever steps are relevant from the following seven:[20]

1 Classify, measure and monitor risk. Understand the stakes, using real examples of what has happened and what could happen. Map the risks and their severity.
2 Make a risk management plan. Define management principles and a process for dealing with the key risks, including goals, objectives and

Supply chain risk factors 7.4

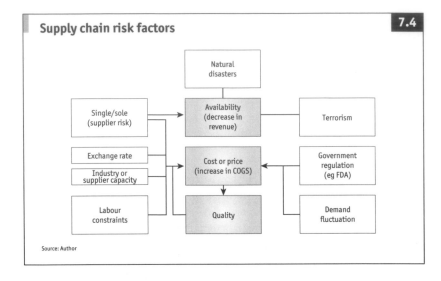

Source: Author

formalised organisational accountability for risk management. Establish risk management metrics and triggers that should stimulate action by managers.

3 Avoid risk by reducing consumption or passing costs on to customers.
4 Hedge risk by buying options (or similar forward contracts) or insurance, or by studying and anticipating market conditions.
5 Diversify risk by buying from more suppliers and dual sourcing.
6 Minimise risk by buying in advance at the current price and/or signing long-term contracts at forecast rates.
7 Mitigate the severity of potential disruption and disasters through contingency planning.

Classify, measure and monitor risk
Classify risk
Risks that could affect the supply chain come from a wide range of sources. Terrorism and natural disasters can lead to physical and property damage, and hence an inability to function. Changes in the regulatory framework can affect costs and prices, as shippers and carriers implement new compliance measures. Volatile demand can be hard to accommodate or may cause cyclical overcorrections, as happens frequently in oil and gas markets. Labour strikes can shut down capacity, as happens repeatedly in the transport sector in France. Reliance on single suppliers can restrict availability, drive up prices or limit innovation. Price risk

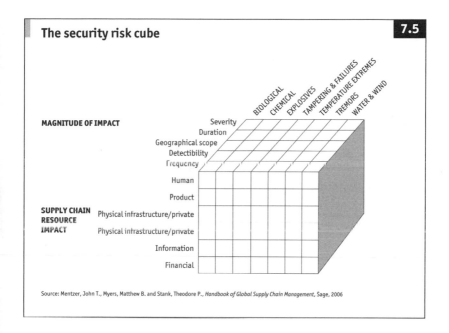

The security risk cube **7.5**

Source: Mentzer, John T., Myers, Matthew B. and Stank, Theodore P., *Handbook of Global Supply Chain Management*, Sage, 2006

– including interest rate risk, commodity price risk and exchange-rate risk – can increase the cost of goods sold.

Demand risk, the risk that demand will change unexpectedly, is increasing, as products have shorter life-cycles and more competition is resulting in more new or updated products. In addition, increases in sales promotions and sales incentives are making it more difficult to manage reorder quantities for consistent replenishment.

Most supply chain risk factors (see Figure 7.4) have a direct impact on cost or price. Some of them can decrease availability, which may affect revenue. Revenue increases are not always good, especially if they are being driven by rising input prices: both carriers and shippers got squeezed by rising fuel costs on the US–Asia container shipping lane in 2008. Cost increases can affect quality, as producers look to substitute materials for ones whose price has risen, and may opt for a less expensive but lower-quality input – for example, auto manufacturers substituting plastic for metal or vinyl dashboards.

Mentzer has elaborated on the terrorism and natural disaster risks cited above in a "security risk cube" that classifies risks (Figure 7.5).

Supply chain risk can be exacerbated by a wide number of company-specific factors. Highly specialised materials are more prone to price volatility since there are narrower markets for them. Long supply chains are more prone to the risk of congestion (which is a form of supplier capacity constraint) and, unless it is removed by hedging or fixed-price contracts, to price risk because of the time that passes between shipment and receipt of goods.

Internal processes can make matters worse. Inflexible organisations take longer to respond, during which time prices may increase, materials may become more difficult to obtain, or quality problems may make their way through the supply chain to an unhappy customer. Flawed information systems or poor data quality make it difficult or impossible to be aware of supply chain problems. Managers at many large organisations do not have access to their prices, costs and logistical or production information. Finally, unusual customer sensitivity to price, quality or availability can make adjusting to supply chain disruptions more difficult.

Lack of transparency in internal processes is a risk that is specifically addressed by the Sarbanes-Oxley Act in the United States and the European Union (EU) Company Law Directive in Europe. Although Sarbanes-Oxley leaves a lot of details unspecified, which has irked many companies, experts and lawyers since its inception, several supply chain aspects are important to note. For example, the act addresses the risk of invalid or improper accounting for inventory write-offs, price escalations in contracts, the promptness of posting of material acquisitions and transfers, lease obligations and contingent contractual obligations with suppliers (such as shared investment of shared risk clauses).

Because of the failure of risk management that contributed to the global financial and economic crisis that erupted in 2008, subsequent legislation has encouraged companies to pay more attention to internal process risk. Under the Sarbanes-Oxley Act, long-term contracts and vendor-managed inventory (VMI) are both technically reportable off-balance-sheet transactions.

Measure risk

At a simple level, risk can be measured in categorical terms. Is the risk present or not (yes/no)? At a more complex level, ratings can capture a lot of the factors in an intuitive sense. The Economist Intelligence Unit and other organisations rate countries' political and economic risk, and some consulting firms measure supplier risk in this way.

Risk can be measured in terms of probabilities (see Figure 7.6). This approach is well-suited to relatively low probability events with high pay-offs, for example drilling for oil.

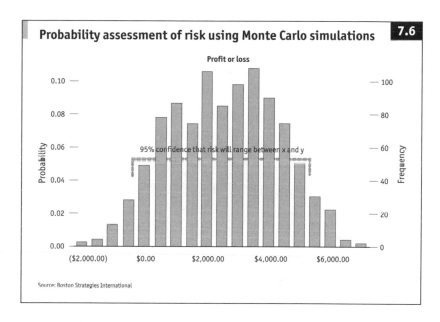

Probability assessment of risk using Monte Carlo simulations 7.6

Source: Boston Strategies International

Risk is the possibility of an undesirable outcome, but there is always some risk, and no organisation will or should try to eliminate all of it, not least because of the insurance cost of so doing. If the oil firms were totally risk-averse, they would never drill for oil. Actuaries often quantify the odds that risky events will happen by using statistical indices. Consultants often use risk models to compare chances with the associated costs, for example the costs of exploration against the chance of a positive payoff, or the cost of avoidance or mitigation against the chance of a negative outcome.

Monitor risk
To manage risk, it needs to be transparent. Intelligence should be gathered at three levels: company-specific supply chain partners; industry-specific supply chain bottlenecks and opportunities; and economic opportunities and risks.

Trading partner data should be managed in a database that is used to score and select suppliers based on ratings, qualifications, performance history, financials, and records of personal interactions and contract negotiations.

Industry data should be monitored to identify risk factors and deal with them. Ongoing monitoring should include capacity utilisation and bottlenecks, order lead time, cost structures, productivity, prices and regulatory developments.

Economic data should be monitored to identify the potential for new markets and for broad-based changes in the composition of demand. Such data should include demand, growth rates, regional conditions, risk factors and the price of broad-based cross-industry input costs such as energy.

Although early warning systems would not have prevented the massive 2004 Indian Ocean earthquake and subsequent tsunami, they could have allowed enough time for people to seek higher ground. This might have saved some of the 225,000 people who died in the disaster.

The value of monitoring supply chain risk is exemplified by the case of a fire in a Mexican microchip plant that supplied both Nokia and Ericsson. The fire, which occurred in 2000, ruined thousands of chips destined for use in mobile phones built by Nokia and Ericsson. Nokia, which had a close relationship with the supplier, noticed the disruption in inbound supply immediately and used top management connections to assure its share of the limited supply of good microchips coming from the Mexican plant. In contrast, Ericsson did not notice the disruption until the delays halted its production, which cost the company $400m of sales, according to its claim in a subsequent lawsuit.[21]

Saudi Aramco monitors about 50 detailed supply markets on a continuous basis to detect emerging conditions that could affect its production capability and its costs. It has developed metrics and models of suppliers, market trends, costs and prices, and technological developments. Early warning systems trigger management involvement based on the severity and timeframe in which an incident may occur.

Make a risk management plan

In conjunction with the business and marketing plans, or other planning process, companies should address risk management and have a plan for measuring, monitoring and executing it. Hasbro, an American toymaker, is one company that has developed an extensive plan for managing and mitigating supply chain risk. The plan articulates the potential dangers and their severity, sets goals and objectives for the risk management programme, and designates a programme leader. It recognises the importance of working collaboratively with suppliers to be successful, and has a budget sufficient for the development of databases (for example, of incidents and risks), tools (for example, risk modelling) and staff (training).

The plan should address specific action needed in order to conform with legislation such as the Sarbanes-Oxley Act.

Avoid risk by identifying substitutes or passing on costs

One way to mitigate the risk of availability or rising costs is to substitute products or services with alternatives. Because of a diminishing supply of barite, a mineral used in drilling for oil, many oil companies shifted to a less pure and less expensive grade of barite in their drilling fluids. The cost of the extra quantities which they had to use was more than offset by the lower price.

Another way to deal with rising prices is to pass them on to the next party in the supply chain. To analyse the best strategies for purchasing energy following a spike in prices, Boston Strategies International simulated the results that a heavy manufacturer and a retailer would have had using each strategy for oil and natural gas. The analysis took into account the actual energy cost and forecast data, the financial and inventory carrying cost of advance energy purchases, the lost sales that companies sustain by passing on price increases, and the increase in sales they would realise from reducing prices. The results showed that adding an energy surcharge resulted in a cost-neutral position, since cost increases were passed through when they occurred and retracted when they went away. However, embedding the cost increase in the base price created a potentially rich profit centre. It not only shielded buyers from price increases but also resulted in windfall gains as energy prices subsequently declined.

Hedge risk

Buyers of long lead-time, expensive items such as capital equipment or multi-year services contracts such as drilling rig construction are highly exposed to changes in prices that affect their revenue and their costs over the period of the contract.

One strategy for managing risk under these circumstances is to agree on fixed prices in advance. However, if the underlying prices are volatile, the supplier is unlikely to agree to a fixed-price contract. For example, on a contract for steel pipe two years in the future, few suppliers may want to commit to a price. Or they may agree, but at a large price premium to cover the risk that the price would escalate significantly over the two year timeframe.

An alternative strategy is to hedge the risk by making financial contracts of equal value. If the commodity in question is traded on an exchange, there may be swaps, options and collars available. A swap provides a one-for-one hedge: if the price of the indexed commodity rises during the contract period, the buyer receives the difference, and vice versa. A call option has a strike price. If the buyer calls the option at the strike price, his hedge is over. If he does not exercise the call option, he receives the difference between the strike price and the market price. A collar has a put and a call strike price: if the price is below the put price, the buyer must pay extra if he still wants the floor price; and if the price is above the call price, he receives the extra amount between the call price and the market price.

Diversify risk

Diversification of risk is a common strategy in financial management: holding a variety of investments minimises the risk that any one of them will decrease in value, and often some will rise while others fall, effectively balancing out the swings.

One of the most relevant applications of risk diversification in SCM is choosing how many suppliers of any particular product or service to have. Having too many suppliers means none of them can achieve economies of scale, given their smaller volumes. However, it does provide assurance in case one or more of them experiences difficulty. Since Asian sourcing became popular in the early 2000s, many buyers have had to choose between a low-cost distant supplier with unreliable lead times and sporadic quality problems, and a high-cost nearby supplier with high prices and reliable delivery. Some companies have responded by using some of both. The solution is called dual sourcing.

Companies like Blyth, a distributor of consumer goods for the home, dual source in Asia and the United States. Blyth dual sources in order to have the flexibility to respond rapidly to demand shifts in the United States.[22]

The decision whether or not to single source remains an issue, as companies increasingly consolidate their supply base. Sometimes there is no choice but to go with a single supplier. A leading US medical-device manufacturer single sources many of its original equipment manufacturer (OEM) buys because of long development lead times and stringent technical requirements. Upfront tooling is sometimes so costly that having two suppliers is prohibitive, as is the case at a US manufacturer of semiconductor assemblies. Appearance considerations, batch specifications, mixing and other technical or customer-driven constraints sometimes force the issue. Suppliers may have patent protection or proprietary designs that cannot be duplicated.

Most companies avoid single sourcing where possible, or at least structure single-sourced contracts carefully, because of the various potential risks of being held captive, including price gouging; quality problems at a sole manufacturing site; product unavailability due to a fire, flood or other natural disaster; equipment unavailability during peak periods; and supplier financial difficulties.

Minimise risk

Buyers can minimise risk by buying in advance at the current price and/or signing long-term contracts. For example, Saudi Aramco bought years worth of drill pipe in advance to avoid anticipated shortages and price hikes. Unisys, a US-based systems integration and IT infrastructure consulting company, in one of the longer contracts executed to ensure supplies at a low cost, signed a nine-year contract for packaging to amortise a large upfront investment. Buying in advance takes capital, however, and while it locks in guaranteed rates, buyers could be worse off in later years if the market price decreases.

Mitigate potential disruption

All the preventative measures in the world make no difference once disaster strikes, and when it does, mitigation and recovery efforts are what counts. Experts' recommendations for best practices for guarding against supply chain disruption include screening cargo, communicating frequently with suppliers and using available technologies to enhance visibility to shipments en route.[23]

Lean supply chain operations help mitigate the adverse effects of disasters. A rationalised SKU base will limit damage by reducing the speed of response. Postponement will limit the damage by ensuring that the average value of the product in the pipeline is of less value than if inventory were kept in finished goods form. Increased communication between partners will maximise the chance of downtime as a result of any threat, and help get security efforts up and running quicker once the decision is made to deploy them.

Beretta: synchronisation strategy

Founded in 1500, according to legend, Beretta is the oldest active gun manufacturer in the world. With 3,000 employees and revenues of €600m ($800m), it is a world leader in such small firearms as pistols, shotguns and rifles, under brands such as Beretta, Benelli, Franchi, Burris, Sako, Tikka, Uberti, Stoeger and MDS. Its headquarters are in Valtrompia, Italy, the largest specialised firearms hub in the world. With its constellation of artisans and specialised micro suppliers, it is to guns what Toyota City or Detroit is to the automotive industry.

The product is relatively simple compared with, say, an automobile: auto manufacturers regularly have thousands of components, whereas firearms have no more than 100 parts. Moreover, the technology has remained essentially unchanged since the 1800s, according to Massimo Marchi, director of supply chain and IT.

If the product is so simple, why is managing its supply chain a challenge? First, the production and transportation lead time is 5–12 months to ensure the necessary quality, performance and aesthetic refinement, so it has to make to stock instead of make to order. The company purchases steel for the barrel and the frame, then hammers the steel via a continuous processing machine in a time-consuming and costly process called cold hammering, which involves hammering sections of the inside and the outside of the barrel 1mm at a time without heat. The laborious process makes the barrels highly shock-resistant. In addition, premium-grade products involve manual fitting and gold inlaying, chisel techniques and artistic engraving.

Second, more than 15 suppliers and affiliates are involved in the production process. Beretta owns distributors in more than 15 countries and manufacturers in Italy, Spain, Finland, Turkey and the United States.

Third, firearms manufacture is highly regulated, so process improvement is subject to regulatory scrutiny. Traceability requirements make standardisation of semi-finished components, final customisation, postponement and cross-docking more complex than in less regulated industries.

Fourth, until recently there were wide differences between the affiliates' inventory management processes. Each company had different barcodes and inventory levels were not available across companies. Furthermore, when they were available, the standard operating definitions were different, so available inventory might not mean the same thing for any two companies.

Lastly, paperwork was in each company's local language; for example, many invoices were in Finnish, which was not understandable to the other companies.

Beretta's synchronisation efforts started with Beretta in the United States, followed by its European affiliates. It consisted of five parts:

1 **Standard operating definitions** of supply chain terminology, including cross-references between product codes. English translations were added to each document worldwide.
2 **An internet-enabled application** to centralise order fulfilment information from each company's enterprise resource planning (ERP) system. The system gathers information on customer orders, sales trends, shipments, delivery schedules and inventory throughout the supply chain, as well as SKU listings and images

of products and components. Because it is centralised, the company can cross-reference barcodes and factories, and each company can look at the system in its own language.

3 **An advanced production scheduling tool** that is linked to the materials requirements planning and master production scheduling tools of its sister companies.

4 **A configurator** to create new product configurations. Orders go directly from the configurator, which has the capability to define 800,000 SKUs – from the trigger to finishes – for production without involving the engineering department.

5 **Executive S&OP meetings** involving monthly videoconferences with supply chain partners and the maintenance of five aggregate levels, comprising 8,000 SKUs. The group defines a consensus forecast on a rolling 12–18-month time horizon.

With all this information available, each distributor can complete the integration of the supply chain information flow and, for example, calculate an available to promise (ATP) date (the date by which the company knows that it can commit delivery, given all the constraints in its sourcing, production and distribution operations) for its customers.

The main benefits of the supply chain planning system have been a reduction in inventory and increases in service levels and fill rates. Historically, each small company tried to minimise inventory locally, with consequently low fill rates and a high cost of excess inventory because of the lack of risk pooling. Now the process is collaborative, and the company's supply chain meets the challenging standards set by its customers, such as Dick's Sporting Goods, Wal-Mart, Cabela's and Bass Pro.

8 Customisation: competing on customer intimacy

For the past decade and a half, companies in every industry have obsessively devoted themselves to managing the supply side of their businesses, from manufacturing through distribution and pricing. We have made enormous improvements in productivity. But opportunities and ideas to drive incremental growth are drying up ... Increasingly, companies will be forced to focus on the top line.

Peter Georgescu, chairman and CEO, Young and Rubicam,
quoted in *You Can't Shrink Your Way to Greatness* by Tom Peters, 1997

Honda's legendary after-sales service operations exemplify a customisation supply chain strategy. While the assembly line focuses on aligning many motions in sequence to deliver a reliably standard product every time, customer service is based on co-ordinating a set of unique customer interactions to deliver a one-of-a-kind product-service experience for each customer, each time.

Customisation strategy emphasises higher gross margins. Being personal increases value to individual customers, and hence brings in higher prices and profit margins.[1] Companies achieve a rapid response capability by better understanding each customer's value equation, and being able to deliver rapidly, reliably, uniquely and profitably to each customer.

Avoiding commoditisation

Customisation helps to avoid commoditisation, the real or perceived state of lack of differentiation except on price, by providing product-specific value, but there is always a finite set of customised options. Mass customisation does better by enabling flexible changeovers between customised product options, thereby eliminating excess inventory of customised product, but from the customer's point of view it still results in a finite set of options. Customerisation,[2] mass customisation combined with customer-specific targeted marketing, offers mass customised products via personalised sales channels such as custom websites. At the extreme, personalisation provides each customer with a unique experience.

Pure non-goods businesses offer fantastic examples of personalisation even if they do not all have supply chains. Google and other search engines and internet service providers offer customised browsers that allow the user to configure the source of their information. For instance, users can view headlines from *The Economist*, the *New York Times*, CNN and Reuters simultaneously and they are updated in real time. Plaxo and other social networking services such as Facebook, LinkedIn, Twitter and Flickr allow people to share information with people they know and meet people through each other's personal networks, and each application is eminently personalisable. Microsoft operating systems learn the users' most frequently accessed programs and provide quicker access to them, thus providing a personalised experience without customers even knowing that the experience is personalised.

Some products facilitate a high degree of personalisation by providing the platform for configurable software, as in the case of the downloadable applications available on mobile phones or personal digital assistants (PDAs). Doug Macmillan of Nokia explains:[3]

> *Personalisation used to be a custom colour case, then a custom ringtone, then the caller's picture instead of a caller-ID phone number, then the sound file of [the user's] children, and now it is moving toward new enabling technologies that allow developers to download content from anywhere.*

Nokia is also offering location-based services that use global positioning systems (GPS) and radio frequency identification (RFID) tags to enable the user's friends and family to track his or her movements through a website. BlackBerry PDAs are also totally configurable, and the more users configure them, the more useful they become.

Mixed product-service businesses can use supply chain management (SCM) to deliver the special customer experience. Manufacturers deliver customisation and personalisation through value-added services that relate to the product, for example:

- customer-specific delivery conditions;
- customised maintenance and repair programmes and interactions;
- customised or personalised value-added services such as warranties and financing;
- customer-specific outsourced services such as integrated supply, where the supplier provides dedicated onsite support.

Success factors

There are five requirements for any customisation supply chain strategy to succeed: customisation, flexibility, intimacy, convenience and speed. These ensure unique value to the customer, and at the same time they provide repeatability and an economically viable execution of the strategy:[4]

- Customisation – the experience must be unique to each customer.
- Flexibility – the personalised nature of the experience must adapt to the changing needs of the customer and the environment, including product configuration and flexible delivery capability.[5]
- Intimacy – the customer must feel that he or she is getting something special, and it must increase the brand awareness.
- Convenience – the customisation aspect must not be a burden on the customer and is ideally invisible.
- Speed – delivery must be fast; the customer should not have to wait longer for a personalised solution than for a normal purchase.

Honda: customer focus

American Honda Motor Co's demand-driven philosophy allows it to flexibly match production to customer demand. Its flexible manufacturing systems allow it to rapidly change production to meet current demand. Manufacturing plants can totally change their product mix in 24 hours if necessary to accommodate shifting demand patterns.

Honda targets an average transit time of less than nine days from assignment to delivery of vehicles, compared with an industry standard of 24 days. It achieves this target by working closely with its transportation partners and placing vehicles in 35 strategic locations. The distribution network allows for high utilisation of rail and truck transport.

The parts division has ten strategically placed warehouses that supply the facing dealerships with replacement parts. The standard for parts supply is two days or less from receipt of order, and 95% of parts are delivered to dealers within 24 hours.

Performance advantages

Companies that follow a customisation supply chain strategy have higher margins than those that do not. McDonald's, whose name may be prone to association with impersonal service more than the opposite, earned a gross margin of 36% in 2007. Starbucks, which prides itself on recognising its frequent patrons by name, earned a gross margin of 52% during the same period. In fact, a benchmark of personalising companies[6] averages 34.6% gross margin compared with 31.8% for a broad cross-section of industries and companies (see Table 8.1). In addition, survey results show that customisation-focused companies earn net profit margins of 16%, compared with 14% in other companies. The higher profits come from price premiums, higher sales volumes, cross-selling, up-selling and referrals to other customers.

Table 8.1 **Benchmark gross margins of customisation-focused companies**

Industry	Benchmark gross margin of companies with customisation focus, %
Household & personal products	63.4
Diversified financials	62.2
Software & services	59.4
Telecommunications services	42.7
Utilities	37.8
Hotels, restaurants & leisure	37.3
Energy	35.3
Technology, hardware & equipment	34.6
Materials	31.1
Transportation	28.5
Capital goods	25.5
Food & drug retailing	18.8
Insurance	10.1
Average	**34.6**

Source: Boston Strategies International, based on an analysis of data from Thomson Reuters and Boston Strategies International's 2008 supply chain performance benchmark study

They also have more satisfied customers than those that do not. In a 2008 survey, companies that followed a customisation strategy reported 79% overall customer satisfaction, compared with those that did not, which reported 75% overall customer satisfaction. Companies that pursue a customisation supply chain strategy get 15% more customer mindshare, which may be defined as the presence of the brand in the mind of the customer, than those that do not.

How do they do it? They are more focused on meeting the customer's delivery schedule. They make the customer's requested delivery date 84% of the time, compared with 81% for the companies that are not trying to personalise. They are much more flexible, able to increase output by 20% more than twice as fast as those that follow rationalisation or synchronisation strategies.

Elements of customisation strategy

Companies can use the supply chain to realise the major elements of customisation strategy:

- Control of the customer relationship
- Value analysis
- Customer knowledge management
- Linking the customer data to all interactions
- Customer profitability management
- Mass customisation
- Available to promise/on-demand availability
- Personal interactions
- Design for configurability
- Lifetime services

Control of the customer relationship

Control of the customer interface is critical to executing customisation-based supply chain strategies. Companies often choose to outsource customer call centres, which are one of the most frequently outsourced activities. However, many companies took them back in-house after offshore customer service representatives failed to deliver the expected levels of quality and service. Netflix, a US online movie distributor, runs a 24-hour, seven days a week customer call centre in Oregon rather than offshore, so that it can stay close to its customers. Road Runner Sports, a US distributor of running shoes, does not plan to shift its call centre to India for this reason. "[Customer service] needs to be so well-executed that you can't get it overseas. You can't fool Americans on this," says Mike Gotfredson, president. Dreams, a UK mattress retailer, keeps control over its delivery personnel even though it would be less costly to outsource them, because it values the control over the customer interface that this provides. Customer "touch-points", interfaces between company representatives and customers, are strategically valuable and needed to gain and maintain control of the customer relationship, which is in turn needed to execute a customisation strategy.

Whether to go through a value-added reseller (VAR) or a distributor – that is, which distribution channel to serve – is also an important decision that affects the ownership of the customer relationship. The company that serves the customer is the one to collect data on every transaction, and therefore has the ability to mine that data to better understand the customer and offer more relevant and higher-margin products and services. Dunhill, a luxury brand, is taking more ownership of its retail supply chain through both increased ownership of retail outlets and enhanced collaboration with the retailers to better monitor the moment of customer interaction.

For some companies, the channel decision will be a strategic one: all or nothing. Others may decide to split the business. Deciding how much revenue to put through distributors – in other words, how much value to sacrifice for what is usually easier revenue – can require analysis. Since the decision hinges on risk and return – the risk of not being able to sell direct as against the lower return from selling to an indirect partner – decision tools such as real options may be used to determine the optimum split.[7]

Value analysis

Some may describe value analysis in terms of the voice of the customer. Regardless of the name, understanding the customer's underlying needs is central to avoiding commoditisation and moving up into premium segments of the market. Customisation-focused companies devote more than three times as many resources to value analysis as those that focus on other supply chain strategies.

Value analysis segments customers based on their preferences, sometimes at the broad level and often at the detailed (feature or attribute) level. It presupposes that the marketing department has segmented the customer base. It also assumes that there is a mechanism, usually through the sales force, to gather data on customer transactions and interactions, for which a direct relationship with the customer is often needed.

Quality function deployment

There are many tools for structuring value analysis, including segmentation tools such as cluster analysis and quantitative market research tools such as conjoint analysis. Quality function deployment and its hallmark

The house of quality 8.1

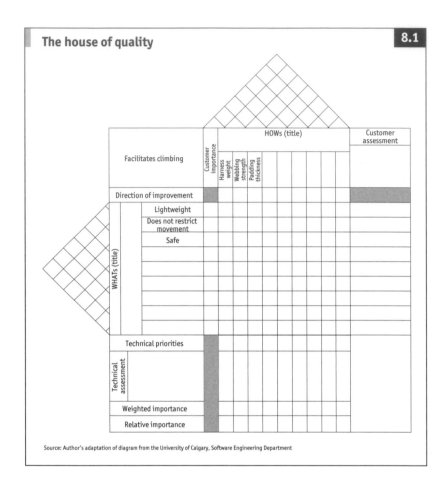

Source: Author's adaptation of diagram from the University of Calgary, Software Engineering Department

diagram, "the house of quality" (see Figure 8.1), are useful because they are easy to understand and adaptable to most products and services. The product characteristics are listed across the top and the potential dimensions for improvement are listed down the side. The strength of the interrelationship between the two goes in the grid, and the strength of the relationship between the product characteristics and between the potential dimensions for improvement is marked in the diagonal grids. Sometimes space is left at the right and/or at the bottom for comments and action plans.

The makers of the film *Jurassic Park* used a diagram of the house of quality to help design a more lifelike model of a dinosaur than had never been used before. The dinosaur needed to breathe, make facial expressions and flare its nostrils, for example. Quality function deployment was used to get the dinosaur ready for prime time.

Customer knowledge management

Customer knowledge management, as used here, is the gathering and use of customer data to enrich and enhance the delivery of the product or service on a customer-specific basis. It is tightly related to customer relationship management (CRM), which is essentially about differentiating between customers and treating each one differently.

CRM's objectives are to enable the customer management process. US companies lose half their customers every five years, according to Donald Peppers and Martha Rogers.[8] The prescription is a customer relationship management process which, according to Roger Baran,[9] a CRM expert, involves ten steps: identifying prospects, acquiring customers, developing customers, cross-selling, up-selling, managing migration, servicing, retaining, increasing loyalty and winning back defectors.

Gathering data on customers, their behaviour and their interactions with the company is the first step in CRM. To gather data, customers must first be identifiable and have a retrievable data record, which is not always the case. For example, if they have been inactive recently, their data record may be inaccurate or purged from the customer database.

A US drugstore, CVS/pharmacy, gathers information through its ExtraCare loyalty card as customers shop. The loyalty card is structured so the buyers benefit: they get a 2% rebate and $1 back for every two prescriptions filled when they spend a minimum quarterly amount. But CVS benefits as well by having access to customer-specific data, from which it can precisely – individually – target coupons, discounts and promotions.

A European department store, Galeries Lafayette, has a sister company that offers loyalty cards. Because it has proprietary access to the data, it can mine the data for customer-specific purchases and purchase patterns. By correlating the information across family members who have cards, it can even predict the buying habits of one family member (say, a daughter) based on the buying habits of another (say, her mother) and use that information to develop special promotions.[10] Tesco, Sainsbury and Marks & Spencer are not blind to the potential and introduced loyalty cards; Tesco spent £1 billion in cash giveaways between 1995 and 2002 on the programme, and it claims to have increased profits by 100 times that.[11]

Netflix uses its online ordering system and back-end data mining to compile extremely detailed knowledge of individual customers' preferences. It uses that information to determine customer priorities in fulfilment operations, so as to achieve a 95% fill rate on next-day deliveries and simultaneously make sure that customers who order different kinds of movies, from new releases to old classics, get equitable treatment despite variations in stock availability.

Customer data management in business-to-business environments is equally important. Sales force automation (SFA) software helps gather and analyse contact and correspondence history.

Privacy issues are a substantial concern in customer data-gathering. Permission-based marketing has gained popularity as a way of ensuring that customers feel they benefit from the process rather than are abused by it. By using opt-in and opt-out provisions, customers have a say in their own involvement.

Because the highest-quality customer data are often gathered through a company representative who delivers the last article of the supply chain to the customer (such as the airline ticket, the box of shoes at the store, the package with the purchase inside), the supply chain should play a critical role in value analysis. The individuals who touch the customer should be involved in the analysis of the data to improve the delivery mechanism, which inevitably involves stepping back in the supply chain to remedy problems.

Data mining

Fair Isaac is a US-based services firm that specialises in customer data enrichment and analysis for retailers. It gathers customer data from all the touch-points that its customer have with their customers, cleanses it, aggregates it and enriches it with data from third-party sources. The external data pick up information such as birth dates and addresses (the postal code says a lot about income and demographics). Then it mines the data for patterns and priorities. One of the biggest challenges is simply aggregating the data from the customer, since such data normally come from many different sources, such as point-of-sale data from the customers' stores, call-centre calls and e-mails.

Linking the customer data to transactions

The information is good only if it enhances the customer's experience and the customer increases his sales with the company. For that to happen, the company must link the customer-specific data to all transactions that the customer makes with the company.

Ahold, a Dutch supermarket chain, is experimenting with "smart carts" that have RFID chips and electronic displays. Based on the customer's location in the aisle, the display can project personalised announcements (for example, "Are you aware this product has gluten in it?"). Although early stages have not been linked to actual customer purchase history and/or demographic data, this can be imagined as part of an ultimately very different shopping experience.

Depending on the data, the linkage may or may not be transparent to the customer. A guest staying at the Ritz Carlton who asks for a hypo-allergenic pillow will never have to ask for it again. The Ritz does not even tell the guest that it has memorised the preference; it gives the guest the same pillow next time he or she stays there.[17]

Linking customer data to transactions involves technology that collects data on events throughout the supply chain. RFID, for example, can be used to link customer-specific data to real-time transactions, inventory availability and order processing. The steel shopping cart of today will be dwarfed by the intelligence of the data system, just as the engines of most cars today have become more about electronics than about pistons.

Customer profitability management

Since a customisation supply chain strategy is about increasing margins, an important element is the ability to know the profitability of each customer. Companies that do this usually divide the customers into tiers – for example A, B and C customers, with A customers being the highly profitable ones. For example, Brown Shoe, maker of brands such as Buster Brown, Naturalizer and Dr Scholls, uses software called ProfitLogic to determine the profitability of various products to help it drive price decisions that lead to higher margins. Some companies go further and quantify customers' lifetime value: the amount they will contribute if the company can retain them indefinitely.

Customer-specific costing

To ascertain customer profitability, customer cost and customer revenue are needed, but most companies' cost accounting systems are not sophisticated enough to allow accurate cost accounting by customer.

For consumer goods, cost allocation is less of an issue since the fixed costs get spread across large quantities of items. However, in industrial environments and capital-intensive plant environments, the methods used to allocate fixed cost often determine whether customers are considered profitable or loss-making. A particular challenge is determining which customers should bear the burden of unutilised or under-utilised capacity. In a plant operating at 70% capacity utilisation, there is a lot of overhead allocation to be done, and the method of allocation can significantly affect customer profitability results.

Therefore, customer-specific or activity-based costing, a process of apportioning costs based on the frequency, volume or cost of usage, is usually the way the cost of the fixed assets is allocated. But the methodology is complex and the process can be challenging. The data are not always available and may be fragmented between multiple departments, and stakeholders may have conflicting interests in the outcome. For example, the sales department might want to shed a high-volume, low-margin customer that loses money to make room for a new sale if it is compensated on profit, but the plant management might want to keep the customer if it is measured according to the volume produced. Therefore, a consultant is frequently involved in activity-based costing exercises.

Customer-specific pricing approaches
Differential classes of service
American Airlines created differential classes of seats for full-fare and for discount passengers and put People Express, a budget airline, out of business by offering a similarly priced alternative without sacrificing revenue – indeed, it actually increased it. One of the early concerns about the approach was that by creating two classes of seats, the full-fare customers would buy discount seats instead, thereby cannibalising the revenue. However, the airline limited this risk by making the full-fare seats available only during weekdays, when most business travel takes place. American Airlines' Sabre business unit was so successful that Sabre sold its system to other airlines, and Sabre has flourished as a stand-alone company operating in other industries in addition to air travel. In recent years, differential classes of service have become an accepted pricing approach across many industries such as hotels and online media.[13]

Demand management
Demand management (also called yield pricing) is the process of adjusting pricing to influence demand and thereby increase sales and margins. In periods of excess demand, a high price encourages customers to seek non-peak periods. In periods of low demand, a low price encourages customers to book slots, typically anywhere above marginal cost. The combination of category profitability management, yield pricing and customer data can be used to offer timed and targeted promotions to individual customers.

Manufacturers have been adopting yield management pricing approaches, techniques and software in order to shed obsolete inventory and control demand during successful new product launches or seasonal surges. Companies that have implemented yield management pricing include Emerson, Honeywell, Sun, Hewlett-Packard, Seagate, Owens-Corning, Grainger, Eastman Chemical, Georgia-Pacific and British Petroleum.[14] Wal-Mart uses a form of yield management when it updates its prices in real time based on demand patterns observed through its worldwide system of point-of-sale scanners.

Load time and other order criteria can be used in addition to or instead of price to stimulate sales or to shift sales from one product to another. For example, if laptops with the latest processor are not available, customers may opt to buy a slightly older model with a less powerful processor for less money.

Revenue management

Revenue management goes a step beyond demand management by determining the profitability of individual customers and transactions before committing to an order. Software computes the marginal cost of capacity and the marginal revenue that would be earned by the transaction and if the marginal revenue exceeds the marginal cost, it proceeds with the transaction. If the profit margin is below a predetermined threshold, it calculates the probability that another order will arrive that is more profitable. And if there is not enough capacity to fill the order or if the customer is not willing to pay a profit-making price, it directs the customer service agent to ask if customers could defer the commit date, effectively preserving orders that otherwise might have been lost.

In the business-to-business environment, air cargo carriers use software to decide whether or not to accept off-contract shipments. In the business-to-consumer environment, Travelocity, an online travel reservations system, asks the introductory question: "Are you flexible on your dates?"

Product life-cycle management (PLM) can be combined with revenue management to maximise yield over the life of the product or category. Using a form of yield pricing that is specifically related to product life-cycles, some companies lower prices at the end of the product life-cycle to clear out merchandise that is no longer profitable to keep in stock.

The ultimate goal of revenue management is for the staff who perform management analyses "to disappear", says Jamison Graff, solutions director for JDA Software, a US company. As scientific management is now simply called management, Graff sees revenue management eventually blending into the information systems of all businesses.

Mercator, the IT division of the United Arab Emirates-based Emirates Group, provides revenue management services to Emirates SkyCargo, the air cargo division of Emirates Airline.[15] It linked 19 different data systems together into one application with 31 modules. The system combines revenue planning, with capacity and cost management, and cargo rating (pricing). It also interfaces with the online reservation system and tracking and tracing systems. The system has improved response times to booking inquiries and communication with the airline. It has also helped the carrier introduce new products to market more quickly, reduced underpricing and enabled Emirates SkyCargo to look at profitability by individual freighter aircraft.

Mass customisation

As part of a growing trend towards mass customisation, companies have increasingly been customising their products and services to generate more sales, more loyalty and higher margins.

Sampo Bankas, a Lithuanian bank, trains its branch personnel to ask potential customers a sequence of questions in order to tailor financial products to their circumstances. Sales of new products to existing customers have grown sevenfold since it began the process. According to a 2007 Economist Intelligence Unit survey, nearly two-thirds of senior executives said that customisation of their products or services had resulted in "somewhat higher" or "much higher" revenues.[16]

A personalised supply chain must be capable of delivering one-off orders quickly and efficiently to many customers, so it needs to be capable of producing unusually high volume with unusual configuration flexibility. The problem is that lean – that is, efficient – supply chains and agile (flexible) supply chains are normally viewed as polar opposites. Efficient supply chains are often inflexible because they are engineered to provide a consistent throughput level, and flexible supply chains are often costly because they are built with enough capacity to handle the peak workload.

Different customers generate different demand patterns, and some companies have demonstrated a good ability to increase customers' satisfaction by tailoring service characteristics for each type of demand pattern and establishing operations to serve each one separately. For example, customers with few but large orders and long lead times are usually handled through a separate process from the one handling customers

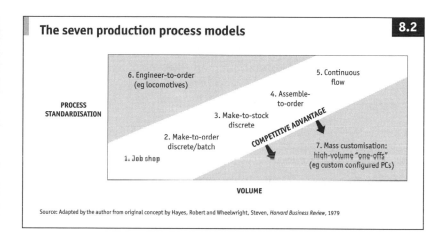

The seven production process models   8.2

PROCESS
STANDARDISATION

6. Engineer-to-order
(eg locomotives)

5. Continuous
flow

4. Assemble-
to-order

3. Make-to-stock
discrete

COMPETITIVE ADVANTAGE

2. Make-to-order
discrete/batch

1. Job shop

7. Mass customisation:
high-volume "one-offs"
(eg custom configured PCs)

VOLUME

Source: Adapted by the author from original concept by Hayes, Robert and Wheelwright, Steven, *Harvard Business Review*, 1979

with one standard order placed at a constant rate. By treating these flows differently, companies can plan production more efficiently, set different internal process expectations and meet customers' expectations more effectively. They do this by establishing different order types, terms and conditions and customising the product or service.

In conventional production operations, high production requires standardised processes. There are seven sets of processes that align revenue per order, the speed of information flow, the production process, performance measurements and a corporate culture that consistently satisfies customer demands at minimal cost as laid out in Figure 8.2:

1   **The job shop model,** for low volumes, produces a series of individual, customer-specific products or services. Each job contains information that is exchanged once at the outset of the project. The objective is to satisfy the order criteria.
2   **The make-to-order (MTO) model,** for slightly higher volumes, processes a higher volume of inputs and outputs and has more standardised processes and information flows. The objective is to fulfil each order within predetermined cost, quality and lead-time parameters.
3   **The assemble-to-order (ATO) model,** also for slightly higher volumes, prefabricates components and assembles the right combination of components when an order is received. The objective is to fulfil orders rapidly and cost-efficiently.
4   **The make-to-stock (MTS) model,** for high and consistent volumes, produces products or services for consumption by multiple

customers. The product is standard or occurs in a discrete number of configurations. The objective is to replenish inventory to the target levels.

5 **The continuous flow model**, for extremely high and consistent volumes, produces a standard product without stopping. The objective is to maximise asset utilisation.

Outside the conventional relationship between volume and production organisation and offering special solutions are the following:

6 **The engineer-to-order model** produces individual customer orders, but often involves complex, long lead-time products such as locomotives, aircraft and ships. The objective is to manage the order book to smooth the workload over time.

7 **The mass-customisation model**, for very high volumes, produces many varieties of the same core product or service in mixed sequence. The objective is to produce the right number of items of the right configurations within the target lead time.

Dell popularised the configurability of computers and electronic equipment during the ordering process. Since then, other companies have established web-based ordering interfaces that allow customers to easily custom-order their product.

Jabil Circuit, a US manufacturer of semiconductors, uses sales patterns by industry and customer segment to design tailored global supply chains for its customers. "We use a volume-mix matrix," says Courtney Ryan, senior vice-president of global supply chain. By dividing its customer orders into quadrants (high-volume low-mix, high-volume high-mix, low-volume low-mix and low-volume high-mix), it has been able to treat each type of flow differently and achieve a better service for all of them. For example, for high-volume low-mix products it sources at low cost and routes production in a straight line to keep material moving quickly. For low-volume high-mix products, it sources opportunistically and organises its assembly in a square, so that workers at every station can access material at every other station. Jabil's revenues grew by 20% per year between 2004 and 2008.

Well-known companies regularly adjust their production strategies in search of the optimal positioning on this chart, as these two examples show:

- Harley Davidson, an American motorcycle manufacturer, moved from a MTS to a mass-customisation operations model. The move allowed it to tap into latent customer satisfaction enough to increase the market for motorcycles. Harley-Davidson's revenue increased by 11% per year on average from 2001 to 2005 in a market that most people thought was mature in the 1960s.
- General Motors failed to move from a high-volume low-mix MTS model to a high-volume high-mix mass-customisation model while attempting to become competitive with the Japanese production system that had been popularised by Toyota.

Modularisation

Modularisation and postponement, which were introduced in Chapter 7, are essential tools in achieving mass customised products. Don Peppers says:[17]

> For agile manufacturers that wish to become continuous inventors, the path is clear. It begins by embracing the principles of mass customisation.

Modular design, also called component modularity, is a critical element of mass customisation because it enables people to customise at minimal cost. This is especially feasible for software because, as Peppers succinctly explains, "anything that can be digitised can be customised". This explains why internet products have led the way in customisation. But modularisation is common in manufacturing environments as well. Kitting, the assembly of pre-prepared sets of material in a midstream process, is an example of modular production. Auto companies have assemblies and sub-assemblies ready to bolt together to speed up the production of vehicles. IKEA and The Container Store, Swedish and American home furnishing products retailers, respectively, sell modular furniture that consumers can quickly assemble and configure in whatever combinations they please.

Modularisation is also a form of postponement in which final assembly is delayed until the details of individual customers' orders are clear. For complex production sequences, anticipating the demand for SKUS at varying levels of assembly comes down to a gamble on probabilities. Electronics can consist of hundreds of parts and intermediate components. This is partly why electronic contract manufacturers (ECM) have become so dominant in this field. For complex situations,

Monte Carlo simulations (see Figure 7.6 on page 119) and "real options", a financial decision analysis tool that uses methodologies invented for financial options to make decisions about real assets, can be used to help determine the cost and benefit of varying levels of build-up.

Available to promise/on-demand availability

"Available to promise" is a term that stems from materials requirements planning (MRP) in the 1970s. It refers to the mathematical calculation of when any given order can be promised for delivery to the customer. It was originally based on algorithms that considered the production backlog and cycle time as well as the availability of raw materials and inventory of intermediate components or parts.[18]

Today, the notion of available to promise has been reborn as on-demand logistics. It is no longer the manufacturer telling the customer when the product can be available, but the customer saying when he wants it and the supplier (often of services) producing it by that time. This short lead time, instant production approach requires highly integrated logistics and a can-do customer-focused attitude. To claim on-demand availability, companies must have one-piece flow, flexible manufacturing and total quality management (TQM) in place.

IBM led the way with its on-demand supply chain strategy. According to Ian Crawford, vice-president of global procurement sourcing, IBM acts as an intermediary to link its customers to its suppliers. "This completely changes how you put the supply chain together," he said in a 2005 interview with the author. By using the principles of rapid, on-demand response, IBM was able to help a customer avert a shortage while its competitors could not obtain enough supply for the next six weeks. IBM's rapid response gave it an important competitive edge.

Personal interactions

Mass marketing is to rationalisation and synchronisation as one-on-one relationships are to personalisation strategies. If the objective is greater customer mindshare, then personal interactions are definitely the right choice. A Singapore-owned shipping line, APL, segments its customers into high-touch and low-touch customers. It addresses the high-touch customers through a direct sales force and the low-touch customers via a web portal, according to David Noe, vice-president sales and marketing at APL logistics.

For the high-touch customers, three aspects of the customer interaction are the most critical, according to a study by the Economist Intelligence

Unit: the moment of customer enquiry, service delivery and post-sale support.[19]

Personalisation is not only nice; it also helps get the job done better. Being able to get logistical questions answered quickly is important to delivering packages efficiently, and it is usually a lot easier to get a quick answer from a friend than from a stranger. That is why the most productive UPS drivers know their customers' employees at each location by name – and maybe their birthdays and a few other personal things.

Responsive delivery can make valuable connections with customers. Delivery drivers for bed specialist Dreams place a mint on the newly delivered mattress and take away the old mattress. Road Runner Sports finds out which running races its customers will be taking part in, and then calls them to find out how they did. Life Fitness, an American sports equipment manufacturer, connects with its customers during the delivery of the product. A delivery for Life Fitness often provides opportunities for interaction with the customer, by including not only a delivery, but also installation, servicing and removal of pieces of equipment from a gym. Therefore, the company plans the visits carefully.

Companies in higher-value, longer-term relationship industries such as consulting, financial services and systems integration go beyond the interaction. IBM, Siemens and other large multinationals working under multi-year contracts use relationship marketing. Baran specifies criteria for fruitful interactions in a relationship marketing setting:[20]

- individuals on the supplier and the customer side are clearly identified;
- all parties can participate in the dialogue;
- all parties want to have the dialogue;
- dialogues can be controlled by anyone in the exchange;
- there is certainty that the dialogue will result in actionable change;
- a dialogue should pick up where it last left off.

Personal interactions are critical means of gathering customer feedback that helps to up-sell, cross-sell and continuously improve the relationship. This would meet two customer relationship management[21] goals: having a high percentage of customers with more than half of their needs data collected; and having a high percentage of customers providing customer service feedback within the last year. If the staff are responsive and customer-focused, they can also contribute towards a third metric: a high percentage of customer enquiries that resolve the customer's concern at the first contact.

Document management customisation

DSTS, a spin-off of the Portuguese national postal service, is a direct-mail third-party document management service in the United States. It offers full document life-cycle management for electronic and multimedia documents through infrastructure and information management of the documents. DSTS develops personalised document programmes such as individually packaged promotional inserts for a major retailer. As an outsourced provider in the supply chain, it uses a mass-customisation process to execute personalised fulfilment for its clients.

On-demand availability

Having products and services ready when customers demand them is an important element of customisation strategy.

The Wilh. Wilhelmsen (WW) group makes about 6,500 products for the marine market, especially for the maintenance of vessels and cleaning tanks. It also provides on-board fire and rescue safety items, environmentally focused services, ship agency and logistics services. As a logistics company, its principal benefit is responsiveness, so management started from the premise that all parts should be available worldwide at any time. The problem was that the overall delivery service level was only 87–90%. After studying the issue, the company differentiated between customers and items with different frequency of demand.

"You have to differentiate," says Sten Vedi, director of supply chain, echoing one of the core principles of customisation. SCM identified key customers' "core" products based on total global demand, frequency of ordering, the number of locations they are used in, profit margins and sales. All the high-demand products are tagged in the system and are available to customers 97% of the time they are ordered. For non-core products and low-volume customers, the company looks at available stock and determines whether it can promise availability or not. It differentiates availability by customer site and location, and makes strategic items available everywhere, but others available only locally. It uses its ERP system to hold the right level of inventory of each part type in different locations to support the programme.

Design for configurability

Product design can allow customers to shape their own personal version of the product, and can even embed auto-personalisation into the working of the product.

At a simple level, a toy manufacturer can allow a child to personalise a toy by including sheets of stickers to apply wherever he or she wants. Even painting the toy is a form of personalisation.

At an intermediate level, telephony products are particularly well-suited to personalised configuration. France-based Popular Telephony manufactures and distributes electronic PBX systems that allow customers to configure their personal version of the system with hundreds of customisable features and options. Sometimes customers need assistance to learn the intricacies of the systems. Customer support like this can be viewed as an added cost, but it also represents an opportunity to interact with customers and build customer loyalty.

At an advanced level, the product can learn about the customer's usage patterns. BlackBerry's SureType feature learns the user's vocabulary based on the names and addresses in the device's address book and e-mail history.

Lifetime services

Having an intelligent product in the hands of a customer is an opportunity for enhanced loyalty through value-added subscription services. If the product has a means of gathering usage data, for example through a cookie on a computer or an RFID device on a vehicle, there is an opportunity to deepen the relationship by learning more about the customer's needs and through interactions based on actual usage history.

For example, condition monitoring can be offered as a value-added service to equipment sales from farm equipment to oilwell drill bits, because it can reduce user downtime. Deere & Company has filed a patent application to predict the failure of an in-vehicle communications network for its farm tractors. Varel, a manufacturer of oilwell drill bits, offers run and post-run analysis services.

Usage history can also serve as a springboard into more solution-based revenue models. In addition to selling jet engines, manufacturers such as Pratt & Whitney and Rolls-Royce offer turnkey solutions such as power-by-the-hour on long-term contracts.

Netflix: customisation excellence

Netflix, a US online movie distributor that gives its members access to over 100,000 DVD titles online and has a growing library of over 10,000 downloadable titles, tracks more customisation metrics than most companies, including:

- percentage of customers for which the profit margin is known;
- customer satisfaction relative to expectations for cost, delivery, quality and overall;
- percentage delivered by the time the company commits to;
- standard deviation of order cycle time;
- revenue per supply chain management employee per year.

Netflix makes personalised movie recommendations and ships more than 2m DVDs on a typical day, with delivery next day from more than 54 distribution centres to more than 95% of its 8.4m members. It also knows its competition well: almost all its employees can name the firm's top three competitors.

As well as customisation-oriented metrics, the company uses other important supply chain metrics, including:

- the percentage of obsolete or inactive inventory;
- orders entered accurately;
- shrinkage and stock accuracy;
- the average age of available metrics (in months);
- the order fulfilment cost per order;
- the percentage of perfect order fulfilments.

9 Innovation: competing on revitalisation

Innovation is a necessary response to globalisation and competitive pressure. Product life-cycles are shortening for everything from toys to mobile phones. Information technology has had a big influence on the trend, but has not been the only driver. Technology and globalisation in general have been driving faster new product introduction.

The nature of innovation is changing rapidly and reshaping industries. Product life-cycles are getting shorter, increasing the need for quick and reliable new product introduction as well as smart tools for knowing when and how to best retire products that have matured and are at the end of their life-cycles. Also, new technologies can change industry structures. The telecommunications industry has changed dramatically in response to the massive popularity of wireless communications and internet telephony, as per-minute phone service is being replaced by multimedia information, communications and entertainment services.

The traditional view of innovation has been that it starts in research & development (R&D), but competing on innovation through supply chain management means the opposite: innovation begins with the customer. The role of the supply chain is to serve as an antenna to sense customers' needs, to transmit them all the way back to R&D, and to push seductive new products back out to the customers rapidly, frequently and reliably.

Supply chains needs to be dynamic to meet the challenge. This chapter articulates a strategy for creating dynamic supply chains. The innovation stage comes after customisation because the user feedback that is gleaned through value-added services offered (see Chapter 8) on customisation can be used to create new technologies and improve existing ones. Even seemingly minor product updates and new features for existing products can be valuable to customers.

Success factors

Timing is crucial in launching new products, especially if they are seasonal. They are usually timed to be accompanied by costly promotions and advertising, and supply chain management missteps can cause physical shipments to miss advertised time windows.

The tremendous pressure for timely new product launches should not result in unwise risks, however. Sony had problems bringing its Playstation

3 (PS3) to market when it decided to use Blu Ray technology which offered higher definition and greater storage capacity, but it could not deliver half of the needed volume. Sony was forced to delay the launch.[1]

Timing is also important in pulling products out of markets when they have matured and are in decline. But gradually withdrawing them from sale requires co-ordinating on appropriate levels of maintenance inventory, as well as the management of other SKU assets after the items have gone out of active production.

Performance advantages

Companies that focus on innovation generate higher revenue growth than others, at 26% annual revenue growth over a five-year period, compared with 16% for their peer groups, for the companies ranking in the top 15

Table 9.1 **Benchmark one-year revenue growth rate of innovation-focused companies**

Industry	Benchmark one-year revenue growth rate of companies with innovation focus, %
Materials	32.5
Diversified financials	30.9
Banks	29.1
Energy	27.5
Telecommunications services	24.2
Software & services	23.7
Capital goods	22.7
Food & drug retailing	19.7
Technology, hardware & equipment	19.1
Transportation	17.5
Household & personal products	16.2
Hotels, restaurants & leisure	12.8
Insurance	10.3
Utilities	9.3
Average	**21.7**

Source: Boston Strategies International, based on an analysis of data from Thomson Reuters and Boston Strategies International's 2008 supply chain performance benchmark study

positions in Boston Consulting Group's study of the most innovative companies of 2007.[2] Another study on innovation by the Economist Intelligence Unit also showed a differential in performance.[3] The companies in this study – 3M, Bell Labs (Lucent), British Telecom, Cemex, Cisco, Dell, JetBlue, Lockheed Martin, Netflix, Procter & Gamble, UPS and Wal-Mart – grew 2.4% per year faster over a five-year period than their industry peers. Table 9.1 shows revenue growth benchmarks for companies that focus on innovation supply chain strategies in a range of industries.

Supply chain innovation strategies continually result in newer products and services by dramatically faster new product development and introduction cycle times, according to the author's 2008 analysis of survey responses from 102 companies worldwide. Innovation leaders[4] get 62% more of their sales from new products[5] by launching 55% more new products[6] in nearly half of the time that others take.[7]

Elements of the innovation supply chain strategy

How can companies best achieve innovation through SCM? Certainly, high R&D spending would seem to make a company more innovative, or vice versa. Most companies spend 2–6% of their sales on R&D (see Table 9.2).

More important than R&D spending, however, is the ability to speed a product through the design and prototype stage on through commercial

Table 9.2 **R&D as a percentage of sales, by industry group**

Industry group	R&D expense as % of sales
Discrete manufacturers	3.8–6.2
Process manufacturers	2.7–5.3
Pure service companies	2.6–4.5
Fast-moving consumer goods	2.0–3.4
Extraction	0.7–1.5
Distributors/value-added service providers	0.3–0.4
Value-added service providers	0.2–0.4
Average	**2.1–3.5**

Source: Boston Strategies International, based on an analysis of data from Thomson Reuters and Boston Strategies International databases

delivery, since this relies on the proper definition and smooth functioning of multiple processes.

A set of eight best practices leads to an innovation advantage:

- Continuous market feedback
- Concurrent product development
- Rapid and early prototyping
- Product life-cycle management (PLM)
- Early supplier involvement
- Forward branding
- Designing for the supply chain

Continuous market feedback

No matter where you are in the value chain, you will be more powerful if you know how the end-customer really feels about the product. This principle is so important that it reverberates through the supply chain. The final link in the supply chain is the customer, so establishing a feedback loop completes the chain.

Procter & Gamble (P&G), which sells through major retailers like Wal-Mart, increased its bargaining power with Wal-Mart significantly when it got a closer handle on consumers' wants and desires. A.G. Lafley, P&G's CEO, created a position called vice-president of design, innovation and strategy. Resources were focused on getting close to customers – in their bathrooms actually watching them clean. P&G created an "innovation gym" to learn how to gather rapid feedback on new product ideas. The effort helped it successfully launch Mr Clean MagicReach, a bathroom cleaner on a 4ft (just over 1m) pole.[8]

Jeff Immelt, GE's CEO, commissioned more than $5 billion in 80 initiatives under the umbrella of innovation, designed to lead the company's growth into new markets and world areas. Its newly defined creativity process starts with observing consumers while they shop, eat and take care of other daily activities. Understanding consumers' behaviour in the context of their environment is central to the innovation process.

Concurrent product development

When pitching a ball, the wind-up makes all the difference. Similarly, in product development and launch a product launch builds momentum throughout its conception, development and testing; a strong process maximises the chance of a fast and accurate pitch.

The serial model of product development takes too long for today's rapidly evolving markets. To keep products coming to market at a rapid pace, design and engineering have to work concurrently in designing the product. After the prototype has been approved for production, engineering and manufacturing should work closely to ensure a least-cost, best-manufacturing process (which is called design for manufacturing). And after that, manufacturing, logistics and distribution should work together to ensure seamless order fulfilment. Innovation-driven companies spend twice as much time in cross-functional teams as companies that do not focus on innovation.

The challenge is especially large with complex products in long supply chains. Electronics often involve many components, making the upstream processes (procurement and manufacturing) complex, and long supply chains, making the downstream processes (distribution and merchandising) complex. M&C Specialties China, a manufacturer of mobile phone components, designs products concurrently with Motorola to help speed the phones to market. Many electronics manufacturing companies set up web portals to manage the collaboration needed to ensure adequate and balanced resource allocation and inventory levels.

Rapid and early prototyping

Rapid prototyping, whereby product development organisations produce many early examples of products or services under development, speeds products to market faster than the more traditional, slower "stage-gate" process, which requires new product ideas to pass a series of go or no-go approvals at defined milestones. Like concurrent design, rapid prototyping accelerates the introduction of products, and thus also profits and margins. Companies worldwide have used rapid prototyping to secure a competitive edge in otherwise declining industries.

Nypro gained a reputation for rapid product development that was based on rapid prototyping as well as a culture of innovation and a related ability to manufacture in low-volume, high-mix operations. Nypro's rapid innovation has kept it in the leading position in its industry for the last 15 years.

Minteq, a US minerals company specialising in refractory products used for lining steelmaking furnaces, incubates custom-new refractory solutions on-site at customers' locations. A continuous evolution of customised products, each with a slightly different formulation from the other, is the essence of rapid prototyping. The company put in place a process where it solicits ideas from staff on a routine basis, then set up a committee to look at those ideas and make business priorities.

Product life-cycle management

To a marketing person, product life-cycle management (PLM) means aligning the pricing and promotions with the stages of the product's life-cycle: its introduction, growth, maturity and decline. To an IT person, PLM means a software application that is used to make engineering change orders (formal changes to the design specifications of products) and to maintain and update bills of material (BOM) that define the composition of products or services that the organisation produces. To an inventory person, it means an inventory approach that builds inventory during the growth stage and withdraws it in the decline stage.

To a supply chain expert, PLM means modulating the level of activity involved in each activity in SCM (R&D, engineering, production, logistics and customer service, for example) to suit the needs at each stage of the product life-cycle. Picture a mechanical snake of linked segments, each one rising immediately after the previous one, and then falling again, as the volume of sales rises and falls. Each functional area is like one of the segments of the snake, connected to the others and rising or falling sequentially.

Seasonal peaks and troughs are like product life-cycle stages, but much shorter, so seasonal businesses like iParty, a party supplies store, and Christmas Tree Shops, a home goods retailer, have particular challenges managing their supply chains. For them, one season is the entire life-cycle of some products. Consequently, many of their SKUs have no historical purchasing, sales or inventory performance to use as a gauge for making purchasing and logistical decisions. Three strategies can help to deal with this unpredictability: diversifying into non-seasonals to reduce the volatility; balancing the mix of SKUs so that the stability and predictability of old ones offsets the volatility and unpredictability of new ones; and applying statistical methods to reduce the forecasting errors.

The introduction of a new product usually involves pushing it to customers rather than pulling it from orders. The push supply chain is common not only in innovation-driven supply chains as part of the new product introduction cycle, but also in fast-changing industries such as fashion (sports apparel or jewellery), technology (phones or laptops) and seasonal merchandising (holiday paraphernalia), where production and inventory decisions must be made long before the customer ever sees the product.

Early supplier involvement

In the past decade there has been a transformation of conventional wisdom on relations with suppliers. Companies that had previously treated their supplier relationships as transactional and even antagonistic began to realise the benefits of making the suppliers part of their team.

While the partnerships used to be driven by cost reduction, buyers have more recently begun looking at suppliers as important innovation partners. Some have even begun expecting suppliers to participate equally in innovation, on the basis that the suppliers will benefit equally through the sales of new products. These examples demonstrate how three companies integrate their suppliers in their innovation activities:

- CLP Power, Hong Kong's major electric utility, has codified the precepts of rapid prototyping in its documented message to suppliers: "We consider our suppliers to be an integral part of our business, and believe that there are mutual benefits in working co-operatively and collaboratively using a shared vision and common goals."
- Toyota and Honda value innovation from their suppliers more than low cost, and are consequently reluctant to source from low-cost countries such as China.[9]
- Blyth, an American consumer products company, sees the long-term future of SCM as more about product innovation than about logistics. "Retailers that don't let their suppliers help them are losing out," said Bruce Crain, a senior vice-president.[10] Blyth aims to leverage supply chain management for innovation by stimulating creative collaboration with its suppliers so they add "design power, not just less expensive arms and legs".[11]

Forward branding

Forward-looking supply chain strategies seek to brand all the way to the end-customer, even if they do not control the distribution channel. Forward branding[12] can strengthen the brand image of both the supplier and the original equipment manufacturer. For example, Intel has run a campaign called "Intel Inside" for years. Consumers have come to associate Intel chips with a superior chip compared with chips from AMD or no-name suppliers. Google and other search engines use the term "Powered by Google" in their customers' websites. Bose sound systems are branded Bose in the vehicles in which they are sold, and while their owners may not be able to remember what brand of tyres is on the car or what company made the seats, they will remember that their stereo is a Bose. Forward branding creates the impression of a more innovative company in end-users' minds, which reinforces the value of following an innovation supply chain strategy. Having a strong brand image also allows these companies more flexibility to sell through parallel channels directly to the end-customer.

Designing for the supply chain

Design used to be done independently of logistics and the supply chain, and only the largest companies had packaging departments to figure out the optimal packaging specifications, stacking and nesting capabilities and vehicle load plans so as to be able to ship the most product at the least cost. However, in today's world of energy consciousness and environmental concerns, green concepts and shipping prices have necessitated forward planning. In addition, short product life-cycles make it necessary to have a standardised and repeatable design for the supply chain process.

The forward planning should consider not just physical logistics, however. An effective design-for-supply chain programme should consider the total supply chain costs, including taxes and drawbacks.

HP has had a very successful design-for-supply chain programme for its all-in-one printer. It tightened linkages between its packaging, R&D and supply chain groups. Designing for the supply chain resulted in the cube-shaped printer that is so common today. The size of the outer box is smaller nowadays, since many of the small peripherals are tucked inside the printer itself. Key parts are standardised, such as the power cord. Configuration is standardised so that the only thing that changes is the language; all other aspects are identical.[13]

Zara: innovation through supply chain management

A Spanish clothing retailer, Zara, can bring new products to market in three or four weeks by holding materials in undyed form and regularly feeding information about market demand back to its suppliers. This allows it to react quickly to changing demand patterns. When it figures out which items are the most popular, it applies the right colour and pattern to the garment and ships them to stores. Retailers that source entirely from faraway low-cost countries have to issue firm orders long in advance due to the long shipping lead times, so Zara sources from locations closer to its stores.[13]

---

10 Organising, training and developing staff

O rganisational structure should support the corporate strategy, at least according to the 1962 work of Alfred DuPont Chandler,[1] a Harvard professor of business history whose work chronicled the emergence of large industrial conglomerates in the UK, the United States and Germany. Until recently, ambiguity concerning the definition and scope of supply chain management (SCM) created a challenge for business leaders. To the extent that it is unclear whether functions such as procurement are within SCM or separate from it, it is difficult to decide whether they should be stand-alone departments or part of an integrated SCM group.

Designing supply chain organisation
During the evolution from rationalisation through synchronisation, customisation and innovation, supply chain organisation must adapt to the requirements of each stage of evolution: first, functional; second, order fulfilment; third, the supply chain; and fourth, integration. Shoshanah Cohen and Joseph Roussel outlined a similar progression in their book *Strategic Supply Chain Management*.[2] The principal difference between that framework and this one is that they describe the development of supply chain organisations over time, whereas this is a life-cycle model that describes the evolution of the supply chain organisation within a company as it progresses through the four stages of supply chain strategy.

Stage 1: the functional organisation, focused on rationalisation
The functional organisation disperses supply chain activities throughout the organisation (see Figure 10.1 overleaf). Transportation, customer service, production control, procurement and product development are all in individual functional silos. Operations/procurement and order fulfilment/logistics each carry out rationalisation initiatives relatively independently of one another. The fragmented organisation makes it almost impossible to execute an end-to-end strategy.

Companies that pursue a rationalisation strategy concentrate their resources in activities that generate cost reductions such as auctions, cost analysis, gain-sharing, global sourcing, outsourcing, standardisation, supplier consolidation, total cost of ownership (TCO), total quality

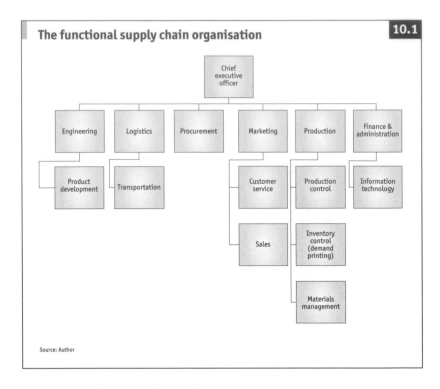

The functional supply chain organisation   10.1

Source: Author

management (TQM), value engineering and vendor-managed inventory (VMI). They devote more than twice as many staff to these activities as those that pursue other supply chain strategies, according to Boston Strategies International's 2008 survey of 58 companies across Asia, Europe, the Middle East/North Africa and the Americas.[3]

Stage 2: order fulfilment organisation, focused on synchronisation

The formation of a group responsible for order fulfilment is the major change that leads to stage 2 (see Figure 10.2). An order fulfilment department demonstrates a process focus rather than a functional focus. Production control, inventory management and customer service move from the production area into order fulfilment to allow this function to work more effectively with distribution and transportation. Inventory control may be renamed demand planning in recognition of that process.

Companies that synchronise devote more headcount to channel design, collaborative inventory management, cross-docking, demand management, pull, sales and operations planning (S&OP) and Six Sigma

The order fulfilment supply chain organisation   **10.2**

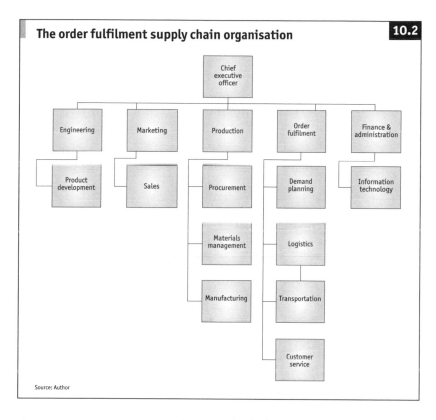

Source: Author

than companies following other supply chain strategies.[4] Most notably, they have more than three times as many resources dedicated to S&OP than the other companies.

Organisation at the New York City Housing Authority[5]

Recognising the benefit of centralised SCM, the New York City Housing Authority (NYCHA) integrated its former materials management department into a more modern supply chain operations organisation that draws on many of the leading practices in the private sector. Its organisation marries procurement, warehousing and logistics under one umbrella (see Figure 10.3 overleaf). This allows it to obtain synergies between those functions, and also to optimise decisions that cross functional boundaries, such as whether to centralise or decentralise warehousing, which requires a total supply chain cost assessment.

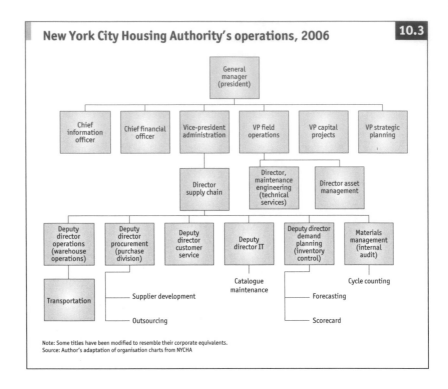

New York City Housing Authority's operations, 2006   10.3

Note: Some titles have been modified to resemble their corporate equivalents.
Source: Author's adaptation of organisation charts from NYCHA

Its centralised supply chain structure is the result of many years of consolidation. In 1985 the organisation had 22 local warehouses that were distributed throughout the boroughs (Bronx, Brooklyn, Manhattan, Queens and Staten Island). It consolidated those to three by 2000 in order to streamline logistics. Since suppliers offered more attractive pricing if they could also consolidate deliveries, NYCHA created a central warehouse in 1998.

The resulting high level of co-ordination has allowed the NYCHA to implement many leading practices from private-sector companies. This includes ABC inventory management, direct shipment, cross-docking and automated procurement transactions; 75% of its material expenditures are on blanket orders, reducing the processing time and cost per order dramatically.

As a result, the organisation has accurate and efficient purchasing operations, very good customer service and the lowest warehouse labour intensity out of nine public housing authorities in the United States. Customer confidence in the supply chain operations is up, according to the results of customer service surveys and unsolicited feedback from stakeholders. "Supply chain operations are getting more responsive," according to the head of technical services, which is responsible for maintenance and engineering.

The NYCHA still has progress to make towards integrated supply chain operations. For example, its purchasing group sometimes opts for low price when the maintenance engineering section believes that more durable and technologically advanced products would incur less maintenance and have a lower life-cycle cost. "You can throw out poor-quality tools if they don't work, but you get hurt working with bad tools, which costs money in medical claims," says the head of technical services. Also, capital equipment purchasing is handled in the asset management group and is not co-ordinated with the purchases for ongoing operations, which sacrifices purchasing leverage. Finally, field inventory information is not accessible to the supply chain operations inventory management group.

Gary Smith, director of supply chain operations, knows the organisation's strengths and weaknesses and is enthusiastic about its prospects. In addition to becoming more efficient and lean, the NYCHA has programmes in place that will help it to become more customer-centric and innovative:

> We're making progress here. The new category management structure, whereby buyers and planners work together, and end-to-end processes like storeroom pilot [which allows the local stocking locations to sell back excess inventory] and automated supplier scorecarding [whereby inventory information systems will be programmed to generate periodic supplier performance reports] will help us be even more responsive to our customers.

Stage 3: the supply chain organisation, focused on customisation

In the transition to stage 3, organisations integrate supply chain processes across business units through information systems and matrix management structures and incentives in order to focus on more top-line activities geared towards revenue growth and profitability, such as yield pricing, revenue management and value analysis.

Elevation of the supply chain leadership from the post of director to that of vice-president, executive vice-president or c-level leader (whose title starts with "chief" at, for example, the highest level in the organisation; these executives sit above directors, whose reports are managers) is typical of the transition. Over time, various chief operations positions have waxed and waned in popularity, including chief operations officer (coo), chief procurement officer (cpo), chief logistics officer (clo) and chief supply chain officer (csco). For example, Ann Taylor, an American

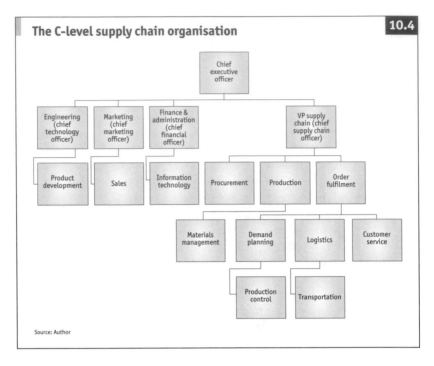

The C-level supply chain organisation   10.4

Source: Author

women's clothing retailer, named an executive vice-president, chief supply chain officer in September 2008. The addition of a vice-president or C-level position that has jurisdiction over all supply chain issues is the passageway from a stage 2 to a stage 3 organisation (see Figure 10.4).

Creation of the C-level supply chain post facilitates the sharing of information among all the relevant departments. Colin Smith, director of marketing for WebEx, a US-based web conference facility, says:

> You can't just link up databases and expect the business relationship to thrive. You have to link up the databases and then allow people in your business ecosystem to collaborate. That's the way the next generation is going to grow.

WebEx feeds back information from its customer care group to its product development group. The customer care group conducts business reviews, some via WebEx itself and others on the phone, with the main user at the customer company. Based on questions about how the respondents are using the product, the company determines if they are getting the value they should be getting, and if they are they using new features and products that have been available since the last customer service interaction.

Stage 4: integrated organisation, focused on innovation

In stage 4, cross-functional teams integrate supply chain processes across functional areas, particularly processes that offer synergy in the conception, design, testing and commercialisation of new products, and report to senior executives. Standardisation, value engineering and early supplier involvement are all used to simplify and expedite the new product process (see Figure 10.5).

Marketing shares market research with R&D so that the organisation

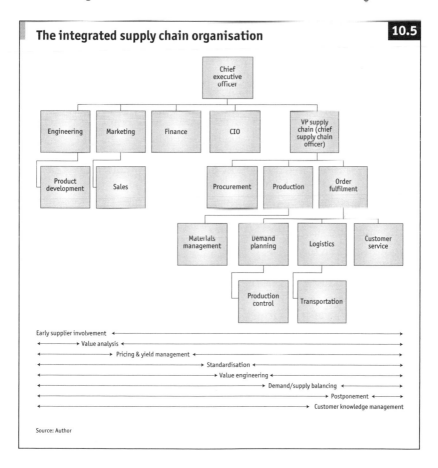

The integrated supply chain organisation `10.5`

Source: Author

can deliver new products that are sought by the market rather than be pushed from the company outward. Marketing plans jointly with product development, procurement and manufacturing on the rapid ramp-up of new products. Distribution shares market insights with sales to enhance customer knowledge and feed customer relationship management (CRM) systems. Sales shares inventory levels with procurement and production through S&OP to jointly agree on pricing strategies such as demand management and revenue management. Finance works with production and distribution to determine customer profitability. IT works with multiple areas of the company to provide applications that support collaboration, such as CAD/CAM, supplier relationship management (SRM), demand planning, advanced planning systems (APS), warehouse and transportation management systems (WMS and TMS), CRM, pricing, e-commerce and product lifestyle management (PLM).

Innovation-focused companies devote twice as many resources to new product introduction as other companies and spend twice as much time as others in cross-functional teams. The co-ordination between the supply chain department and other departments ensures the strategic connections that ensure success.

Despite the multitude of interfaces, innovation does not need extensive resources, as illustrated by these two examples from "pure service" companies. Wikipedia, a continually morphing encyclopedia that has practically become the definition of innovation, employs only 15 people. Plaxo, a social networking service that facilitates one-to-one interactions among 20m registered users, employs only 50 people.

Developing a world-class skill base

As functional silos have disappeared, supply chain managers have needed to work more in cross-functional teams, rotate between departments to become cross-trained and learn new technical skills.

Today, average supply chain managers spend more time (30–40%) working with external partners, and usually deal more with strategic relationships rather than transactional ones. They need more decision analysis and financial skills, since there are more strategic and less transactional decisions to be made. They also operate on a decision time horizon of between three and five years, compared with around one year in 2001 (see Table 10.1).

To be successful, the new role requires individuals with a different profile than in the past. As a result of cross-functional teaming, interdepartmental rotation and the need for new technical skills, professionals

Table 10.1 **The change in CPOs' backgrounds**

Function	CPO average no. years of experience in functional areas	
	2003	1987
Purchasing/supply	12.7	17.0
Operations/production	4.3	4.2
Finance	2.5	0.8
Management information systems	1.3	0.5
Other	0.9	0.7
Engineering	0.8	1.3
Marketing	0.8	1.6
Accounting	0.7	0.6
Transportation/distribution/logistics	0.5	1.0
Total (years of experience per respondent)	24.7	27.8

Source: Rudzki, Robert, Smock, D.A., Katzorke, M. and Stewart Jr, S., *Straight to the Bottom Line*, J. Ross Publishing, 2006

rotate through functional areas, spending less time in any one supply chain area. For example, the average number of years spent in the purchasing function decreased from 17 to 12 years between 1987 and 2003 (see Table 10.2).

Table 10.2 **Illustrative profile of a category manager in a large industrial company**

Supply chain metric	1997	2007	2017
% time working with supply chain partners	20%	30%	40%
% time working cross-functionally	60%	75%	90%
Decision horizon (years)	1	3	5
No. active suppliers accounting for 80% expenditure	5–20	2–8	1–3

Source: Boston Strategies International

Success factors[6]

The success factors for future supply chain leaders are IT skills, comfort with and aptitude for doing international business, interpersonal and cross-cultural skills, financial skills and functional experience.

They need to be familiar with and able to make decisions about new hardware and software applications, for example the selection of communications equipment and the encryption of communication with virtual private network (VPN) security. Mobile solutions and technologies such as voice over internet protocol (VOIP) and click-to-talk that are designed to increase the volume and the richness of customer contact will become an increasing part of supply chain management.

International capabilities are a career advantage. Formulating the right manufacturing and sourcing strategy requires context, education, information and wisdom from experience, and sometimes hard-learned failure. Some companies are bringing manufacturing back onshore or trying to decide what combination of products and services to offer to win today's new and more competitive game. Other important success factors are language skills, and a sense of humour and flexibility to accept and appreciate cultural differences along the way.

A supply chain executive needs the clout to redirect the cost focus of rationalisation and even synchronisation to the other side of the supply chain matrix, to customisation and innovation. He or she will need strategic vision and a willingness to lead multi-party initiatives in order to accomplish bold bottom-line and top-line improvements.

Financial skills are highly important in the world of collaborative SCM. Extended SCM crosses business units and boundaries between divisions, regions and companies. Instead of each player having a clear territory, many have smaller, shared roles in longer supply chains. Costs and benefits are distributed among multiple trading partners. For example, in a long supply chain where upstream and downstream partners benefit from radio frequency identification (RFID), which one(s) should bear the burden of investing in the tags and software?

Volatility has also magnified the need for financial skills. Volatile fuel costs have led carriers, especially airlines, to become experts at hedging, analysing profitability by customer and route, and deconstructing budget variances. Manufacturing firms need to decide how much supply chain risk to take. For example, how much quality risk or supply chain risk is acceptable for a lower unit cost? Financial and risk management tools are becoming a more important part of the supply chain professional's toolbox.

Structuring a staff development programme

Executive development should combine mentoring, rotation outreach and training. Mentoring can be formal or informal; models exist for both approaches. Job rotation is needed to successfully reach the integrated stage, since people need to understand the job responsibilities of the departments with which they must deal. There are several forms of outreach. John Deere, Honda and Harley Davidson have had academic outreach programmes. Saudi Aramco sends its executives on one-year externships to learn best practices from other leading organisations.

There are numerous certification programmes for staff development, for instance those offered by professional associations such as APICS, CSCMP and ISCEA (see Appendix 3 for a list of abbreviations). Table 10.3 overleaf shows the coverage of some of these programmes.

Engaging suppliers

A crucial part of sourcing is suppliers' engagement. Partner suppliers help to achieve cross-enterprise supply chain improvements and increase value for money paid. The first step in a supplier performance management programme is to stratify the suppliers and clearly outline the standards that they must meet in order to gain more business. Most buying organisations classify their suppliers into at least three categories: transactional, preferred and partner.

- Transactional suppliers have no established criteria. They meet some basic minimum level of acceptability to be able to register as a supplier, but have no better likelihood of being selected for a given assignment than any other registered supplier. They must compete via requests for proposal (RFP) or requests for quotation (RFQ).
- Preferred suppliers have a history of delivering high-quality work. They share more information about their business, for example about their technology development plans, than transactional suppliers. They have an established basis for acceptable cost based on historical rates or costs, and have clearly defined their market positioning compared with competing firms.
- Partner suppliers are the chosen, sometimes single source for vital products or services. Buyers feel comfortable enough with their quality to share their target cost levels, and suppliers feel comfortable enough to share technical information with the buyers. Buyers and suppliers share plans and other information

Table 10.3 **Topics addressed by selected professional supply chain certification programmes**

Awarding body	Institute for Supply Management (ISM)		APICS – The Association for Operations Management		American Society of Transportation and Logistics (AST&L)	International Supply Chain Education Alliance (ISCEA)
Certification	Certified purchasing manager (CPM)	Certified professional in supply management™ (CPSM)	Certified in production and inventory management (CPIM)	Certified supply chain professional (CSCP)	Certified in transportation and logistics (CTL)	Certified supply chain manager (CSCM)
Procurement, strategic sourcing and replenishment	•	•		•		•
New production development		•		•		
Production, lot sizing			•		•	
Quality	•	•	•	•		
Logistics and inventory management	•	•	•	•		•
Network design			•		•	•
Transportation	•		•		•	•
Demand management, including S&OP		•	•	•	•	•
Integrated SCM	•			•	•	•
CRM, customer service				•		•
Pricing						•
Risk management		•	•			
Project management		•	•			
Leadership, people management	•	•	•			
IT	•			•	•	•

Source: Boston Strategies International

well in advance to increase the chances of continued work together on major initiatives.

A comprehensive partner supplier programme guides suppliers from being mere commodity suppliers through five levels of partnership arrangements towards establishing what is a strategic partnership, which involves value-added, alliance and strategic suppliers – a simplification of the five-step partnering continuum developed by a leadership specialist, Michael Maccoby (see Figure 10.6). Value-added suppliers have a framework agreement to provide a focused service, as FedEx has with the US Postal Service (USPS) to handle airport-to-airport mail delivery (leaving the USPS with the local last-mile delivery). Alliance suppliers participate in joint development with the buyer, such as that of an oil contractor, Halliburton, with companies for the development of oilfields. Strategic partners establish a common vision based on mutual needs and strategies, as Northwest Airlines and KLM had for 15 years under the Wings Alliance before they merged in 2008. Companies that form true partnerships collaborate closely with suppliers to achieve not only lower total cost, but also faster speed to market, more innovation and better quality. One example of such a partnership (according to Maccoby) is between a Swedish-Swiss automation technology manufacturer, ABB, and a Canadian mining producer, Cominco. Through the partnership,

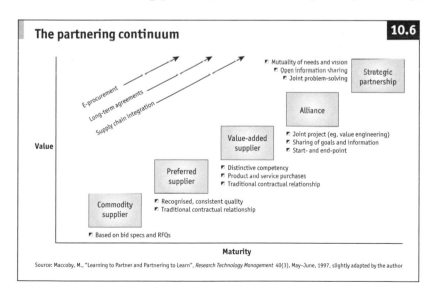

The partnering continuum | **10.6**

Value

E-procurement
Long-term agreements
Supply chain integration

Strategic partnership
- Mutuality of needs and vision
- Open information sharing
- Joint problem-solving

Alliance

Value-added supplier
- Joint project (eg, value engineering)
- Sharing of goals and information
- Start- and end-point

Preferred supplier
- Distinctive competency
- Product and service purchases
- Traditional contractual relationship

Commodity supplier
- Recognised, consistent quality
- Traditional contractual relationship

- Based on bid specs and RFQs

Maturity

Source: Maccoby, M., "Learning to Partner and Partnering to Learn", *Research Technology Management* 40(3), May–June, 1997, slightly adapted by the author

ABB was able to avoid the costs of bidding and get lower-cost solutions by engaging the creativity of Cominco staff on how best to implement a complex project. The two companies claim business process improvements, lower life-cycle costs and enhanced innovation. Unlike some partnerships, the companies have no written contract, instead relying on senior-level commitment and vision.[7]

Supply chain organisation maturity model

In summary, organisations progress through four stages of maturity, each one corresponding to one of the supply chain strategies. In addition, they are characterised by the progression of sophistication in the articulation of the strategy (see Table 10.4):

- The mission, vision and values progress from being informal to being documented, known throughout the organisation and motivating employees.
- The structure moves from the pre-supply chain format to rationalisation, synchronisation, customisation and innovation.
- Career paths advance from on-the-job training inside the company to external and internal training programmes, and later on include alliances and externships.
- The culture moves from being hidden and based on historical power relationships, to being rational and transparent in the synchronisation stage, and then on to being a learning organisation and a creative self-regenerating one during the innovation stage.

Table 10.4 Supply chain organisation maturity model

Organisational element	Pre-supply chain (siloed)	Stage 1 Rationalisation	Stage 2 Synchronisation	Stage 3 Customisation	Stage 4 Innovation
Mission, vision and values	Informal	Documented	Consistent with corporate culture	Mission and vision known inside department	Mission and vision known inside and outside department
				Values consistent with mission/vision	Employees rewarded for acting on values
Structure	Decentralised and unco-ordinated	Rationalisation	Synchronisation	Customisation	Innovation
Career paths	On-the-job training	External training	Internal training	Mentoring	Alliances and externships
				Job rotation	Supply chain is axis of advancement in company
Culture	Shadow culture influences most decisions	Rational	Transparent	Learning	Creative
			Collaborative		

Source: Boston Strategies International

11 Leveraging information technology

Supply chain management has become more about the management of information than the movement of goods, especially given the much greater customer interaction that comes in the customisation and innovation stages. Data and information exchange define the discipline, through electronic data exchange (EDI), extensible markup language (XML), networks and wireless access. Data security is a requirement. Value-added services – and more specifically value-added information services – are becoming an important part of every business.

Many companies have built their supply chain success on information technology (IT) and accessibility. FedEx and UPS know where millions of small packages are at any point in time and manage the flow as they move around the world. The price of a package delivery is indirectly related to the confidence that it will get there on time (which is in turn related to information capabilities) and partly to the ability of a consumer to track and trace it (which is directly related to information capabilities). Iron Mountain does likewise in the United States with millions of business and hospital records. Jabil Circuit is able to create custom supply chains for its clients because it has excellent information flow.

A complete supply chain information system has 11 components, which are outlined below. They are generally built on the framework of enterprise resource planning (ERP) (see Figure 11.1). ERP applications come with an SCM module for demand planning, but the SCM module typically only contains part of the analytics that are needed to successfully execute the four SCM strategies (see Table 11.1 on page 172). Therefore, many companies supplement their ERP systems with best-of-breed software applications for their supply chain activities. These are independent applications for which interfaces are often built to link them to the ERP data set.

The components of a complete SCM IT capability are:

◪ Computer-aided design and manufacturing (CAD/CAM)
◪ Network design
◪ Supplier relationship management (SRM), including auctions and electronic requests for quotation (eRFQs)
◪ Demand planning, including distribution resource planning (DRP)
◪ Advanced planning and scheduling (APS)

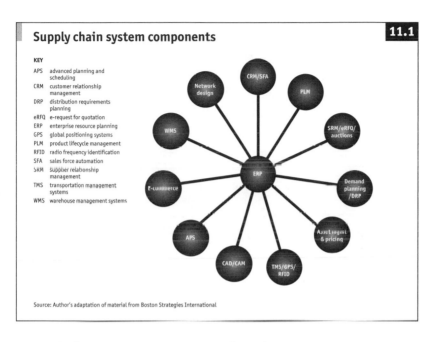

Supply chain system components 11.1

KEY

APS advanced planning and scheduling
CRM customer relationship management
DRP distribution requirements planning
eRFQ e-request for quotation
ERP enterprise resource planning
GPS global positioning systems
PLM product lifecycle management
RFID radio frequency identification
SFA sales force automation
SRM supplier relationship management
TMS transportation management systems
WMS warehouse management systems

Source: Author's adaptation of material from Boston Strategies International

- Warehouse management system (WMS)
- Transportation management system (TMS)
- Customer relationship management (CRM), including sales force automation (SFA)
- Financials, including asset management and pricing
- E-commerce
- Product life-cycle management (PLM)

Computer-aided design and manufacturing

Computer-aided design and manufacturing (CAD/CAM) supports SCM by working out how products can be manufactured for the least cost. Most waste in downstream SCM processes is created in the early stages of a product's conception and development. Architects and design engineers regularly use CAD to develop and refine their work, and automakers use CAM to monitor and adjust machine speed and increasingly control advanced robotics.

As organisations progress towards synchronisation, CAD can be used to create modules for low-cost manufacturing and assembly, including modular inputs. CAM can be used to identify plant bottlenecks using constraints management and throughput analysis. At the customisation

Table 11.1 **Supply chain IT requirements at each supply chain stage**

Application	Rationalisation (low cost)	Synchronisation (low assets)	Customisation (high margin)	Innovation (high revenue)
CAD/CAM	Design for manufacturability	Design for assembly/modularisation	Design for operability	Design for prototypeability
		Design for maintainability		
Network design	Rationalisation	Cross-docking	Forward stocking	Continuous market feedback mechanism
SRM	Auctions	Supplier event management	Supplier performance rating	Supplier qualification/ partnering
		Delivered cost TCO		
		Event management		
Demand planning	Consignment	Collaborative planning, forecasting and replenishment	Available to promise	Precise timing of new product launch
	VMI	Network design what-ifs		
APS/PC	Lean (waste reduction through optimised scheduling)	Pull (ECR, JIT, etc)	Mass customisation	Rapid and early prototyping
		CMMS		
WMS and TMS	Scheduling	Cross-docking	Time windowing	Dynamic routing
		Honeycombing		
CRM	Value analysis	Order cycle time compression	Personalised delivery	Data mining
		E-commerce		
Finance, cost and pricing	TCO	Risk management	ABC	Revenue management
			Yield pricing	
E-commerce	Virtual fulfilment	Back-end WMS and ATP	Amazon-like interface ("if you liked this...")	Web portal
PLM	SKU rationalisation	S&OP	Lifetime services	End-of-life planning

Source: Boston Strategies International

stage, design for configurability makes the product customisable by the end-user. At the innovation stage, CAD/CAM ensures that the design can be easily prototyped, which will accelerate new product launch.

Network design

At the rationalisation stage, companies often consolidate the number of warehouses and distribution centres that they operate to reduce total logistics cost. At this stage, the network design tool must have total cost modelling capability. At the synchronisation stage, network design applications help set up cross-docking operations that reduce pipeline inventory and compress end-to-end cycle time. At the customisation stage, forward stocking is needed to accommodate finish-to-order operations, so traditional network design tools may need to be supplemented with another tool that can model the finish-to-order operation and the outbound distribution in order to get end-to-end total cost. At the innovation stage the tools forward-integrate to get closer to the customer in order to receive continuous market feedback. At this stage, the modelling of extended operations all the way to the customer will be required, especially if the trunk line and the "last mile" had hitherto been handled by a different carrier.

Supplier relationship management

At the most basic level, the SRM module handles transactional purchase order (PO) processing. As the company's needs advance, SRM often features auctions, which may help reduce cost in the rationalisation phase. In the synchronisation phase, SRM should help track and compute the delivered cost and the total cost of ownership (TCO) so as to reduce the inventory of spare parts needed to operate and maintain the unit. At the customisation phase, SRM is needed to rate suppliers' performance by customer and order or delivery. And at the innovation phase, SRM is needed to rate and qualify potential partner suppliers according to their historical design collaboration performance.

E-procurement

Although in the 1990s many e-procurement initiatives ran over budget due to cataloguing and data management processes that proved to be overwhelming, electronic procurement is a necessity for cost-efficient SCM. A European company reveals a success story. The number of personnel creating purchase orders had doubled in the past ten years to the point where 80% of the staff initiated purchase orders. Furthermore, most of these (80%) were low-value purchases. The company established e-procurement in two stages. First it created catalogues that provided it with access to 40,000 SKUs, which it viewed as virtual units of storage. At first, its ability to update prices from suppliers and to tie purchased materials to end-products were limited, so it embarked on a second round of improvement and increased the number of available SKUs to 170,000. The experience allowed it to negotiate lower prices as a result of the higher volume of purchases of common items.

Competitive bidding and auctions

Most markets are imperfect. Cost differences stem from differences in manufacturing processes, production volume[1] and quality. Costs also vary geographically because of domestic resource costs and natural competitive advantage.[2] As a result, some companies pay more than others for comparable purchases. In the 1980s, Brazilian automakers were paying more than automakers in other countries for parts because of Brazil's import barriers.[3]

Bidding and auctions level the playing field:

- Sealed bid tenders where the item/s go to the lowest bidder. The US and some other governments use this approach.
- Reverse auctions, the most common types of auction relevant to SCM, are conducted by buyers to engage the sellers. They start high and are awarded to the lowest bidder.
- Combinatorial bids ask for multiple price options from sellers –
  including bundles of goods or services that the seller proposes
  – and computes the optimal allocation of business based on the
  sellers' proposed bundles as well as the lowest-cost option for
  each item or service. Companies like The Home Depot, Sears
  Logistics Services, Wal-Mart and Ford Motor Company have
  used combinatorial auctions to source transportation services.
  In transportation, carriers may bid different amounts on a given
  route, or lane, depending on which other routes they are awarded,
  since the combination of routes, rather than the number of routes,
  determines their average vehicle payload and therefore their profits.

Demand planning

Demand planning systems help match demand with supply. For companies at the rationalisation stage, these systems should enable the determination of requirements for all types of inventory, including consigned inventory, which does not have to be paid for until it is consumed, and vendor-managed inventory (VMI), which is paid for but managed by the vendor. Demand planning systems should also monitor the status of inventory by stage of postponed finishing if postponement is being used as a management method. For companies in the synchronisation stage, demand planning modules should also accommodate collaborative planning, forecasting and replenishment and help to design the network by using what-if analysis. For companies in the customisation stage, demand planning systems need to additionally provide accurate available-to-promise information by customer and order to help customer service representatives make commitments that can be met and that meet the customer's delivery expectations. For companies at the innovation stage, these systems need to help match raw materials and finished goods inventory with demand during new product launches in order to stay synchronised with the pace of products' introduction.

Advanced planning and scheduling and production control

In most operations, a master schedule establishes the production plan for a certain time horizon (the decision timeframe of handling orders). Production control is the day-to-day execution of the advance plan. APS consists of the range of systems that provide master scheduling and production control capabilities. The production scheduling system should include logic for determining the most economical lot sizes (planning) and for sequencing and prioritising jobs for maximum efficiency and profitability.

For companies at the rationalisation stage, APS supports lean waste reduction by tightening up the slack in production schedules. For companies at the synchronisation stage, APS needs to interface with pull systems such as JIT. Since APS is driven by schedules and JIT is driven by demand, APS should be used as a guide rather than the rule. Furthermore, computerised maintenance management systems (CMMS) help prevent downtime, thus supporting supply chain synchronisation.

In companies at the customisation stage, APS should be able to layer on the unique supply chain requirements of specific customer segments or even individual customers in order to deliver customised service and even order-specific service. Jabil Circuit, CVS, mail-order fulfilment houses, and gift companies that imprint logos and personal artwork on items like pens and shirts, use APS in this way.

For companies at the innovation stage, APS should help with rapid and early prototyping by allowing pilot production runs under real conditions, so it needs to be flexible enough to handle new product introductions.

A UK call-centre operator uses APS to manage streams of customer calls, e-mails, web chat and web support services from around the world, and it personalises its response to every enquiry. Operations like this need APS to determine appropriate staffing levels and shift structure and work assignments, given the peaks and valleys of traffic and the varying profit margin of the different types of orders that come in at different times of the day.

Materials requirements planning and production scheduling

Materials requirements planning (MRP) determines the right amount of material needed when demand is triggered by an item that requires a component. MRP explodes the original demand into the items contained in its bill of materials, and then orders each component or part within the lead time needed so that all the parts arrive in time for assembly. This leads to the right amount of production and therefore fewer inventory imbalances. Since MRP became popular in the 1970s, its penetration has deepened, and today even most small manufacturers have implemented MRP systems.

Warehouse management systems

Warehouse management systems (WMS) help make pick-pack operations more efficient and reduce the required footprint of the warehouse. They determine the routing that minimises the resources required to pick (or put away) material in a warehouse. To do that, they optimise the storage plan of the material based on its velocity. Like TMS, storage plans can be either static or dynamic. In large warehouses, WMS work in conjunction with automated guided vehicles (AGVs), conveyors and other equipment such as automated storage and retrieval systems (ASRS) in order to co-ordinate materials' flow in and out of the shelves using the least amount of resources. Large auto part warehouses, such as those for Ford or GM, and high-volume third-party warehouse companies also use their WMS to plan waves of picking.

Transportation management systems

Transportation optimisation solutions fall into seven broad categories, and sometimes interface with wireless communication technologies, optical character recognition systems and resource planning systems:

- **Carrier management systems** help shippers that do not own their own fleets to interface more efficiently with their transportation providers. These systems can provide rating, tendering, payment and freight bill auditing capabilities. The abbreviation TMS is often used to refer to this type of carrier transportation management system.

- **Routing and scheduling systems** offer features such as territory planning, load consolidation planning and execution, dynamic and static vehicle and driver assignment (the difference is whether or not the routing solution is limited to a fixed assignment of certain drivers to certain trucks or certain trucks to certain routes, or whether it can find the optimal solution without these constraints), routing, scheduling around time windows, mapping and in some cases what-if modelling capabilities. Some vendors of these offer planning systems that are used only when the network configuration changes, while others offer execution systems that are meant to be run every day or every time the route is run. Some systems offer both territory or area planning and dynamic route generation capabilities.

- **Real-time dispatching systems** include some capability to balance loads, either inbound and outbound, or from vehicle to vehicle. Some have the capability to edit routes manually once they are created, while others do not. Some high-end systems offer vehicle tracking after the route has begun, while others only generate the route itself.

- **Tracking and communication systems** involve a wireless hardware device, which can be on the vehicle or on the driver, as in a handheld device or PDA (personal digital assistant such as a mobile phone or BlackBerry). The cost of the hardware can be balanced against the benefits of improved service and the ability to divert and change orders once the vehicle is in transit.

- **Order verification and reporting systems** allow central dispatchers or customer service managers to see the real-time status of orders as they are delivered.

- **Fleet management systems** monitor equipment as a whole, or components of the equipment, such as engine performance, fuel consumption and compliance with local requirements to pay fuel and mileage taxes based on places driven to.

- **Trade compliance systems,** applications that help to determine the duties and documentation required when shipping internationally, can also provide real-time information about the economics of end-to-end supply chains. Trade compliance systems increasingly provide landed costs and the ability to view breakdowns of shipment costs showing fuel costs, labour rates, real-estate and facility costs, cross-dock economics, customs clearance preferences and handling import/export paperwork. Some of these tools allow shippers to recalculate the cost of end-to-end supply chains by changing parameters such as the port or shipment size.

The right choice of a TMS depends on factors such as service requirements, fleet size (if there is proprietary equipment), time spent on the road versus at drop-off locations, and the flexibility of the workforce to implement change.

Wireless technologies such as RFID and optical character recognition interface with TMS systems to deliver real-time positioning information that enhances transportation security and efficiency.

Wireless communication technologies

Technologies such as radio frequency identification (RFID), a microchip-based signalling system whereby readers are used to identify items that are tagged, are increasing the ability of companies to track inventory flowing through the pipeline, and to personalise their relationship at the moment of delivery with their customers. If and when it is used at the item level on a large scale, shoppers may trigger the replenishment of grocery store items when they pick up the item from the shelves, and they could be recognised when they come through the door by an RFID chip in their loyalty card. Airline passengers could walk nonchalantly through the airport if an RFID chip designated them as low-risk passengers to automated inspectors. Many airlines and airports, from Amsterdam to Tokyo to Las Vegas, are testing RFID for baggage handling. Applications will focus on high-value transactions (such as expedited cargo) and convenience.

In retail supply chains, RFID has had some success with companies such as Wal-Mart, Tesco and Marks and Spencer, and has in some cases displaced the electronic article surveillance tag. RFID has also started to replace the barcode in libraries and document applications. Nederlandse Bibliothek Dienst, the Netherlands library service, piloted RFID at the public library in Eindhoven in 2002. The Vatican has tagged 30,000 items. Other libraries using this system include the Catholic University of Leuven in Belgium, Olin College in Boston, MA, and the University of Nevada at Las Vegas.

Optical character recognition

Optical character recognition (OCR) is being used to track cargo and improve operational efficiency.[4] China's Dalian Dayaowan Port used to experience lengthy loading and uploading and could process only 40 containers per hour. Moreover, its data input error rate was high. It implemented an OCR reader to read the licence plates on the trucks entering and departing. The system increased throughput to 180 containers per hour, lowered operating cost and achieved 95% data accuracy.

Distribution resource planning

Distribution resource planning (DRP) systems plan the amount of inventory that is needed in multi-tier distribution networks, for example where there are two warehouses between the source and the customers. Similar to MRP, DRP uses the demand (in this case, a forecast) to calculate how much product needs to be resupplied and in what timeframe. Then, based on that information, it places orders on the warehouses. DRP systems are often viewed as a cause of the bullwhip effect for two reasons: first, in a multi-tier warehouse network, one of the warehouses has larger order quantities than the others, so one small order at the point of consumption creates larger orders at the farther warehouse; and second, DRP is based on a forecasting approach, as opposed to efficient consumer response (ECR) principles.

Customer relationship management

CRM systems gather and manage data on customer interactions in order to increase the quality of future interactions. At a minimum, CRM is just a mechanism for gathering and maintaining customer transaction data, especially for web transactions since they are increasingly common. However, a robust CRM system should help realise each supply chain strategy. During rationalisation, CRM should provide a comparison of the customer profile, or needs, with the product purchased, to facilitate a gap analysis that sheds light on which features of the product are most useful. In the synchronisation phase, CRM should connect with back-end order fulfilment applications to allow flawless and timely execution. In the customisation phase, it should allow for customers to include personal information such as their credit card details, addresses and notes in their order, and for this to be remembered the next time if they wish. Finally, in the innovation phase, CRM should provide a creative user interface and a base of data that can be mined to identify new and creative product offerings.

Amazon has extraordinary CRM capabilities in the four ways mentioned above. It creates a detailed transaction database. It tracks what people buy compared with what people like them buy, thereby allowing a value analysis. The value analysis is presented directly to the consumer, who can decide how to best spend his or her money, rather than to Amazon personnel. The system connects with back-end order fulfilment operations; it even offers different shipping times and announces the cut-offs by which the shipping dates will change, which allows customers to decide when to make their purchase. Lastly, it offers a wide array of continuously changing choices to the customer.

Cost, pricing and risk applications

SCM needs five cost and pricing capabilities that extend beyond the normal capabilities of the classic enterprise resource planning (ERP) financial and accounting modules. In the rationalisation stage, companies need to know the total cost of ownership (TCO) in order to reduce lifetime cost. Heavy equipment that is routinely overhauled is one example of lifetime cost.

FedEx calculated the cost per cycle (take-off and landing) and the cost per operating hour of its jet engines in order to reduce total lifetime cost. Since each overhaul basically restores the engines to brand-new condition, it is tricky to separate a cause of failure between the original equipment manufacturer (OEM), the overhaul vendor and the severity of the flight mission (for example, repeated take-offs and landings are more stressful on the engines than a long cruise at high altitudes). FedEx developed maintenance and failure analysis models, and analysed the cost by type of overhaul and repair vendor to ascertain the normalised cost per cycle and cost per hour.

At the synchronisation stage, companies need to measure and manage risk to avoid supply chain disruption. Supplier risk, economic risk, input cost risk and others need to be reported to shareholders as part of the Sarbanes-Oxley legislation. A market intelligence system can help mitigate the impact of imbalances between supply and demand by providing visibility to shortages and price abnormalities.

At the customisation stage, companies should use activity-based costing (ABC) and practise yield pricing. ABC helps to allocate overhead to the prime consumer, thus helping to compute customer profitability. Yield pricing helps to simultaneously satisfy multiple customer segments.

At the innovation stage, systems are needed to support revenue management, that is, deciding how to price and prioritise orders or shipments based on their individual profitability. Priceline, an online airline ticket reseller, has a web interface that allows customers to place bids and each offer is evaluated on its own merits by the airlines.

E-commerce

At the basic level, e-commerce requires order fulfilment through an unseen warehouse. Such virtual fulfilment is based on HTML and XML protocols interfaced with a WMS. An important improvement is the proper functioning of available-to-promise features, a hallmark of the synchronisation stage. Amazon and most other e-tailers offer specific promise dates for shipping and delivery, thanks to back-end inventory availability data and interfaces with logistics providers' cut-off and delivery times. Additional customisation features include, for instance, Amazon's referral features ("readers who bought this book also bought this other book ..."), which can increase sales considerably. The accumulated mass of customisation data can be used to rapidly develop and introduce new products (innovation).

EDI/XML

Electronic data interchange (EDI) has been the standard for e-commerce and other transaction set transfers between trading partners for decades. The American National Standards Institute (ANSI) and UN/EDIFACT protocols have specified the protocols for the transfer of everything from requests for quotations (ANSI 840) to advance shipping notices (ANSI 856). XML is replacing these protocols as web-based transactions dominate offline transactions. For example, when the European company mentioned on page 181 embarked on the second round of its e-procurement transaction efficiency programme, it chose UNSPSC item classification codes and XML messaging and ordering protocols. The number of SKUs covered rose from 40,000 to 170,000, costs decreased and ordering fill rates increased.

Product life-cycle management

As mentioned in Chapter 9, a key function of PLM is to process and facilitate easy storage and retrieval of changes to the product design and specifications. At the rationalisation stage, PLM systems need to be able to help identify and reduce product complexity to facilitate cost reduction through simplification. At the synchronisation stage, the PLM output should be used in the S&OP process to plan for emerging (new) and declining (old) items and services. In the customisation stage, PLM should be used to plan value-added after-sales products and services related to the item(s). And in the innovation stage, PLM should be used to facilitate rapid and repeated product design changes.

Cochlear, a global hearing solutions provider, implemented a PLM solution from Parametric Technology Corporation to accelerate its design review process and streamline the process of administering engineering change orders. The company considers the programme to have had a significant impact on its ability to share documents globally and therefore enhance its speed to market with new products. By replacing manual processes with automated ones, the company works more collaboratively and concurrently than in the past, when paper documents needed to be assembled and passed from one department to another. It relies on its PLM solution to help it manage the stage-gate product development process more tightly, transmit complete sets of documentation to manufacturing for pilot programmes and reduce the potential for errors throughout the entire process.

Integration of the components

Effective supply chain support relies foremost on full functionality and integration between core ERP modules such as finance and engineering. Several particularly important transactional modules are as follows:

- Purchasing and accounts payable need to be complete and up to date to permit supplier spend consolidation in the rationalisation stage.
- The quality of order management and APS data needs to be high to allow collaborative inventory planning in the synchronisation stage.
- Finance and in particular cost accounting (cost of service) need to be fully functioning to allow ABC to support customer profitability analysis in the customisation stage.

In addition, best-of-breed applications (those that are not a part of the core ERP system) should be integrated with each other to allow the full success of critical initiatives at each stage. These typically include marketing, sales, CRM, SCM, SRM, WMS and engineering components.

Marketing applications such as yield pricing need to link with production planning and scheduling to permit the rapid introduction of new products. Aramex, a Middle Eastern transportation and logistics company, can introduce new products particularly quickly because of linkage of scheduling and pricing databases.

Sales applications need to link with distribution information systems to allow customer-specific handling in the customisation stage.

CRM, SCM and SRM need to be tied together to allow end-to-end supply chains to become a reality. A leading oil company helps its suppliers process its customers' orders by operating both its call centre and its accounts payable via the same ERP system.

WMS picking status, which indicates what stage of processing orders are in as they move from picking through packing and shipping, must be integrated with TMS and cross-docking applications to provide timely inventory availability information. Georgia Pacific designed a custom application to link its WMS to order management in its ERP system, enabling it to transform its warehouse into a cross-dock and thereby reduce inventory.

Engineering, APS, purchasing and distribution modules all need to be working properly to permit concurrent engineering. David Hastings, CFO of US company Incyte Pharmaceuticals, explains that "siloed organisation can kill productivity". Chemists and biologists are often in different parts of the country, whereas at Incyte they are down the hall from each other. Cross-enterprise collaboration accelerates new product development. Incyte and Pfizer collaborated to improve the research process. This improved IT interfaces and enhanced communication between the two companies to make a seamless partnership.

12 Measuring success

"**Y**ou get what you measure," goes the adage. This chapter is about which metrics are good barometers of supply chain management effectiveness, and what target levels make sense.

Until the mid-1960s, metrics for measuring supply chain processes were uncommon. In 1966, only 58% of companies surveyed even measured inventory turnover or obsolete stock.[1] The cost of overproduction was rarely counted in companies' books, so the velocity of material as it flowed through the supply chain did not matter.

The growing awareness of supply chain concepts, combined with ambiguity over the boundaries of SCM, led to a proliferation of low-level process metrics whose linkage to value creation was tenuous. Initially, supply chain metrics focused on inventory levels. Then, when life-cycle cost became a popular concept, the focus shifted to total supply chain cost. When the theory of constraints became popular, metrics such as throughput and inventory dollar-days gained currency. When lean accounting became popular, metrics focused on activity-based costs (ABC).[2] The "plan-source-make-deliver" model introduced by the Supply Chain Council brought hundreds of metrics. The cumulative pile of metrics was so extensive that many people began to categorise them, in many cases by the old (pre-supply chain) functional boundaries.

The top-level metric: economic value added

Economic value added (EVA) is an all-inclusive metric for measuring the impact of SCM performance improvement since it captures revenue, cost and asset effects.[4] When SCM generates incremental revenue (for example, through lower pricing or rapid new product introductions) EVA is the profit after tax less the true cost of capital employed. It is calculated as:

EVA = net operating profit after taxes (NOPAT) − (capital × cost of capital)

Martin Christopher[5] proposes a variant on EVA that accumulates the value of EVA into the future and discounts it back, as in a net present value (NPV) calculation, where market value added (MVA) = NPV (EVA)). Another way of calculating MVA is akin to measuring the company's market premium over book value (stock price × issued shares − book value of total capital invested). EVA may be approximated by after tax free cash flow, which is net operating income less tax less working capital investment and fixed capital investment. This, however, is harder to measure at the level of the supply chain, so figuring out the supply chain's impact on after-tax free cash flow is quite tricky.

Primary (CFO-oriented) results metrics
At the highest level, each supply chain strategy delivers certain financial benefits that can be measured, as shown in Figure 12.1 overleaf.

Rationalisation efforts have been demonstrated to result in a 1–4% improvement in the net margin (for example, going from a baseline of 10% to 11–14%), which corresponds to a 4–6% improvement in EVA. (Note that all correspondences of performance to EVA results are based on a company with $1 billion in revenue and a multi-industry average rate of asset intensity and profitability.) Supply chain initiatives in the rationalisation phase focus on reducing supply chain cost, which in turn increases the net margin.

Synchronisation efforts have shown also to have a 1–4% improvement on return on net assets (RONA) – for example, the capability to move from 7% RONA to 8–11% RONA – which equates to a 5–7% improvement in EVA. Supply chain initiatives in the synchronisation phase typically achieve the improvement in RONA by reducing forecast error, and thus achieve level production both within the enterprise and across trading partners, which decreases the need for inventory and fixed assets.

Customisation can lead to 5–7% higher gross margin (for example, the potential to increase from 32% to 37–39%), which translates to a 6–10% improvement in EVA. The principal catalyst of higher gross margin in the customisation stage is greater customer mindshare, which is achieved by increasing customisation at customer touch-points.

Innovation can lead to 10% incremental revenue growth (for example, moving from 13% growth rate to 23% growth rate), equivalent to about 15% or greater increase in EVA. The revenue growth comes mainly from new product introductions, and a key subsidiary metric of revenue growth related to innovation is the percentage of sales derived from new products over the previous 12 months.

Subsidiary results metrics
Table 12.1 on page 194 lists the key metrics that are most appropriate for each supply chain strategy. It is divided into three categories of metrics: primary results, subsidiary results and top-level process. This organisation

12.1 Supply chain balanced scorecard

	ECONOMIC VALUE ADDED			
	Rationalisation: operating cost	Synchronisation: asset utilisation	Customisation: margin	Innovation: revenue
PRIMARY RESULTS METRIC	Net profit margin	Return on net assets (RONA)	Gross profit margin	Revenue growth
SUBSIDIARY RESULTS METRIC	COGS Reduction in COGS Cost per unit Customer segment profitability Direct labour Direct product profitability Inbound freight Order fulfilment costs Order fulfilment lead times Outbound freight Overhead cost Total landed cost Total product costs Total supply chain management costs	**FIXED ASSETS** Asset turns Return on capital employed Asset utilisation Capital productivity Return on investment **WORKING CAPITAL** Cash flow to sales FG inventory carry cost Inventory carrying cost Inventory value	Overall satisfaction Customer complaints	Revenue growth rate % of sales from products introduced in last 12 months % of total SKUs introduced in last 12 months Customer share NPI cycle time NPD cycle time Decrease in NPI cycle time Decrease in NPD cycle time
PROCESS METRICS	% spend sourced in 2 years % spend outsourced % SKUs value-engineered Decrease in no. of parts per unit Inventory turns Cost per delivery Visibility to end customer Cost per ECO No. black belts at core suppliers % materials on consignment % excess cost designed in % transactions paperless	% production lines on JIT Frequency of S&OP meetings No. black belts on staff Frequency of sharing demand forecasts with suppliers Time since constraints review % SKUs on ELDP % perfect orders % peak % transactions via EDI or XML Standard deviation of delivery time Mean standard error % direct ship	% SKUs with house of quality % interaction history accessible % transactions with customer data % customers segmented % customers known profit % % prices dynamic % product line customised % product line personalised % transactions cross-sale offered % transactions up-sale offered Customer data integration? Time to flex up 20% Order to ready for shipment time On-time vs customer request time On-time delivery vs promise time Duration of late orders Response accuracy Response time to enquiries	Time to feedback test market information First prototype % of EVA % overlap design and engineering Stage of supplier involvement Stage of customer involvement Total marketing cost Response time from break point % SKUs via assortment planning % SKUs designed with supply chain involvement

Source: Author. Compiled from experience and sources such as Bowersox (*Logistics and Supply Chain Management*), Carroll (*Lean Performance ERP Project Management*), Christopher (*Logistics and Supply Chain Management*), Cohen and Roussel (*Strategic Supply Chain Management*), Frazelle (World-Class Warehousing presentation), Hugos (*Essentials of Supply Chain Management*), Lambert (*Strategic Logistics Management*), Meltzer (*Handbook of Global Supply Chain Management*), Monczka (*Purchasing and Supply Chain Management*, p. 202), Poirier (*Business Process Management, Advanced Supply Chain Management*, pp. 124, 146), Rudzki (*Straight to the Bottom Line*), Woods (*Supply Chain Yearbook*)

facilitates the selection of the appropriate metrics depending on the purpose.

Rationalisation subsidiary results metrics
At the next level down, functional executives need to track the components of net profit margin in order to ensure that operational changes end up in financial results. The principal components that should be tracked at this level are:

- total supply chain management costs;
- cost of goods sold (COGS);
- cost per unit;
- customer segment profitability;
- direct labour;
- direct product profitability;
- inbound freight;
- order fulfilment costs;
- order fulfilment lead times;
- outbound freight;
- overhead cost;
- total landed cost;
- total product cost.

Synchronisation subsidiary results metrics
Companies following the synchronisation strategy will find that one of two sets of subsidiary metrics will be appropriate.

If the company's supply chain has a high turnover of goods and/or services, it should measure working capital:

- cash flow to sales;
- finished goods inventory carrying cost;
- inventory carrying cost;
- inventory value.

If the company is asset-intensive, it should measure the asset performance of its fixed assets, for example:

- asset turns;
- return on capital employed (ROCE);
- asset utilisation;

◾ capital productivity;
◾ return on investment.

Customisation subsidiary results metrics
The most effective subsidiary results metrics for the customisation strategy are:

◾ overall customer satisfaction;
◾ customer complaints.

Innovation subsidiary results metrics
Innovation through SCM is best measured by the share of customer's attention that the brand receives, which can be measured directly or inferred from repeat purchases and customer penetration rates (up-selling, cross-selling, etc). A short list of level 2 metrics for innovation-driven SCM should include:

◾ percentage of total sales from products introduced in last 12 months;
◾ percentage of total SKUs introduced in last 12 months;
◾ customer share;
◾ cycle time for new product development and delivery;
◾ decrease in cycle time for new product design and development.

The next level down: key process metrics

Below the top level there are hundreds of additional metrics that can be used to track the effectiveness of SCM processes and sub-processes. Since each company is extremely different at the operational level, the selection of metrics below needs to be evaluated on a company-specific basis.

Rationalisation process metrics

The success of rationalisation strategies can be affected by metrics such as:

◾ percentage of spend sourced in last two years;
◾ percentage of spend outsourced;
◾ percentage of SKUs value-engineered;
◾ decrease in number of parts per unit;
◾ cost per delivery;
◾ visibility to end-customer;
◾ cost per engineering change order (ECO);
◾ number of Six Sigma black belts[6] at core suppliers;

◪ percentage of materials on consignment;
◪ percentage of excess cost designed in;
◪ percentage of transactions paperless.

Synchronisation process metrics

The success of synchronisation strategies is affected by two process metrics related to scm's struggle against the bullwhip effect: first, the variability of order volume over time and through the supply chain; and second, the assets needed to support that variability.

The variability of order volume over time measures the extent to which supply chain partners fail to co-ordinate, resulting in peaks and valleys of capacity and prices over time. The variability of order volume through the supply chain – for example, the standard deviation of order volume at the finished goods level, divided by the standard deviation of the volume of raw material purchases – measures the counterproductive reverberation of the overcorrection on an order or shipment basis. Many people measure forecast error as a proxy for this since it measures the extent to which the bullwhip effect has been avoided.

Measuring the variability of order volume over time (cyclicality) is like measuring the business cycle. It can only be done over a long time horizon, so it tends to be measured mostly by large companies that are in cyclical industries and are at the raw material source, so get the worst of the bullwhip effect, being at the tip of the whip.

Recent economic patterns and globalising markets have demonstrated the propensity for overcorrection. Therefore, long-term decisions that involve substantial investment and risk often hinge on an accurate forecast of industry conditions. Which markets to buy from, which suppliers have capacity, what is the right price to pay and whether to partner, enter into a joint venture or acquire are questions that all depend on a reasoned and accurate view of future conditions (see Figure 12.2 overleaf).

Saudi Aramco measures the variability of order volume over time through a sophisticated supply market intelligence initiative. For 50 categories of purchased materials and services, it estimates the future demand, order lead times, capacity utilisation and prices quarter by quarter, with forecasts three years forward. It tracks prices and projections to determine the peak of the cycle and proactively works with suppliers to avoid shortages and price spikes.

Companies that measure long-term cyclical trends and forecasts in an attempt to mitigate the costs of a bullwhip effect establish market intelligence and risk management at three levels: supplier, supply market and

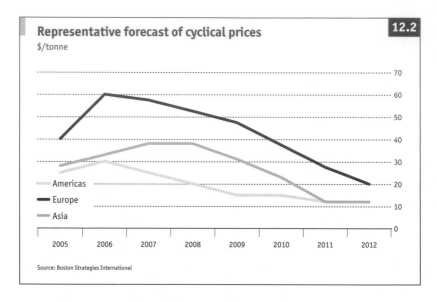

Representative forecast of cyclical prices   12.2
$/tonne

Source: Boston Strategies International

macroeconomic. At the supplier level, they should monitor supplier ratings and qualifications, performance history, financial results and news. At the industry level, they should monitor capacity utilisations, lead times, costs, prices, regulatory changes and productivity. At the macroeconomic level, they should monitor demand, growth rates, regional conditions, risk factors and prices for underlying commodities.

Other tier 3 synchronisation metrics include: percentage production lines on JIT; frequency of S&OP meetings; number of black-belts on staff; frequency of sharing demand forecasts with suppliers; time since constraints review; percentage SKUS on ELDP; percentage market share of end customer; percentage perfect orders; percentage peak; percentage transactions via EDI or XML; standard deviation of delivery time; mean standard error; and percentage direct ship.

For simplicity, many companies measure demand forecast accuracy, or actual versus forecast sales. Forecast error, if converted to a supply chain results metric, would equate to the reduction in inventory or working capital, which contributes about 5–7% to EVA, as previously mentioned.

Customisation process metrics
While the success of the customisation strategy is ultimately measured in gross profit margin, many processes need to be aligned in order to yield the financial results. Here is a sampling of some process metrics that

would provide a snapshot of the health and adequacy of customisation supply chain processes:

- on-time delivery performance to customer request time;
- on-time delivery performance to the time that the sales representative promised the customer;
- percentage of transactions where up-sale offered;
- percentage of transactions where the sales representative offers to sell products or services of a type that the customer is not currently buying (cross-sale);
- percentage of SKUS that have been reviewed using the "house of quality" approach (see page 132 and Figure 8.1);
- percentage of interaction history accessible on demand;
- percentage of transactions using customer data;
- percentage of customers segmented;
- percentage of customers with known profitability;
- percentage of prices that are dynamic;
- percentage of orders via formal profitability assessment;
- percentage of product line customised;
- percentage of product line personalised;
- customer satisfaction;
- percentage of transactions for which available-to-promise (ATP) used;
- time required to increase volume by 20% in response to a customer's request or surge in demand;
- complete manufacture to order ready for shipment time;
- degree of demonstrated flexibility;
- response accuracy;
- response time to enquiries.

Innovation process metrics

Generating revenue, the level 1 innovation metric depends on a range of sub-processes coming together. Specific supply chain processes that need to be fully functional in order to generate innovation include the following, which should be measured:

- percentage of sales from new products;
- percentage of SKUS new in last 12 months;
- time to feed back test market sales information;
- first prototype stage as percentage of EVA;
- percentage overlap between design and engineering;

- stage of first supplier involvement;
- stage of first customer involvement;
- total marketing cost;
- response time before/after the postponement point;
- percentage of SKUs via assortment planning;
- percentage of SKUs designed with supply chain involvement;
- customer share;
- new production introduction (NPI) cycle time;
- new product development (NPD) cycle time;
- decrease in NPI cycle time;
- decrease in NPD cycle time.

Additional detailed process metrics

Companies use close to 700 additional process metrics to measure supply chain success.

More than 200 tier 2 metrics are more detailed versions of the primary results metrics (one degree of separation from the original metrics). An example is the cost per mile of trucking operations. This can be linked to corporate performance via the cost per delivery, which in turn affects the total supply chain cost, which in turn affects the net profit margin. Assuming that the company's supply chain strategy is at least partly focused on rationalisation, this level 2 metric makes sense.

Nearly 500 highly operational level 3 metrics are at least two degrees of separation from the top-level metrics. Some of these are extremely helpful in achieving incremental improvements in cost, flexibility, cycle time or customer service. For example, back orders tie to fill rates, and fill rates tie to customer satisfaction, and customer satisfaction ties to pricing and margin strength. So if the company is following a customisation strategy, it makes sense to track back orders, even though the relationship to corporate financial performance is indirect.

The risk with allowing tier 3 metrics to proliferate is that the logical and quantitative link to high-level value-creating metrics used at the C-level can become obscure. One of the principal responsibilities of a supply chain leader is to champion a select number of metrics that logically and intuitively connect SCM to supply chain strategy, and supply chain strategy to corporate value.

A metrics maturity model

Stage 1 companies without a supply chain focus usually have a hard time collecting the data to compile the metrics. As a result, when they need to cut costs, they do so by executive mandate. There are wide inventory variances as a result of not only the bullwhip effect, but also shrinkage (theft, damage and obsolescence). Returns are handled chaotically, customer service provides one uniform response to all customers, and each new product introduction (NPI) shakes the company. The chief procurement officer at a UK-based mining company expressed dismay at the quality of the master data on external expenditures. Even after years of centralised management of the procurement function, poor data quality was still an impediment to implementing supply chain programmes. Moreover, budgets and estimated savings did not meet expectations, and the combination of bad baseline data and erroneous and unaudited projections created a culture that defied accountability. An Economist Intelligence Unit study reports:[1]

> Fully 31% of respondents say getting accurate and timely spend data is a top challenge to achieving overall success in purchasing strategies and initiatives. An inability to measure company-wide expenses accurately means "indirect [spend] for BAT until very recently has been ostensibly a virgin area, significantly larger than direct spend, and is spread across disparate profit centres, without good spend visibility or strategic sourcing," says Andrew Brock of BAT in South Korea.

As companies approach stage 2, they often experience a decrease in profitability or a loss, and hire a supply chain professional to institute processes and detailed metrics that help to contain costs. A US pharmaceutical company launched an SCM initiative to align its cost base when its stock price performance slipped behind that of its principal rivals. This usually results in a programmed cost reduction, the establishment of commodity management teams and the implementation of information systems that automate order entry (as in e-procurement systems, MRP and better materials control systems to track and manage SKUs through their life-cycles. Still, at this stage they usually measure cost on a first-cost basis (as opposed to life-cycle costs) and they focus on getting high equipment or plant utilisation (as opposed to balancing loads in lean style).

Stage 3 is often brought on by volume growth or new shareholder-oriented management. IBM significantly beefed up its internal SCM by buying PricewaterhouseCoopers Consulting in 2002 as it faced new market realities in the PC market. Typical steps in stage 3 include instituting externally (supplier and customer) focused metrics and processes

Table 12.1 **Supply chain metrics maturity model**

	1	2	3	4	5
Overall/ integrated supply chain strategy	No supply chain focus	Internal focus	External (supplier and customer) focused metrics and processes Tier-skipping	Chain leadership	Supply chain network hub
Rationalisation (source)	Cost-cutting by mandate	Programmed cost reduction Commodity management teams First cost orientation	Collaborative supplier initiatives Landed cost orientation Activity-based costing	Integrated IT systems make virtual supply chain Total cost orientation	"Lifecycle total cost" centre of excellence
Synchronisation	MTP; no strategy Wide inventory variances High obsolescence Returns are handled chaotically	Focus on high equipment or plant utilisation Inventory controls and procedures MRP Available to promise	Focus on ROA Compliance Global demand forecasting Lean initiatives in place	Public-private partnership (PPP) co-ordination Capacity synchronised across multiple tiers Flexibility Risk measurement	Portfolio approach to risk management Dynamic capacity Revenue management prevents excess inventory

	1	2	3	4	5
			Performance-based agreements	Lean extends to customer (VA/House of Quality) and suppliers (lean supply)	
			Pull or JIT systems	Electronic visibility and transaction clearing with all trading partners	
Customisation	One size fits all	Customisation by customer segment	Data mining	Personalisation/configuration for all customers	Personalisation/configuration for all customers one unit at a time
		Automated customer order entry	Mass customisation enables rapid changeovers	Continuous customer access to status information	Margin premium due to extraordinary service
			Ability to adjust supply chain parameters for "A" customers		
Innovation	Each NPI shakes the company	Codified new product introduction (NPI)	R&D and field feedback and synergy	Market leadership through New product development (NPD) and new product introduction (NPI)	Brand allure ("glow") as an innovative company
		PLM part management		Suppliers are integral to NPD	

Source: Boston Strategies International

that support collaborating with suppliers and customers on demand planning, negotiating with suppliers' suppliers (tier-skipping) and structuring performance-based agreements that favour customers' needs over internal needs.

Stage 4 comes as companies reach a size where they exert such influence that their actions affect the public at a national or international level. It engages with stakeholders on labour agreements and public–private partnerships. It measures and manages risk because of the potential for loss not only to itself but also to its customers. For example, Wal-Mart's store locations affect hundreds of millions of consumers, many of whom feel emotional about the company's presence. Because of its dominant position, it exerts supply chain leadership, and so invests in information systems to allow it to have extended visibility across the chain, measuring its supply chain performance from one end of the supply chain to the other. Its momentum in NPD leads Wal-Mart to introduce more products more rapidly than most of its competitors.

In stage 5, the CEO – for instance of companies such as Dell, Wal-Mart and HP – recognises the value of SCM as a competitive weapon and as a lever for moulding a new and innovative business model. Countries also recognise the value of SCM as a competitive weapon. The Saudi Arabian General Investment Agency defined "economic cities", of which one (Hail) is a logistics hub. The hub plan is an innovative way to make Saudi Arabia worth more than the sum of its parts by connecting the cities inside the country to each other, by linking Saudi Arabia to Jordan and Iraq, and by potentially diverting some east-west traffic from the Suez Canal.

Companies – and countries – in stage 5 use supply chain metrics and tools to decide when to accept profitable work and when to turn down loss-making business; when to add capacity for specific customers and when to stretch with the existing capacity; and how much to collect as a premium for customer-specific value-added services.

Qatar Fuel: supply chain excellence by the numbers

Qatar Fuel, based in Doha, Qatar, distributes and sells fuels including diesel, petrol (gasoline) and aviation fuel in Qatar. Rated one of the country's top ten companies, Qatar Fuel strives to integrate supply chain excellence in everything it does. As a result, it is a leader in customer and employee satisfaction as well as shareholder earnings. This produces high levels of cost accountability, reliability, customer service and innovation.

In Boston Strategies International's 2008 benchmark study, which received 500 responses from around the world to a questionnaire, Qatar Fuel came top in 15 different supply chain metrics. Measures of its operational success covering the range of supply chain strategies include the following:

- Rationalisation
  - >95% first pass yield
  - 5.6% cost of order fulfilment as % of order value
  - >99% stock accuracy
- Synchronisation
  - >97.6% uptime
  - Six Sigma order and delivery cycle time reliability
  - >99% of orders delivered by the time committed to
- Customisation
  - >99% orders delivered by time customer requests
- Innovation
  - >95% of items introduced in the last 12 months
  - >95% of sales from new products or services

Its supply chain is an important contributor to its outstanding financial performance. In 2007 the company earned a 58% return on capital employed (ROCE) and a 46% return on net assets.

BASF's balanced supply chain scorecard

For BASF, the North American arm of a German chemicals manufacturer, measurement is a process rather than a set of numbers.[8] It has outlined a nine-step process to ensure organisational alignment, facilitate a cross-functional view, motivate the organisation towards continuous improvement, and provide a means to link individual and organisation performance to reward systems.

BASF follows a nine-step process for measurement that it continues to roll out throughout its business units as the company grows:

1 Develop a project plan.
2 Form the team and kick off the project.
3 Provide performance measurement education on SCOR and balanced scorecards.
4 Identify and assess existing key performance indicators (KPIs).
5 Design a balanced scorecard.

6   Develop and document the SCOR level 1 and supporting KPIs.
7   Develop and document roles and responsibilities for formulating and assembling the metrics.
8   Establish targets and tolerances for each KPI.
9   Incorporate the use of metrics in business planning and control processes.

Using the SCOR framework, BASF tracks:

■   delivery reliability, including on-time delivery, fill rates and perfect order fulfilment;
■   responsiveness, as measured by order fulfilment lead time;
■   flexibility, as measured by supply chain response time and production flexibility;
■   costs, including distribution and transportation, manufacturing and supply chain costs as a percentage of revenue;
■   asset management, including inventory days of supply, capacity utilisation and cash-to-cash cycle time;
■   financial indicators, including revenue, profitability and cash flow;
■   status of enablers such as new processes and technologies, knowledge sharing and suggestions, as leading indicators of the ability to successfully implement the metrics, and to identify and troubleshoot problems.

BASF uses a detailed profile for each KPI to ensure thorough and internally consistent metric development. The characteristics include:

■   business process category that specifies which business process is being measured (customer service, inventory management, forecasting, production planning, warehousing, distribution, freight, training, procurement, etc);
■   name of the owner of the metric, which specifies who is accountable for the result of the KPI;
■   name of the data co-ordinator, which specifies who is responsible for gathering the data for the KPI;
■   source of the data (financial systems, controller's book, etc);
■   purpose of the metric;
■   frequency of measuring (hourly, daily, monthly, quarterly, annually, etc);
■   level of detail available (product, project group, business, business group, country, customer, customer segment, supplier, location, etc);
■   calculation method, that is, the formula and any special methods for calculating the figure, including averaging method, which elements to count, how much mean absolute deviation is acceptable, etc);
■   what year, month, or other time period is used as the baseline;

- performance targets, including the timeframe by which these are expected to be achieved, as well as the source of the target (demonstrated historical performance level, business plan target, benchmark, etc);
- tolerance for error in measuring the metric;
- frequency of updating the source data and the metric value.

L'Oréal's supply chain cockpit

L'Oréal, a French cosmetics company, established a "supply chain cockpit" of KPIs and targets after it standardised its packaging and raw material supply processes in Europe. The cockpit was part of a supply chain information system that linked production planning information among 13 European plants, and then extended its inventory visibility by linking to over 100 suppliers via both a web portal and direct data exchange from the suppliers' ERP systems to its own.[9]

13 Challenges for the future

Supply chain management is in a golden age of its history. Globalisation, fast product cycles and choosy consumers have made supply chains more complex, and those same pressures have simultaneously increased the cost of failure. While for many years theory outpaced the practical implementation of many concepts, that theory is being called upon today to solve the most complex and challenging operations management problems. Companies are consuming all the applied theory that academics, consultants and software providers can deliver in order to enhance their competitive positions.

Is SCM past its prime?

However, some might argue that SCM – or even the movement of goods – is becoming irrelevant as manufacturing shrinks from 27% to 10% of developed economies such as that of the United States, and services overwhelmingly replace products in the global economy. Are tools such as materials requirements planning, design for maintainability, design for operability and profit life-cycle management for bills of material becoming marginalised as financial services, health care and other services become today's growth engine?

Some concepts have already been largely implemented by most companies. For instance, over two-thirds of companies already outsource their major logistics activities, and manufacturing and procurement are not far behind.[1] Small and large companies alike have consolidated their supply bases by 50% or more; many are now single-sourcing. Lean methodology has become more or less ubiquitous since Japanese automakers demonstrated the beauty of the Toyota production system after the second world war. The popularity of Six Sigma has waned as the recent volatility in raw material and energy markets and sharp growth in Asia have made statistical variability reduction less urgent.

The savings from some of the more mature SCM techniques are diminishing as well. Companies' savings from RFX – requests for information (RFI), quotes (RFQ) and proposals (RFP), collectively called RFX for short – dropped from over 6% in 2005 to slightly over 4% in 2007, as the technique's popularity made it less effective for stimulating competition among suppliers.[2] The value of techniques to reduce inventory has also diminished as declining interest rates have reduced inventory carrying costs. Product simplification has been increasingly implemented since the days when automakers blazed trails by de-contenting their vehicles (engineering them to cut out any excess weight and complexity) to save costs.

As well as becoming fully implemented, many of the process improvements have been built into enterprise resource planning (ERP) systems, best-of-breed applications or internal information systems. ERP systems have embedded SCM, product life-cycle management (PLM), customer relationship management (CRM) and supplier relationship management (SRM) modules. Transportation and warehouse management systems (TMS and WMS) have downscaled to the point where most are available at a price that can be afforded by even small companies. Applications have migrated from the costly in-house or legacy architecture to internet-based processing and even software as a service (SAAS) for "pay-as-you-go" on-demand intelligence.

Where will SCM ultimately settle in the body of knowledge? Will it be subsumed by a grander movement, or will it last for 150 years, like the Industrial Revolution?

So far we are halfway through the life-cycle of SCM and it has contributed potential for a 33% increase in EVA. Between 2008 and 2015, it will provide another 12% potential improvement to EVA for companies that ship goods or provide services with supporting goods.

New conditions will provide fertile ground for the continued expansion of SCM. These include the Asian retailing boom, increasing trade and global sourcing, better customer analytics, increased availability of event management data, more standard data transfer protocols, green initiatives, and the extension of operations management principles and best practices to service industries.

The Asian retailing boom

As western-style retailing spreads throughout Asia and Chinese personal wealth accumulates, Asian retailers and western retailers based in Asia will transform Asian business with SCM. Metropolises like Kuala Lumpur, Shanghai and Ho Chi Minh will provide a model for smaller, more rural areas, providing the fuel for the trend to continue for many years. This will extend the product life-cycle of SCM considerably.

The expansion towards Asia is happening vigorously. M&C Specialties, a mid-sized American company, set up a plant in China 12 years ago and it is working at fever pitch to produce mobile phone components for Motorola, Nokia and Ericsson. A third-party logistics (3PL) provider, DB Schenker, is developing tools for calculating the cost of inland transportation in developing economies. In addition, "the whole oil industry is moving eastward – both production and consumption," says a product manager at Baker Petrolite, a maker of oil and gas production chemicals.[3] Electrical manufacturers are rushing eastwards. For example, an electrical equipment giant, Schneider, is making a massive investment in China, Caterpillar opened a new generator plant in China, and Siemens' Lighting division added capacity in Malaysia.

The Middle East is also booming. HP is manufacturing in Riyadh, Saudi Arabia, and local companies like Saudi Advanced Electronics Company (AEC) are partnering with major western companies.[4]

Increasing trade and global sourcing

Continued globalisation will increase the need for collaborative inventory management and global sourcing. US imports and imports as a percentage of GDP doubled (from 17% to 35%) between 1990 and 2008. Moreover, Chinese and other Asian sources are increasingly making goods of a quality that is acceptable to western companies. Although the Asian sourcing boom has decelerated because of the exchange rate and the economic downturn that started in 2008, the quality of Asian goods is nearing that of western products and the simple volume of trade will keep Asia the focus of sourcing efforts.

Better customer analytics

With the pervasive availability of data gathered everywhere from credit card transactions to bank loans to grocery stores, enormous amounts are accumulating. The opportunity is not lost on data mining specialists, who are developing methods and technology that will allow better customer analytics and pricing. The data should provide the basis for far better targeted marketing campaigns and the ability to establish direct one-to-one relationships with customers. The trends towards more customer power over the supply chain will make value analysis more important, furthering the state of the art in yet another dimension of data mining and analysis.

Enhanced data capture and transfer capabilities

Advances in wireless communication, especially RFID, will generate more data about supply chain events and product life-cycles than can be absorbed. For high-value shipments, it will support event management: the capture, monitoring and management of the status of production steps or shipments throughout the value chain from order to delivery. The internet enabled what had previously been uneconomical, since creating virtual private networks between companies before 1995 was expensive and risky. Moving forward, increasing acceptance of standards such as XML will facilitate more collaboration, which will in turn reduce the bullwhip effect. In addition, post-sale opt-in value-added features involving the RFID chip may offer customers and sellers valuable benefits such as customised shopping experiences based on the tags embedded in what they are carrying or wearing. Penetration along both vertical (at various points along the value chain) and horizontal (across industries like credit cards and convenience stores) lines will give RFID the capability to generate volumes of data, thereby accelerating the pace of data-mining tools.

Green initiatives
The strong basis of waste reduction in the science of SCM will allow companies to mitigate the wasteful use of natural resources. They can use SCM practices to reduce air and water pollution, trash (through smarter packaging), electrical consumption (through better conservation techniques for lighting and energy consumption in buildings) and junk (through the "four Rs" – return, repair, reuse and recycle). For example, ink-toner companies use this technique by establishing green rules for returns.

Product-services
Services have dominated goods-producing industries for decades. In the United States, wholesale, retail and government employment grew from 75% to 86% of total employment between 1940 and 2000, and will reach approximately 96% of the total in 2020.

The importance of the service sector does not only apply to the West; it also applies to a large number of economies that are generally considered to be based in manufacturing. For example, China's tertiary (service) sector grew from 24% to nearly 40% of GDP between 1978 and 2007.[5] In other countries, the tertiary sector represents between 28% of GDP (Nigeria) and 91% (Hong Kong), as shown in Table 13.1 overleaf.

As the shift towards more make-to-order manufacturing, distribution and reselling occurs, more companies will offer value-added services to complement their products and to increase their customer mindshare. These will increase the connection with customers, which will encourage the adoption of customisation and innovation strategies that minimise the commoditisation of their products and services.

Table 13.1 **Tertiary sector as percentage of GDP**

Country	%	Country	%
Hong Kong	91	Poland	64
US	78	Turkey	60
France	77	Czech Republic	58
Greece	76	Russia	56
UK	75	Argentina	56
Belgium	75	India	55
Netherlands	74	Philippines	54
Japan	73	Bangladesh	52
EU	71	Egypt	48
Australia	70	Morocco	46
Mexico	69	Chile	45
Italy	69	China	39
Germany	69	Ethiopia	39
Canada	69	Cambodia	39
Austria	68	Vietnam	38
South Africa	66	UAE	35
Switzerland	65	Saudi Arabia	33
Brazil	64	Nigeria	28
World	64		

Source: CIA *Factbook*, various years: 2006 basis except India (2005) and World (2004)

As supply chains shift their focus towards the customer, distribution companies will jockey for position to own the customer relationship. Port Said in Egypt is offering value-added logistics services so as to become more important to ocean shipping lines and their customers. The list includes, for example, stripping/stuffing, bulk storage, general and conditioned warehousing, truck maintenance and repair, container repair and maintenance, cleaning, tanking, quality control, repacking, assembly, trailer renting and leasing, information and communication services, safety and security services, and hotels, restaurants and shops.

They will also bundle and integrate services across the channel of distribution in their quest to increase sales and customer mindshare. Even in traditional manufacturing and industrial markets like that for compressors, companies that had been selling through value-added resellers that packaged the units together with air exchangers, engines, pumps and electrical circuitry, are starting to package the units themselves since this saves time and money, and also engages them in a direct relationship with the end-customer. Industry leaders are focusing on service agreements to hedge against downturns in the new equipment market. For example, Dresser Rand, a supplier of heavy industrial equipment, earns over half its revenues from the aftermarket.

The shift towards services is changing business models as companies offer pay for performance deals. Oilwell drill-bit providers are offering to be paid according to length drilled. Aircraft engine manufacturers are offering power by the hour instead of selling engines for a fixed price. Software providers are now offering software as a service (saas), whereby customers rent the time they use the software rather than purchase the software outright.

Chief supply chain officers: link supply chain initiatives to corporate strategy

Senior executives should set the stage for their companies to move to the next stage on the RASCI (rationalisation, synchronisation, customisation, innovation) framework. They should pay particular attention to the following techniques, which are rising in importance:

- Strategic sourcing (currently capable of increasing EVA by up to 8%), which will become more important as global sourcing and international trade become more embedded in everyday commerce.
- Customer knowledge management and customisation, which will become even more vital as more companies move up the supply chain strategy life-cycle from synchronisation to customisation.
- Perfect order fulfilment, which will become more important because most companies do not come close to perfect today.
- Clear anchor players, which will become more important because more supply chains will need public–private partnerships to resolve infrastructural problems, and will require strong leadership to achieve benefits.
- Every day low price (EDLP), which will become more common as retailing along the Wal-Mart model spreads to Asia, in recognition that it is one of the best ways to reduce the bullwhip effect.

- Collaborative and simplified interfaces, which will exert a major influence on supply chain efficiency as data protocols are increasingly standardised and adopted worldwide.
- Concurrent design and engineering, frequent new product development, and early prototyping and supplier involvement, which will figure more largely as product life-cycles continue to shorten and global competition intensifies, and as more companies move from customisation to innovation.

Other techniques that are not as widespread today will become more important, such as design for the supply chain, as awareness and penetration of SCM work their way back through the chain into design and engineering, and as high energy costs have a greater impact.

Corporate decision-makers will need help from solution providers, governments and academics to provide IT, physical and intellectual resources to implement these SCM tools and techniques.

Solution providers: develop new tools for managing data

The widespread implementation of ERP systems and applications to gather and optimise supply chain operations has led to a proliferation of data. To the extent that the data are shared among supply chain partners, data wealth of new capabilities will emerge, including association of product, supplier and customer data with tactile conditions (movement, light, and so on) and far more precise event history at the pallet, case and item level. This will provide the basis for post-sale tracking and value-added services. The abundance of data even has the potential to generate innovation organically, by providing information to trading partners who can apply their creativity and perspectives to it. It also has the ability to stimulate collaborative selling across trading partner boundaries, and to convert supply chains into supply networks where shared information flows encourage all the parties in a supply chain to collaborate for mutual gain. Over time, this could result in a common language for addressing supply chain issues and more standardisation of components and information, which will itself yield economic benefits.

The potential is not lost on MIT's research laboratories. Ultimately, the vast amount of information and the benefits of sharing it could result in a different organisation method and even a different way of organising our thinking process. Stephen Miles, a research engineer at MIT's Auto-ID Labs, explains:

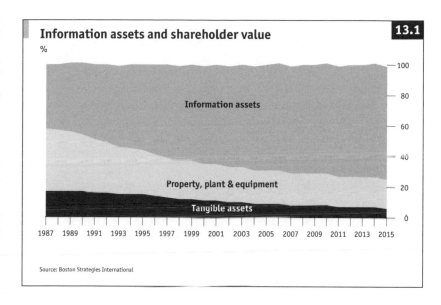

Information assets and shareholder value `13.1`

%

Information assets

Property, plant & equipment

Tangible assets

100
80
60
40
20
0

1987 1989 1991 1993 1995 1997 1999 2001 2003 2005 2007 2009 2011 2013 2015

Source: Boston Strategies International

We're moving towards a world where operations are network-centric. There used to be vertical silos, [but in the future we'll] have horizontal businesses that can integrate with each other.

The ability to manage data and information will be a key determinant of shareholder value in the future, as hard assets will decrease in importance (see Figure 13.1). Accordingly, the tools to manage this information flow will become vital competitive advantages in scm. Companies that apply these tools effectively will have a competitive advantage by delivering better service (matching organisation of resources to demand, segmenting and prioritising orders, and customising product and service delivery); by launching products more frequently and faster; and by increasing margins through rapid response, postponement and dynamic pricing. They will apply the same information to reduce costs through lean manufacturing and lean distribution, inventory management, supplier partnering, cross-docking and fleet rationalisation, quality management and e-procurement.

Governments: ensure adequate physical infrastructure
The march towards more efficient supply chains presupposes an infra-structure that can support inventory movement as fast as companies can make it move. Unfortunately, bottlenecks and unreliable connections are causing shippers to hold more inventory than in the past, jeopardising

years of efforts to create lean supply chains. A recent study by the US Chamber of Commerce uncovered deficiencies in all modes:[6]

> Gridlock on major metropolitan roads during peak travel hours is adding costs to the operations of trucking firms in terms of time and the operational expenses (e.g. fuel consumption, vehicle wear and tear, driver costs) of sitting in traffic. Rail freight is operating at capacity, leading to congestion on major corridors and gridlock in and near major rail hubs and ports. Increased private capital investment may not be able to meet future needs without public investment. Ports are constrained by channel depth, which limits the size of ships that can call. The largest of the modern megacontainerships and tankers can be accommodated at only a limited number of US ports, for example. Severe congestion in major airports ripples through the air traffic system, causing delays nationwide. These capacity problems are caused by both airside and landside traffic bottlenecks. Investment in new airports is lagging.

The infrastructure gap will force more public–private collaboration. This will take three forms: private investment, public policy and shared public and private infrastructure investment. Public and public–private partnerships in large investments will fill the gap. Although physical infrastructure investments have historically come from the public sector – most bridges and tunnels were built with purely public financing – recent investments are relying increasingly on co-operative investment between the private and the public sectors. The volume of investment supported by the Multilateral Investment Guarantee Agency (MIGA), which guarantees private-sector investment to facilitate growth in developing countries, has more than tripled since 2003.[7] Intelligent transportation networks, which use information technology to determine optimal routing and operation of vehicles, have attracted research grants but need to be stepped up in order to have an impact on supply chains.

What can be done? Private shippers can only do so much to restructure their networks and improve their processes. BNSF has lengthened its trains departing from US West Coast ports and simplified their make-up by reducing the number of destinations on each to preferably just one, in order to improve the capacity, velocity and consistency of its service. Public policy will tend towards more congestion pricing, for example greater use of night and weekend deliveries. The PierPASS programme at the port of Los Angeles is alleviating congestion by shifting demand to nights and weekends. Just as companies have recognised that transportation is only one link in scm, so should governments, which may want to consider renaming their departments of transportation as departments of supply chain.

As part of the movement towards the supply chain, government agencies responsible for transportation investment decisions should incorporate collective benefits and supply chain effects in their decision-making. This will involve identifying and reviewing high-cost and high-profile investments that are especially likely to generate supply chain benefits, and working with private-sector companies to agree on economically sound bases for quantifying and sharing their costs and benefits.

Academics: link SCM concepts to system dynamics to dampen business cycles

While business leaders are developing the tools and technology to manage supply chains through *space* (in particular, inventory collaboration, waste elimination and data exchange), researchers and economists need to be working on managing supply chains through *time* by eliminating the bullwhip effect in capital investment, capacity investment and pricing.

Economies oscillate over the short and the longer term according to the business cycle, which hits peaks and troughs every 3–10 years and is driven in part by production and inventory cycles, but also by factors such as levels of demand and available finance and social and political events. Production-inventory lags, which vary directly with supply chain management practices, are a major cause and aggravator of business cycles. Economists have proposed various theories to explain business cycles, including the lag between changes in demand and changes in production due to inventory buffers, multipliers and accelerators (people spend the money some time after they earn it, and withhold from spending for some time after the good times return), monetary and fiscal policies, and external shocks like wars. Jay Forrester's simulations using the National Model show that the business cycle can be flattened and the length between peaks reduced considerably by reducing or eliminating these lags.[9]

Academics, consultants and policymakers can help minimise cycles by highlighting early indications of gaps between supply and demand, thereby allowing decision-makers to make informed investment decisions and avoid overinvesting, overacquiring and overpaying at the peak. Accurate and timely information on industry-specific trends in lead times, productivity, capacity utilisation and similar metrics can help signal potential inflection points. Therefore, these relationships should be measured, modelled and forecasted and the results disseminated to private- and public-sector policymakers.

The benefits of improving supply chains are directly linked to macroeconomic performance and national competitive advantage. This connection is likely to ensure a long-lasting focus on improving the state of supply chain management.

Notes and references

Introduction

1 Kransdorf, Arnold, "High Stock Levels – not the Answer to Volatile Demand", *Financial Times*, June 4th 1982, p. 16.

2 CSCMP's definition of SCM is: "Supply chain management encompasses the planning and management of all activities involved in sourcing and procurement, conversion, and all logistics management activities. Importantly, it also includes coordination and collaboration with channel partners, which can be suppliers, intermediaries, third-party service providers and customers. In essence, supply chain management integrates supply and demand management within and across companies."

3 Characteristic of the evolution, the American Production and Inventory Control Society, a manufacturing-focused operations management group, rebranded itself – first, as the Educational Society for Resource Management, and later as the Association for Operations Management – after 47 years because production was increasingly becoming viewed as only one function of an extended supply chain.

4 Handfield, Robert and Nichols, Ernest, *Supply Chain Redesign: Transforming Supply Chains into Integrated Value Systems*, Financial Times/Prentice Hall, define supply chain management as: "Supply chain management is the integration and management of supply chain organizations through cooperative organizational relationships, effective business processes, and high levels of information sharing to create high-performing value systems that provide member organizations a sustainable competitive advantage." (2002)

5 Christopher, Martin, in *Logistics and Supply Chain Management*, Irwin, defines supply chain management as follows: "Logistics is essentially a planning orientation and framework that seeks to create a single plan for the flow of product and information through a business. Supply chain management builds upon this framework and seeks to achieve linkage and co-ordination between the processes of other entities in the pipeline, i.e., suppliers and customers, and the organization itself ... The management of

upstream and downstream relationships with suppliers and customers to deliver superior customer value at less cost to the supply chain as a whole." (2005)

6 For instance, Mandyam Srinivasan, a professor at the University of Tennessee, as quoted in David Blanchard, *Supply Chain Management Best Practices,* John Wiley & Sons, 2007, lists 14 guiding principles for lean supply chains.

7 For example, Blanchard, David: "top-performing companies have top-performing people working for them. That's the competitive advantage supply chain professionals offer." Blanchard, op. cit., p. 276.

1 A historical perspective on trade and transport

1 A new edition of Greene, James H., *Production and Inventory Control Handbook,* McGraw-Hill, first published in 1970, was published in 1997.

2 Lieb, Robert C., *Labor in the Transportation Industries,* Praeger, 1974.

3 Lambert, Douglas and Stock, James, *Strategic Logistics Management,* Irwin, 1993.

4 Charlene Barshefsky, US trade representative, in a speech on US–China Trade Relations at the Economic Club of Washington, Washington, DC, March 16th 2000.

5 Boston Strategies International analysis of Economist Intelligence Unit WorldData. WorldData combines the economic and industry forecasts of the EIU with updates throughout the day from EcoWin.

6 Data from Shanghai International Port Group (SIPG) website, 2009.

7 Container Security Initiative (CSI) Fact Sheet, US Department of Homeland Security, March 29th 2006.

8 The beer game has been passed on in folklore style through repetitive replaying. Those desiring to learn more about Jay Wright Forrester's contributions to the field of system dynamics may want to read his *Industrial Dynamics* (Pegasus Publishing, 1961) or consult the *System Dynamics Review.* Copies of the "beer game" board are available through the System Dynamics Society.

9 These examples are described in more detail in "Freight Transportation Bottom Line Report: Freight Transportation Demand and Logistics," prepared by Cambridge Systematics for the American Association of State Highway and Transportation Officials (AASHTO), Washington, DC, forthcoming, 2009.

10 Hickey, Kathleen, "Retailers: Starting to Get it Right – at the Store Level", *Global Logistics and Supply Chain Strategies*, April 2005, p. 56.

11 Source: Thelwell, David and Ritson, Christopher, "The International Competitiveness of the UK Cereals Sector", paper prepared for presentation at the 98th EAAE Seminar, "Marketing Dynamics within the Global Trading System: New Perspectives", Chania, Crete, June 29th–July 2nd 2006.

2 The bullwhip problem

1 By Kurt Salmon Associates (KSA), cited in Poirier, Charles C. and Reiter, Stephen E., *Supply Chain Optimization: Building the Strongest Total Business Network*, Berrett-Koehler, 1996.

2 "Tesco's Supply Chain Management Practices", ICMR India. Available online at: http://www.icmrindia.org/casestudies/ catalogue/Operations/Tesco%20Supply%20Chain%20 Management%20Practices.htm (accessed January 22nd 2009).

3 Cecere, Lora, Newmark, Eric and Hoffman, Debra, "How Do I Know That I Have a Good Forecast?", AMR Research Report, January 2005, p. 9.

4 Ouyang, Yanfeng, "Taming the Bullwhip Effect: from Traffic to Supply Chains", in Carranza Torres, Octavio A. and Moran, Felipe Villegas, *The Bullwhip Effect in Supply Chains: A Review of Methods, Components and Cases*, Palgrave Macmillan, 2006, p. 123.

5 Lee, Hau, "The Bullwhip Effect: Reflections", in Carranza Torres and Moran, op. cit., p. 2.

6 Sterman, John, "Operational and Behavioral Causes of Supply Chain Instability," in Carranza Torres and Moran, op. cit. Figures 2.1 and 2.2 are based on similar graphs presented in Sterman's chapter, although they were constructed independently using data from the US Federal Reserve.

7 Lee, op. cit., p. 2

8 J.S. Thomsen and John Sterman modelled tens of thousands of iterations of the beer game and identified chaotic patterns. See Thomsen, J.S., Mosekilde, E. and Sterman, J., "Hyperchaotic Phenomena in Dynamic Decision-Making", *Journal of Systems Analysis and Modelling Simulation* (SAMS), 1992, Vol. 9, pp. 137–56.

9 This synopsis is based on a case study provided by Hau Lee and Seungjin Whang in "The Bullwhip Effect: A Review of Field Studies", in Carranza Torres and Moran, op. cit.

10 From a presentation by David McGowan (vice-president of World Wide Security Services for Tiffany & Co) to the International Air Transport Association (IATA), Rome, March 2008.
11 Based on a December 2007 interview with Gary Maring, Cambridge Systematics.
12 Based on the author's analysis of trade and economic data from Global Insight, 2009.
13 Based on the author's analysis of trade and economic data from the Economist Intelligence Unit WorldData, 2009.
14 Based on the author's analysis of trade and economic data from the US Bureau of the Census foreign trade statistics, 2009.

3 What supply chain management is and where it is going

1 "The Emerging Supply Chain Management Profession", *Supply Chain Management Review*, February 2006.
2 This phrase comes from an e-mailed meeting announcement (June 9th 2008).
3 Quayle, Michael, ed., *Purchasing and Supply Chain Management: Strategies and Realities*, Idea Group Publishing, 2006.
4 Simchi-Levi, David, *Designing and Managing the Supply Chain*, McGraw-Hill, 2004, p. x.
5 The organisation adopted its original acronym "APICS" as a proper name and added the tagline "the Association for Operations Management".
6 For example, Carreira, Bill, "Lean Six Sigma is ... almost like a religion for which the goal is perfection, which is nearly impossible," *Lean Six Sigma that Works: Powerful Tools for Dramatically Reducing Waste and Maximizing Profits*, AMACOM/American Management Association, 2005, p. 3.
7 Interview with the author, May 13th 2008.
8 For further background on MRP systems, see Orlicky, Joseph, *Orlicky's Material Requirements Planning*, McGraw-Hill, 1994.
9 "Memorable Quotes by Defense Secretary Donald Rumsfeld", by Daniel Kurtzman. Available online at: About.com, http://politicalhumor.about.com/cs/quotethis/a/rumsfeldquotes.htm (accessed January 11th 2009).
10 Reid, R. Dan and Sanders, Nada R., *Operations Management: An Integrated Approach*, Wiley, 2007.
11 Poirier, Charles and Bauer, Michael, *E-Supply Chain: Using the Internet to Revolutionize Your Business*, Berrett-Koehler, 2001, p. 3.

12 Vitasek, Kate,"What Makes a Lean Supply Chain", *Supply Chain Management Review*, October 2005.

13 Ptak, Carol, *ERP Tools for Integrating the Supply Chain*, CRC Press, 2000.

14 Eliyahu Goldratt describes the drum-buffer-rope concept in many of his business novels, such as *Necessary but Not Sufficient: A Theory of Constraints Business Novel*, North River Press Publishing Corporation, 2000.

15 Cohen, Shoshanah, and Roussel, Joseph, *Strategic Supply Chain Management: The Five Disciplines for Top Performance*, McGraw-Hill, 2005.

4 Why CEOs need supply chain management today

1 In a 2008 interview with the author for an Economist Intelligence Unit white paper, "Thinking big: Midsize companies and the challenges of growth", February 2006.

2 Friedman, Thomas L., *The World Is Flat: A Brief History of the Twenty-First Century*, Farrar, Straus and Giroux, 2005.

3 Heinrich, Claus and Simchi-Levi, David, "Do IT Investments Really Pay Off?," *Supply Chain Management Review*, May/June 2005.

4 This set of tools was used in Poirier, Charles C. and Quinn, Francis J., "Survey of Supply Chain Progress: Still Waiting for the Breakthrough", *Supply Chain Management Review*, November 2006.

5 Cleveland, Douglas, "The Role of Services in the Modern U.S. Economy," US Department of Commerce Office of Service Industries policy memo, January 1999.

6 "How Will Western Manufacturers Survive: The Art of High-Cost Sourcing", Boston Strategies International White Paper, 2008.

7 "Benchmarking Your Supply Chain Savings", Boston Strategies International webinar, August 2007.

8 Jackson, Bill and Winkler, Conrad, "Building the Advantaged Supply Network", *Supply Chain Management Review*, May/June 2005.

9 Sahin, Funda, Robinson, E. Powell and Gao, L., as quoted in Mentzer, John T., Myers, Matthew B. and Stank, Theodore P. (eds), *Handbook of Global Supply Chain Management, Flow Coordination and Information Sharing in Supply Chains: Review, Implications, and Directions for Future Research*, Sage, 2006, p. 505.

10 Hugos, Michael, *Essentials of Supply Chain Management*, Wiley, 2006.

11 Robert Metcalfe (born 1946) co-invented Ethernet and founded a US computer network infrastructure company, 3Com.

12 "The Transportation Challenge", National Chamber Foundation, 2008. International logistics analysis prepared by Boston Strategies International under contract for Cambridge Systematics.

13 Presentation by Barry Akbar, general director of APL-NOL (Vietnam) to the Sixth ASEAN Ports and Shipping Conference in Ho Chi Minh City, Vietnam, June 2008.

14 "ADB Loan to Boost Rail Links Between Vietnam and China". Available online at: ChinaGate.com (accessed May 21st 2008).

15 "A Week of East–West Economic Corridor (August 27th–September 1st 2007) – The Big ASEAN Economic Event in Vietnam", VinaTrade USA, July 28th 2007. Available online at: www.vietnam-ustrade.org/cgi-bin/anmviewer.asp?a=641&z=4 5/ (accessed May 20th 2008).

16 WorldTravelGuide.net, www.worldtravelguide.net/country/303/internal_travel/South-East-Asia/Vietnam.html (accessed January 11th 2009).

17 Boston Strategies International analysis of data from Global Insight.

18 Brueckner, Jan and Spiller, Pablo, "Economies of Traffic Density in the Deregulated Airline Industry", *Journal of Law and Economics* 37(2), October 1994, pp. 379–415.

19 "The Transportation Challenge", National Chamber Foundation, 2008.

5 Setting the right supply chain strategy

1 Porter, op. cit.

2 Boston Strategies International, 2008.

3 Michael Treacy and Fred Wiersema developed an alternative generic business strategy triangle in *The Discipline of Market Leaders: Choose Your Focus, Dominate Your Market*, Perseus Books, 1995. They identified operational efficiency (low cost), product leadership (innovation) and customer intimacy (niche) as successful generic strategies.

4 These definitions come from SCOR level 1 metrics; in Cohen and Roussel, op. cit.

5 Author's analysis of Top 100 Retailers' data from Kalish, Ira, PricewaterhouseCoopers, as published by Siam Future Development, www.siamfuture.com/RetailBusCenter/RetailIndus/Top100.asp (accessed May 17th 2005).

6 Rationalisation: competing on low cost

1   Economist Intelligence Unit white papers that conclude that cost is a major competitive dimension include: *The New Face of Purchasing; Thinking Big: Midsize Companies and the Challenges of Growth; Courting the Consumer: Creating Dynamic Brands in Retail and Consumer Goods;* and *Business 2010: Retailing – Embracing the Challenge of Change.*

2   The companies that were considered to focus on cost management include Airbus, Alcoa, BHP Billiton, BNSF, Boeing, BP, British American Tobacco, CSX, ExxonMobil, FedEx, General Motors, Herman Miller, HP, IBM, Philips, Royal Dutch Shell and Sud-Chemie.

3   The supply chain cost framework here integrates viewpoints from various authors, including this author's. Handfield and Nichols in particular cover supply chain cost in their work *Supply Chain Redesign*, op. cit., p. 29. See also Cohen and Roussel, op cit.

4   This list draws on Cohen and Roussel, op. cit., p. 190, as well as Handfield, op. cit., p. 29.

5   Ferrin, Bruce C. and Plank, Richard E., "Total Cost of Ownership Models: An Exploratory Study", *Journal of Supply Chain Management* 38(3), Summer 2002, p. 18.

6   Boston Strategies International webcast, "On the Cutting Edge: How Industry Leaders are Planning to Transform Supply Relationships over the Next Five Years", August 21st 2007.

7   These examples are from the mid-1990s. See Moore, Nancy Y., Baldwin, Laura H., Cramm, Frank and Cook, Cynthia R., *Implementing Best Purchasing and Supply Management Practices 2002: Lessons from Innovative Commercial Firms*, RAND, 2002.

8   Moore *et al.*, op. cit.

9   Poirier, Charles, "At the Tip of Transformation", *Food Logistics*, April 15th 2001, p. 56.

10 According to a Northeastern University and Accenture study conducted by Robert Lieb and cited in Blanchard, David, *Supply Chain Management Best Practices*, John Wiley & Sons, 2007.

11 Based on "Outsourcing: the Sydney Airport Experience", by Krishan Tangri, manager – airport facilities and planning, presented at an International Quality and Productivity Center (IQPC) Airport Asset Management Conference in Kuala Lumpur in 2006.

12 Carreira, Bill, *Lean Manufacturing That Works*, op. cit.

13 Duffy, Mike, "How Gillette Cleaned up its Supply Chain", *Supply Chain Management Review*, April 2004.

14 Schutz, John D., "Yellow Freight Targets Regional Competitors 'Newest' Regional Leader?". Available online at: MyYellow.com (undated).

15 Based on "The Pooling Concept", by David Harman, CEO of Unitpool, paper presented to the IATA World Cargo Symposium, Rome, 2008.

16 Economist Intelligence Unit, *The New Face of Purchasing*, 2005.

17 The 13 forms are: 1 invoice; 2 packing list; 3 certificate of origin; 4 house waybill; 5 house manifest; 6 master air waybill; 7 export goods declaration; 8 customs release export; 9 flight manifest; 10 export cargo declaration; 11 import cargo declaration; 12 import goods declaration; 13 customs release import.

18 Eggers, Christophe, "Postal Air Waybill Pilot Test" presentation to the IATA World Cargo Symposium, Rome, March 2008.

19 Leger, Frederic and Kentfield, Ian, "Setting the Standards", presentation to the IATA World Cargo Symposium, Rome, March 2008.

20 Syridis, Constantin, "Message Improvement Programme (MIP): What Have We Learned and What Can You Do?", presentation to the IATA World Cargo Symposium, Rome, March 2008.

21 Chin, Jeffrey, "Implementing RFID to Create a Visible Supply Chain Network", presentation to the 6th Annual ASEAN Ports and Shipping Conference, Bangkok, Thailand, 2007.

7 Synchronisation: competing on reliability

1 According to the author's analyses of data from the US Bureau of Economic Analysis.

2 Author's analysis of data from Thomson Reuters.

3 "International, Supply Chain and Freight Drive 4th Quarter Results for UPS", UPS press release, January 30th 2008.

4 Vitasek, op.cit.

5 Carroll, Brian, *Lean Performance ERP Project Management: Implementing the Virtual Supply Chain*, St Lucie Press, 2002.

6 Halverson, Richard, "Logistical Supremacy Secures the Base – But Will it Translate Abroad?", *Discount Store News*, December 5th 1994.

7 Economist Intelligence Unit, *The New Face of Purchasing*, p. 11.

8 Christopher, Martin, *Logistics and Supply Chain Management*, pp. 226–8.

9 Sheffi, Yossi, "Maxing the Gain: The Key is Delaying the Point of Differentiation", *Chief Executive*, August/September 2005, p. 62.

10 "TNT Steps up China–Germany RFID Trial", *RFID World*, December 21st 2005.

11 Womack, J.P., Jones, D.T. and Roos, D., *The Machine that Changed the World*, Macmillan, 1990; Christopher, op. cit., pp. 226–8.

12 Billington, Corey and Johnson, Blake, "Creating and Leveraging Options in the High Technology Supply Chain", in Harrison, Terry, Lee, Hau and Neale, John, *The Practice of Lean Supply Chain Management: Where Theory and Application Converge*, Springer, 2004.

13 TruServ Corporation press release, May 2002, as reported on Logic-Tools website. See www.ilog.com/products/supplychain/ (accessed August 22nd 2008).

14 Fugate, Brian, Sahin, Funda and Mentzer, John T., "Supply Chain Management Coordination Mechanisms", *Journal of Business Logistics* 27(2), 2006, pp. 129–61.

15 Moran, Felipe Villegas, "Causes of the Bullwhip Effect", in Carranza Torres and Moran, op. cit.

16 The other methods were: requesting upstream (RUS), ordering downstream (OUT), constraints management (CSI), unadjusted replenishment (SRS) and demand sharing (FDC). Constraints management methods reduced bullwhip more but required higher inventory levels.

17 Poirier, Charles C. and Reiter, Stephen E., *Supply Chain Optimization: Building the Strongest Total Business Network*, Berrett-Koehler, 1996, p. 41.

18 Fawcett, Stanley, "Supply Chain Trust is Within", *Supply Chain Management Review*, March 2004.

19 The field of forecasting is vast and there are many books on the subject, so the purpose of this section is to introduce the main approaches. For a more detailed understanding of operational forecasting methods (exponential smoothing, curve fitting, etc), a handbook on forecasting is recommended.

20 This list is adapted from material in Lam, James, *Enterprise Risk Management: From Incentives to Controls*, Wiley, 2003.

21 Christopher, op. cit., pp. 250–51.

22 Author's phone interview with Bruce Crain, former senior vice-president, July 28th 2005.

23 This list is a selection adapted from Elkins, Deborah, Handfield, Robert B. and Craighead, Christopher W., "18 Ways to Guard Against

Disruption", *Supply Chain Management Review*, January/February 2005.

8 Customisation: competing on customer intimacy

1 Wal-Mart, for example, does not follow a customisation strategy (because differentiation between customers would run counter to everyday low prices, and it is profitable; however, EDLP and customisation are not mutually exclusive).

2 The word "customerisation" was coined by Jerry Wind and Arvind Rangaswamy in "Customerization: The Second Revolution in Mass Customization", paper published by Penn State e-Business Research Center, 1999.

3 Economist Intelligence Unit, *Personalisation: Transforming the Way Business Connects*, 2007.

4 Ibid.

5 Delivery capability means delivery throughout seasonal peaks and even weather conditions that could cause stock-outs. If a product cannot be changed quickly enough where necessary, a company will divert it en route to make sure it is shipped to where demand is strongest.

6 The companies adopting a customisation strategy, which included Netflix, Nokia, Plaxo, Popular Telephony, Siemens, Starbucks and UPS, were compared with their peer group averages.

7 Billington and Johnson, op. cit.

8 Peppers, Donald and Rogers, Martha, *Managing Customer Relationships: A Strategic Framework*, Wiley, 2004.

9 In Baran, Roger J., Galka, Robert and Strunk, Daniel P., *Principles of Customer Relationship Management*, South-Western College 2007.

10 Economist Intelligence Unit, *Business 2010: Retailing: Embracing the Challenge of Change*, July 2005.

11 "Loyalty card costs Tesco £1bn of profits – but is worth every penny," *The Independent*, October 10th 2003.

12 "Hotels Take 'Know Your Customer' to New Level," *Wall Street Journal Business*, February 7th 2006. Available online at: http://online.wsj.com/article/SB113927947660466836.html (accessed April 2nd 2009).

13 "Yahoo! Selects Rapt's Price Optimization Software for Its Global Business," Rapt press release October 17th 2005. Available online at: *www.rapt.com/news/051017_YahooRelease.html* (accessed November 20th 2006).

14 Bartels, Nancy, "The Price is Right: Airlines and Hotels Have Done it for Years; now Manufacturers are Discovering the Benefits of Optimized Pricing", *Manufacturing Business Technology*. Available online at: www.mbtmag.com/printversion.asp?page=www.mbtmag.com/curr (accessed November 20th 2006).

15 SkyChain and all the associated modules and systems are specified by Emirates SkyCargo, developed by Emirates Group IT and marketed externally by Mercator.

16 Economist Intelligence Unit, *Personalisation*, op. cit.

17 Peppers and Rogers, op. cit.

18 MRP originally stood for materials requirements planning, and was associated with a production planning algorithm pioneered by J A Orlicky that was embedded widely in software in the period 1970–2000. When its scope grew to include a broader view of production management including the real-world manufacturing, logistical, purchasing and financial constraints affecting the ability to deliver on schedule, the abbreviation MRP II, which stood for manufacturing resources planning, emerged and MRP became known as one of the software components of MRP II.

19 Economist Intelligence Unit, *Personalisation*, op. cit.

20 Baran *et al.*, op. cit.

21 Peppers and Rogers, op. cit.

9 Innovation: competing on revitalisation

1 Ferrari, Robert and Parker, Robert, "Digging for Innovation", *Supply Chain Management Review*, November 2006.

2 "The World's Most Innovative Companies", *BusinessWeek*, April 17th 2008; based on Boston Strategies International analysis of the companies, using data from Thomson Reuters.

3 Economist Intelligence Unit, *Innovation: Transforming the Way Business Creates*, May 2007.

4 In the survey, innovators were defined as those companies that reduced their new product introduction and delivery cycle times by more than 50% over the three-year period spanning 2006, 2007 and 2008.

5 70% of sales are from products that are less than one year old at innovating companies, compared with 43% at other companies.

6 64% of innovators' SKUS are less than a year old, compared with 41% at other companies.

7 Innovators introduce new products in 5.2 months, compared with 11.2 months at other companies.
8 "Get Creative!", BusinessWeek Online, August 1st 2005.
9 *Harvard Business Review on Supply Chain Management*, Harvard Business School Press, 2006.
10 Economist Intelligence Unit, *Courting the Consumer: Creating Dynamic Brands in Retail and Consumer Goods*, 2005.
11 Economist Intelligence Unit, *Foresight 2020: Economic, Industry and Corporate Trends*, 2006.
12 Forward branding should not be confused with a concept called "back-end branding" that Rashid Shaikh of Nypro is developing.
13 Cargille, Brian and Fry, Chris,"Design for Supply Chain: Spreading the Word Across HP", *Supply Chain Management Review*, July/August 2006.
14 Heinrich, Claus and Simchi-Levi, David, "Do IT Investments Really Pay Off?," *Supply Chain Management Review*, May/June 2005.

10 Organising, training and developing staff

1 *Strategy and Structure: Chapters in the History of the American Industrial Enterprise*, MIT Press, 1962.
2 Cohen and Roussel, op. cit.
3 Companies were considered to be pursuing a rationalisation strategy if they said that their primary supply chain strategy was "minimising material acquisition and operating costs" or, secondarily, "minimising inventory throughout the pipeline". The other choices were "optimising pricing and customer promising to maximise profit", "improving customer interfaces to improve sales revenue and margin" and "integrating all of the above strategies simultaneously".
4 According to a survey by the author. Companies were considered to be pursuing a synchronisation strategy if they said that their primary supply chain strategy was "minimising material acquisition and operating costs" or, secondarily, "minimising inventory throughout the pipeline". The other choices were "optimising pricing and customer promising to maximise profit", "improving customer interfaces to improve sales revenue and margin" and "integrating all of the above strategies simultaneously".
5 Parts of this section are adapted from Boston Strategies International's report to NYCHA ("Evaluation of the Cost-

Effectiveness of NYCHA's Supply Chain Operation Department's Central Warehousing Practices", November 2006).
6 This section has been adapted from the author's article "Perfecting Your Supply Chain", *Parcel Magazine*, February 2008.
7 Maccoby, Michael, "Learning to Partner and Partnering to Learn", *Research Technology Management*, 40(3), May–June 1997, pp. 55–7.

11 Information technology

1 Mansfield, Edwin, *Economics: Principles, Problems, Decisions*, WW Norton, 1980.
2 Porter, Michael, *The Competitive Advantage of Nations*, The Free Press, 1990.
3 "Importacao transforma setor de autopecas", *O Estado de Sao Paulo*, August 20th 1991, p. 20; "So Vai para a Frente Quem Enfrenta Desafios", *Exame*, July 11th 1990; "Hora e a Vez do Comprador", *Exame Melhores e Maiores*, August 1990; "O Pais Chegou Aos 20 Milhoes", *Brazil em Exame*, 1990.
4 "A New Era of Ports and Terminal Management", C.M. Lee, chairman and CEO, Bangkok Ports and Shipping conference, September 2007.

12 Measuring success

1 The source for the historical benchmark is Greene, James H., *Production and Inventory Control Handbook*, McGraw-Hill, 1970. Note that inventory turnover is also expressed as the inverse ratio (inventory to sales ratio). A high inventory turnover is a low inventory to sales ratio.
2 Lean accounting is based on the concept that standard costing encourages overproduction. Since manufacturing operations are measured on profitability as measured by standard costs, they look profitable when they overproduce because they get revenue credit for production, even if the product is never sold to a customer. This issue is resolved by improvements in costing, specifically the replacement of direct labour with activity-based costs (ABC), including overhead allocations.
3 SCOR metrics are detailed in Hugos, op. cit. The SCOR level 1 metric areas are: plan (demand forecasts, product pricing and inventory management; source (procurement, credit and collection); make (product design, production scheduling and facility management);

and deliver (order management, delivery scheduling and return processing).

4   EVA is a registered trademark by its developer, Stern Stewart & Co. Some have proposed the use of market capitalisation, but this includes so many other variables that the link to the supply chain is lost. For example, a 2003 study co-sponsored by Accenture, INSEAD and Stanford showed that supply chain leaders have a market cap up to 26% higher than other firms. However, based on this correlation it is hard to know whether the SCM practices led to the higher market capitalisation or vice versa.

5   Christopher, Martin, *Logistics and Supply Chain Management: Creating Value-Adding Networks*, Financial Times/ Prentice Hall, 2005.

6   Black belt is a rank in Six Sigma programmes, similar to the ranks awarded in karate.

7   Economist Intelligence Unit, *The New Face of Purchasing*, 2005.

8   Based on a presentation by Alan Milliken at the 2003 APICS International Conference and Exposition in Las Vegas entitled "How to Implement Supply Chain Performance Measurement".

9   "L'Oreal: High Performance Delivered", Accenture. Available online at: https://www.supplychainservices.accenture.com/web/public/client_successes/loreal.htm (accessed January 22nd 2009).

13 Challenges for the future

1   "How Will Western Manufacturers Survive? The Art of High-Cost Country Sourcing", Boston Strategies International, 2008.

2   "Benchmarking Your Supply Chain Savings", Boston Strategies International, 2007 webcast.

3   Interview with the author, July 2007.

4   "Saudi Private Sector Companies Strive for Excellence", online newsletter of the Saudi Arabian Embassy. See: http://saudiembassy.net/Publications/MagWinter96/private.html (accessed January 12th 2009).

5   *http://finance.people.com.cn/GB/8254179.html* (accessed January 12th 2009).

6   Paraphrased from "The Transportation Challenge", National Chamber Foundation, 2008, with permission from the National Chamber Foundation and the US Chamber of Commerce.

7   World Bank, "Private Participation in Infrastructure (PPI)", Database.

8 System Dynamics Society, The National Model, a videotaped conversation between Jay Forrester and MIT doctoral students, 1999.
9 Ibid.

Appendix 1 A brief history of supply chain thought

1 Greene, op. cit., pp. 30–45.
2 For example, Edward Frazelle in *Supply Chain Strategy: The Logistics of Supply Chain Management*, McGraw-Hill, 2001. CSCMP expanded the definition of logistics to: "that part of supply chain management that plans, implements, and controls the efficient, effective forward and reverses flow and storage of goods, services and related information between the point of origin and the point of consumption in order to meet customers' requirements." And specified its "boundaries and relationships" as follows: "Logistics management activities typically include inbound and outbound transportation management, fleet management, warehousing, materials handling, order fulfillment, logistics network design, inventory management, supply/demand planning, and management of third party logistics services providers. To varying degrees, the logistics function also includes sourcing and procurement, production planning and scheduling, packaging and assembly, and customer service. It is involved in all levels of planning and execution – strategic, operational and tactical. Logistics management is an integrating function, which coordinates and optimizes all logistics activities, as well as integrates logistics activities with other functions including marketing, sales manufacturing, finance, and information technology." Available online at: www.cscmp.org/aboutcscmp/definitions.asp (accessed January 4th 2009).
3 Porter, Michael, *Competitive Strategy: Techniques for Analyzing Industries and Competitors*, Free Press, 1980.
4 Lambert and Stock, op. cit.
5 Cohen and Roussel, op. cit.
6 Hammer, Michael and Champy, James, *Reengineering the Corporation: A Manifesto for Business Revolution*, HarperCollins, 1993.
7 Poirier, Charles C. and Tokarz, Steven J., *Avoiding the Pitfalls of Total Quality*, ASQ Quality Press, 1996.
8 Ross, David, *Competing Through Supply Chain Management: Creating Market-Winning Strategies through Supply Chain Partnerships*, Chapman and Hall, 1998.

9 Poirier, Charles, *Using Models to Improve the Supply Chain*, St Lucie Press, 2004.
10 "The Sinking of Bethlehem Steel: A hundred years ago one of the 500's legendary names was born. Its decline and ultimate death took nearly half that long", A Fortune autopsy. CNN Money.com, April 5th 2004. Available online at: http://money.cnn.com/magazines/fortune/fortune_archive/2004/04/05/366339/index.htm (accessed August 8th 2008).

Appendix 2 Strategic sourcing techniques based on supplier competition

1 "Tesco's international sourcing – the machine behind the machine," *Daily Telegraph*. Available online at: www.telegraph.co.uk/finance/newsbysector/retailandconsumer/4788156/Tescos-International-Sourcing---the-machine-behind-the-machine.html (accessed February 24th 2009).
2 Christopher, op. cit, pp. 226–8.
3 Hannon, David, "GSK closes the Loop Using E-sourcing Tools", *Purchasing*, June 3rd 2004.
4 Most of the literature on the impact of auctions on buyer–supplier relationships is qualitative and subjective. For an empirical study, see Pearcy, Dawn, Giunipero, Larry and Wilson, Andrew, "A Model of Relational Governance in Reverse Auctions", *Journal of Supply Chain Management*, Winter 2007, pp. 4–15.

Appendix 1

A brief history of supply chain thought

Early attempts to solve the demand-supply balancing problem focused primarily on reducing or eliminating the supply-demand imbalances that could be optimised with mathematical algorithms such as the optimal economic order quantity (EOQ). Early efforts were rooted in movements such as operations research (OR), total quality management (TQM), business process re-engineering (BPR), lean manufacturing and e-commerce.

The underlying bodies of knowledge

Operations research (OR), which became a standard discipline in business schools in the 1930s, laid the groundwork for SCM by offering algorithms that optimised transportation operations. The most famous OR problem is the travelling salesman, which is used to demonstrate a least-cost routing algorithm for a vehicle or person needing to make many deliveries. Linear programmes (LP) were so useful in solving problems based on an objective statement and multiple constraints that they became widely used across the OR field. Other useful OR tools were simulations (which relied on probabilistic scenarios), optimisations and stratifications (such as ABC inventory classifications, described in Chapter 7). However, as late as 1970, only 8–9% of logistics practitioners used LP for production or inventory management, and only 8–10% used simulation or probability theory.[1]

SCM developed rapidly after 1990, taking its influence from logistics management, value chain management, benchmarking, process re-engineering and best practices.

Logistics management

Historically, most people viewed logistics as a department that managed transportation and warehousing. As awareness and measurement of inventory increased, the boundaries of logistics expanded to cover inventory planning, forecasting and replenishment methods. When it became evident that poor service quality resulted in customer complaints,

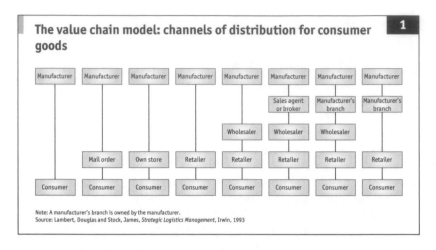

The value chain model: channels of distribution for consumer goods **1**

Note: A manufacturer's branch is owned by the manufacturer.
Source: Lambert, Douglas and Stock, James, *Strategic Logistics Management*, Irwin, 1993

customer service was included. Some included supply in their view of logistics,[2] which usually encompassed transactional purchasing activities such as purchase order processing, buying and payment, and supplier inventory co-ordination.

The classic logistics model is shown graphically in Figure 1. Logistical thought and logistics organisations make an essential contribution to effective SCM by creating competitive advantage through pull-based demand-driven flow.

Retailers such as Monoprix in France reconfigured their logistics networks to improve service levels while reducing inventory by setting up differentiated supply chains. Some warehouses handled only fast-moving goods, while others handled slow movers or heavy products like liquids. They also experimented with cross-docking and direct-to-store delivery that bypassed distribution centres. In the United States, retailers reduced the number of warehouses in their networks in order to benefit from risk pooling by centralising inventory, and numerous consumer products companies conducted best-in-class logistics benchmarks, aiming to improve their service levels and lower costs.

The classic view of logistics included the following areas:

- transportation;
- network design;
- shipment and carrier management;
- fleet management;
- warehousing;

◪ put-away;
◪ picking;
◪ packing;
◪ inventory planning and control;
◪ forecasting;
◪ reorder processing;
◪ customer service;
◪ order entry and processing;
◪ invoicing and collections.

Value chain management

Value chain thinking can be viewed as the first precursor of integrated supply chain theory. Michael Porter, a professor at Harvard University, popularised the value chain as a basic management concept in *Competitive Strategy*.[3] "Value chain" was a relatively simple way of defining a supply chain. Value chain concepts, which became popular in academia in the late 1980s, started being widely applied in corporations in the 1990s. Retailers and consumer packaged goods (CPG) companies in particular started analysing how they could cut costs, layers and cycle time from the heavily intermediated distribution chain. In 1993 Douglas Lambert, a professor at Ohio State University, and James Stock[4] used flow charts and relational maps to show how the processes fit together in sequence as well as in a vertical hierarchy. At this point, more of the flow diagrams began to include procurement, but few touched marketing, engineering or production. Most still indicated that the departments pushed material through the supply chain rather than pulled it.

The plan-source-make-deliver framework

Benchmarking became very popular in the 1990s, and consultants led initiatives worldwide to compare organisations and identify best-in-industry, best-in-class and best-in-world performance.

The supply chain operations reference model (SCOR), developed from 1994 to 1996, is a multi-company benchmarking effort that popularised a four-step view of supply chains. The four steps – plan-source-make-deliver – and benchmark performance levels that went along with them became central to the thought of the Supply Chain Council. The plan-source-make-deliver framework was a convenient way of capturing all the activities included in SCM, but since it mirrored the traditional functions (loosely, plan = logistics, source = purchasing, make = production, deliver = transportation), many companies just used (and still use) the framework to benchmark traditional functional performance. Nonetheless, Shoshana Cohen and Joseph Roussel's book *Strategic Supply Chain Management* made the purpose and elements of SCM clearer.[5] Specifically, their work and the work of the Supply Chain Council clarified the linkage between supply chain management and business strategy, which is reflected in some of the frameworks put forward in this book.

Process re-engineering and change management

Process re-engineering, which was popularised by Michael Hammer and James Champy in *Reengineering the Corporation*,[6] addressed supply chain opportunities by recognising that most of its activities were fragmented in different functional departments of organisations. It exposed the opportunity to redesign corporations around processes rather than functions, with fantastic improvements in cycle times, performance levels and ultimately customer service. Many of these opportunities were found in operations, where gaps existed between departments that shared a common end goal but never talked to each other since they were organised in stovepipe fashion. Some of the ripest opportunities occurred across multiple adjacent organisations in the same value chain; this was analogous to the process re-engineering opportunities that existed inside the companies themselves.

The mid-1990s saw extensive business process re-engineering

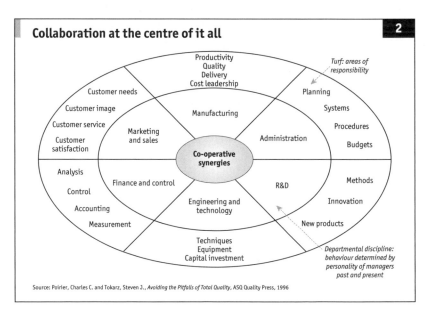

Collaboration at the centre of it all — 2

Source: Poirier, Charles C. and Tokarz, Steven J., *Avoiding the Pitfalls of Total Quality*, ASQ Quality Press, 1996

(BPR), and SCM received its share of BPR attention. In the throes of the re-engineering movement, Charles Poirier and Steven Tokarz[7] acknowledged the importance of organisational change to the success of SCM by placing "co-operative synergies" at the centre of a radial depiction of a variety of aspects of SCM, as seen in Figure 2.

Best practices

Throughout the 1990s, "best practices" thinking pervaded SCM. Robert Handfield (see note 4 on page 211) merged many of the previous concepts into one schema that showed a value-stream flow with best practices overlaid (see Figure 3). A map showing the value chain from suppliers to customers identified relevant best practices such as volume leveraging, design for manufacturing, and global sourcing.

Similarly, but in more depth, Lambert mapped every functional integration and leverage point involved in SCM, showing the contribution that each function could make to supply chain advantage by honing its best practices (see Figure 4 overleaf).

By 2004, the concept was becoming very elaborate, but an increasing amount of descriptive detail was making it harder for practitioners to maintain a common understanding on the central purpose of SCM.

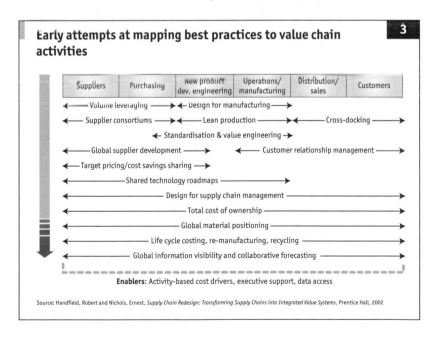

Early attempts at mapping best practices to value chain activities 3

Suppliers	Purchasing	New product dev. engineering	Operations/ manufacturing	Distribution/ sales	Customers

←——— Volume leveraging ———→ ←— Design for manufacturing ——→

←——— Supplier consortiums ——→ ←——— Lean production ———→ ←——— Cross-docking ———→

←— Standardisation & value engineering —→

←——— Global supplier development ———→   ←——— Customer relationship management ———→

←—— Target pricing/cost savings sharing —→

←——————— Shared technology roadmaps ———————→

←——————— Design for supply chain management ———————→

←——————— Total cost of ownership ———————→

←——————— Global material positioning ———————→

←——— Life cycle costing, re-manufacturing, recycling ———→

←——— Global information visibility and collaborative forecasting ———→

Enablers: Activity-based cost drivers, executive support, data access

Source: Handfield, Robert and Nichols, Ernest, *Supply Chain Redesign: Transforming Supply Chains into Integrated Value Systems*, Prentice Hall, 2002

Each function's contribution to supply chain management

Business processes \ Business functions	Marketing	Sales	Research & development	Logistics	Production	Purchasing	Finance
CUSTOMER RELATIONSHIP MANAGEMENT	Marketing plan & resources	Account management	Technological capabilities	Logistics capabilities	Manufacturing capabilities	Sourcing capabilities	Customer profitability
SUPPLIER RELATIONSHIP MANAGEMENT	Capabilities required for competitive positioning	Sales growth opportunities	Material specifications	Inbound material flow	Integrated planning	Supplier capabilities	Total delivered cost
CUSTOMER SERVICE MANAGEMENT	Prioritisation of customers	Knowledge of customer operations	Technical service	Alignment of logistics activities	Co-ordinated execution	Priority assessment	Cost-to-serve
DEMAND MANAGEMENT	Competitors' initiatives	Competing programmes in customer space	Process requirements	Forecasting	Manufacturing capabilities	Searching capabilities	Trade-off analysis
ORDER FULFILMENT	Role of logistics service in marketing mix	Knowledge of customer requirements	Environmental requirements	Network design	Made-to-order	Material constraints	Distribution cost
MANUFACTURING FLOW MANAGEMENT	Differentiation opportunities from manufacturing capabilities	Knowledge of customer requirements	Design for manufacturability	Prioritisation criteria	Production planning	Integrated supply	Manufacturing cost
PRODUCT DEVELOPMENT AND COMMERCIALISATION	Product/ service gaps in market	Customer opportunities	Product design	Logistics requirements	Process specifications	Material specifications	R&D cost
RETURNS MANAGEMENT	Knowledge of marketing programmes	Customer knowledge	Product design	Reverse logistics capabilities	Re-manufacturing	Material specifications	Revenue & costs

CUSTOMERS

SUPPLIERS

INFORMATION ARCHITECTURE, DATA BASE STRATEGY, INFORMATION VISIBILITY

Note: Process sponsorship and ownership must be established to drive the attainment of the supply chain vision and eliminate the functional barriers that artificially separate the process flows.
Source: Lambert, Douglas, *Supply Chain Management: Process, Partnerships, Performance*, Supply Chain Management Institute, 2008, p. 15 (www.scm-institute.org)

The emergence of supply chain strategy

Around 2005, academics were helping to clarify what exactly it was about SCM that contributed strategic advantage to the company above and beyond what excellence in each individual function could contribute. As David Ross explained: [8]

> SCM is about accelerating delivery times and reducing costs; it is also about utilising new management methods and the power of information technologies to achieve order-of-magnitude breakthroughs in products and services that target the unique requirements of the marketplace.
>
> The operational aspects of SCM provide today's enterprise with the ability to stay even with the competition in the struggle for marketplace advantage. On the other hand, the strategic capability of SCM to fashion a shared vision with channel system partners, form co-evolutionary and mutually beneficial channel alliances, and manage complex relationships with suppliers and customers enables today's innovative enterprise to lead market direction, spawn new associated businesses, and explore radically new opportunities.

In response to this, Poirier[9] presented SCM as a set of integrated value-added activities that did more than all the old functional ones. Specifically, it involved a nucleus firm; it used plan-source-make-deliver and had two more dimensions (inventory and technology), and it specified the best practices in categories that made sense to senior management because the benefits were apparent.

Leading-edge companies worked out major SCM programmes based on these frameworks. The world's biggest automaker conducted a large global sourcing programme in Latin America to achieve cost savings on a strategic level. Farm equipment manufacturer John Deere launched a widely recognised lean manufacturing process improvement programme. Steel and metals conglomerates such as KGHM in Poland and Bethlehem Steel in the United States privatised or rationalised their operations to achieve step improvements in shareholder value or stave off decline.[10]

Appendix 2

Strategic sourcing techniques based on competition

Stimulating competition is an important aspect of rationalisation through strategic sourcing, although it falls outside supply chain management in so far as it does not affect the ability to balance demand with supply or reduce the bullwhip effect throughout the supply chain.

For leverage categories, the most effective strategy is generally based on approaches that act to keep suppliers' margins in check. These approaches include, for example, requests for information (RFI), quotes (RFQ) and proposals (RFP), collectively called RFx for short, global sourcing, auctions and payment terms.

Buyers have recently made a significant move from managing supplier price to managing supplier cost. Led by Wal-Mart, buyers know that knowledge of the actual cost is power. When buyers speak knowledgeably and accurately about cost structures in the supply market, sellers are more inclined to share information that proves (or disproves) the buyers' understanding.

In recent years, low-cost country sourcing has proved to be the most effective supplier competition strategy. Studies reveal that global sourcing has saved companies 13% of acquisition cost on their largest-spend categories, compared with an average of 7% for most supply chain initiatives. Both goods manufacturers and service providers do it under different names, for example outsourcing or offshoring, and even small and mid-sized firms are doing it. The arrival of value-priced competitors such as Zara (Spain) and Matalan (UK) has shifted the price expectations of consumers. Tesco buys over 60% of its clothing and 40% of its non-food products through its Hong-Kong based global sourcing centre.[1] Even high-end retailers such as London-based Marks and Spencer have turned to low-cost country sourcing. When it started to make the transition in 1998, textile labour cost $9.50 per hour in the UK, while it cost less than 50 cents per hour in China, Pakistan and Indonesia. Like many retailers, Marks and Spencer began by asking its suppliers to offshore their sourcing and eventually it established some of its own supply relationships overseas. To deal with the challenge of the long import lead times for fashion-oriented clothes, it ordered half of its merchandise well before the season, 40% of it nearer to the season in which it is sold and 10% of it during the season "in response to emerging fashion trends".[2]

Offshoring is a common form of low-cost country sourcing. China became prominent for its low-cost offshore manufacturing capabilities. India also became a hotspot for business process outsourcing (BPO), and other countries are getting in on the BPO game. For example, Gloria Macapagal Arroyo, president of the Philippines, cites BPO as one of the country's growth strategies. Outsourcing and offshoring have been so widespread that international transportation and logistics companies, especially air express carriers such as DHL and UPS, are expanding rapidly on international routes that connect Asia and the West, which is catalysing the spread of SCM concepts in Asia. Even small, privately held firms can participate in the offshoring opportunity. Take, for example, MacGregor, a US financial services software developer that was recently acquired by Investment Technology Group. It operated a development centre in Spain, which was part of the reason it was attractive to Investment Technology Group.

Other ways to engage suppliers in competition include competitive bidding, reverse auctions (which start at high prices and go down), competitive events and structured negotiation.

The traditional mechanism for competitive bidding has been RFX. Charles River Laboratories, a $1.4 billion US clinical research company, uses RFX to source much of its material and service requirements, including lab supplies, animal transportation, and IT hardware and software. The RFX programme was part of a plan to centralise some parts of procurement after years of decentralised purchasing. Procurement decision-making had been fragmented across 40 locations in the United States, Canada, Scotland and Japan as a result of rapid growth through acquisitions.

GlaxoSmithKline, a UK pharmaceutical company, has used reverse auctions extensively for purchasing materials and services. *Purchasing* magazine reports:[3]

> In 2003, the company completed 939 e-sourcing events including 534 e-auctions, pushing more than $3.8 billion through the tools, almost one-third of its total spend. After assuming responsibility for procurement, [chief procurement officer Gregg Brandyberry] was saving an average of 8% before moving suppliers to an online bidding system, when it almost doubled to 15% for sealed bids and sometimes as much as 28% for reverse auctions.

The internet and low-cost computing have spawned many creative variations on auctions. For example, combinatorial auctions allow bidders to choose parts of the whole or the whole bundle in order to increase the chance of a higher bid value. Also, buyers can significantly affect results by controlling the sequence in which the bidders bid and the information is known or hidden from bidders. Today, buyers have polarised opinions on auctions. Some feel that they are the best way to send a hard message to suppliers and get tangible results quickly, while others feel that suppliers are less co-operative when under the auction model than under more relationship-focused supplier management models.[4]

Appendix 3

List of abbreviations

3PL	third party logistics provider
ABC	inventory counting method that stratifies types of inventory into categories according to the frequency of its rotation, or turns; alternative meaning: activity-based costing
AGV	automated guided vehicle
APS	advanced planning and scheduling
APICS	Association for Operations Management. The abbreviation comes from its former name, the American Production and Inventory Control Society
ASRS	automated storage and retrieval system
ATO	assemble to order
ATP	available to promise
BOM	bill of material
BPO	business process outsourcing
BPR	business process re-engineering
CAD/CAM	computer aided design, computer aided manufacturing
CEO	chief executive officer
CFO	chief financial officer
CLO	chief logistics officer
CMO	chief marketing officer
COO	chief operations officer
CMMS	computerised maintenance management system
COGS	cost of goods sold
CORE	clear, objective, relevant and effective
CPG	consumer packaged goods
CPO	chief procurement officer
CRM	customer relationship management
CSCMP	The Council of Supply Chain Management Professionals
CSI	Container Security Initiative
CT/PAT	Customs Trade Partnership Against Terrorism
CTO	configure to order
DC	distribution centre

DIAD	delivery information acquisition device
DMAIC	define, measure, analyse, improve and control
DRP	distribution resource planning
EBIT	earnings before interest and tax
EBITDA	earnings before interest, tax, depreciation and amortisation
ECM	electronic contract manufacturer
ECR	efficient consumer response
ECO	engineering change order
EDI	electronic data interchange
EDLP	every day low price
EFT	electronic funds transfer
ERP	enterprise resource planning
EOQ	economic order quantity
ETO	engineer to order
EVA	economic value added
FMCG	fast-moving consumer goods
GPO	group purchasing organisation
GPS	global positioning system
ISCEA	International Supply Chain Education Alliance
JIT	just-in-time
KPI	key performance indicator
KRA	key results area
LP	linear programme
MECE	mutually exclusive and collectively exhaustive
MRO	maintenance, repair and operating
MRP	materials requirements planning
MTO	make to order
MTP	make to plan
MTS	make to stock
NPD	new product development
NPI	new product introduction
OCR	optical character recognition
OEM	original equipment manufacturer
OM	operations management
OR	operations research
PDA	personal digital assistant
PDCA	plan-do-check-act
PLM	product life-cycle management
PO	purchase order
PPP	public–private partnership

QEC	quick engine change
RFID	radio frequency identification
RFx	requests for information, quote and proposal (RFI/RFQ/ RFP, collectively called RFx for short)
RMA	returned merchandise authorisation
ROA	return on assets
ROCE	return on capital employed
RONA	return on net assets
S&OP	sales and operations planning
SaaS	software as a service
SCM	supply chain management
SCOR	supply chain operations reference (model)
SFA	salesforce automation
SKU	stock-keeping unit
SMED	single minute exchange of die
SRM	supplier relationship management
TCO	total cost of ownership
TMS	transportation management system
TPM	total productive maintenance
TPS	Toyota production system
TQM	total quality management
VAR	value-added reseller
VMI	vendor-managed inventory
VOIP	voice over internet protocol
VPN	virtual private network
WMS	warehouse management system
XML	extensible markup language

Appendix 4

Glossary

All definitions in this glossary are deliberately reduced to the essence of their pertinence to end-to-end SCM. For more detailed definitions, the reader may wish to consult the APICS Dictionary, the CSCMP Glossary and sources cited in the notes.

Assemble to order   Production system in which material is prepared so it can be assembled quickly upon customer request.

Barcode symbology   Logical systems of data storage in barcodes (strips of vertical lines of varying widths designed to be read by optical scanners) that define the amount and type of data that can be stored and how they are transmitted between the barcode and the reader. The UPC code, which is used at most retail checkout counters, is the most popular barcode symbology.

Bottleneck   Point of limited capacity where the flow slows down because of constriction.

Break-bulk   Irregularly-shaped and often oversized cargo that needs to be transported and handled by hand or by specialised equipment. Alternative definition (from the APICS dictionary): division of truckloads of homogeneous items into smaller or more appropriate quantities for use.

Channel design   Architecture of a set of supply chain relationships that defines which actors will trade with which other ones and sets high-level parameters such as which partner will hold inventory and how much, which will face the customer and which will share information with which others.

Close-out   Sale, discount or clearance.

Collaborative inventory management	Co-operation between a buyer and a supplier, usually in the form of shared forecast information and a single unified and reconciled plan, to improve stock availability and reduce its cost.
Concurrent design	Method of product development whereby new product conception is a collaborative and simultaneous process between many functions, such as product development, manufacturing and field service, with the goal of cost effectiveness and customer-perceived value once the product is produced and distributed in large volumes.
Configure to order	Assemble to order.
Consignment	Inventory replenishment mode in which the buyer pays only when he sells the product to his customer, and he may return unsold inventory to the supplier. Alternatively (CSCMP Glossary): a shipment that is handled by a common carrier.
Constraints management	Identifying, reducing or eliminating bottlenecks in an operation; according to the theory of constraints, a five-step process for identifying and eliminating bottlenecks that was developed by Eliyahu Goldratt.
Cross-docking	The process of taking cargo from an incoming vehicle to an outgoing vehicle without storing it in inventory at a warehouse. Cross-docking reduces inventory investment and storage space requirements.
Cross-selling	Offering a customer or prospective customer products or services from parts of the company's offering other than what the customer is currently purchasing or interested in purchasing.
Cycle time compression	Re-engineering of processes to reduce the time, and hence the cost, needed for a product to move through part or all of a supply chain.

DC bypass	Circumventing the distribution centre by routing freight directly to its destination. This requires co-ordination with suppliers and customers to ensure the proper inventory levels and frequency of delivery to achieve the target service level and avoid stock-outs.
Demand chain management	Supply chain management that emphasises the primacy of customer requirements as manifested through the strategy techniques of synchronisation and customisation.
Design for assembly/ modularisation	Engineering a system of components so that they can be easily and quickly assembled as a final product or service when a customer needs it.
Design for maintainability	Engineering a product or service so it can be easily and inexpensively repaired and updated.
Design for manufacturability	Approach to conceiving products that considers the complexity and cost of large-scale production.
Design for operability	Engineering a product or service so it can be easily and inexpensively used.
Design for prototypeability	Approach to conceiving a product that allows it to be easily and rapidly translated into a working model.
Design for supply chain	Approach to conceiving and developing products that considers total supply chain costs.
Disintermediation	Breaking down of an established reseller relationship in a supply chain in favour of a direct relationship between two parties.
Drum-buffer-rope	Lean manufacturing concept in which the drum represents the heartbeat, or *takt* time, of the operation (which is also the pace of the binding constraint); the buffer represents work-in-process inventory in the production operation; and the rope represents the pull of demand limited by the pace of material release.

Early customer involvement	Soliciting input from customers in the product development stage to increase customer satisfaction and implement cost-saving ideas before suboptimal supply chain processes, systems or infrastructure are developed.
Early prototyping	Creation of working models of a product at the initial stages of product development to identify problems while the design is still fluid enough that it can be modified at low cost.
Early supplier involvement	Soliciting input from vendors in the product design and development stages to reveal cost-saving ideas before decisions by others (such as the buyer and the ultimate customer) limit the supplier into suboptimal processes, systems or infrastructure.
Electronic data interchange (EDI) transaction sets	Standardised sets of data that are transmitted, usually between a buyer and a seller, to indicate any number of supply chain events. Advance shipping notices (transaction set 856) and commercial invoices (transaction set 810) are two common EDI transaction sets.
Gain sharing	Splitting benefits achieved (often cost savings beyond a benchmark or target level) with workers, suppliers or customers.
Inventory	Stock. Buffers of raw material, work in process, or finished material designed to hedge against uncertain or erratic demand or supply so as to avoid stock-outs.
Kaizen	Japanese word for continuous improvement achieved through employee involvement.
Landed (delivered) cost	Cost of obtaining a product at its point of use, including transportation, customs duties and fees, insurance, interest and storage.

Lean	Containing no or little waste. Alternatively, a shorthand term referring to an approach towards eliminating waste from production and distribution through the active involvement and motivation of workers and a focus on value to the customer.
Lifts, empty lifts	Taking loaded or unloaded containers (respectively) off a vehicle, usually a ship or train.
Logistics	Co-ordination of flows of funds, information and goods from a supplier to a customer to maximise availability while minimising operating costs.
Make to order	Production system that produces only in response to a customer order.
Make to stock	Production system that replenishes a buffer of inventory independently of customer orders.
Mindshare	Presence of the brand in the mind of the customer, as defined by the proportion of the top customers' attention that is devoted to his or her relationship with the supplier's company.
Offshoring	Producing or sourcing from overseas.
Operations management	Maximising throughput from a dynamic system within constraints (usually time and cost) by adjusting demand and capacity at work centres.
Outsourcing	Contracting of a third party to manufacture or deliver a product or service.
Partnering	Collaboration with suppliers or customers that adds value to each partner's processes, projects or strategy.
Picking and packing	Selecting material from warehouse shelves, wrapping it and palletising it (usually in shrink-wrap or with a band to hold it together). "Pick-pack-ship" includes loading onto vehicles for delivery.

Postponement	Shifting the point of differentiation closer to the point of consumption to reduce out-of-stocks and inventory costs, and increase opportunities for customisation.
Product life-cycle management	Software application that is used to process engineering change orders (formal changes to the design specifications of products) and to maintain and update bills of material that define the composition of products or services. Alternative meaning: modulating the level of activity and resources devoted to SCM activities (such as R&D, engineering, production, logistics and customer service) during product introduction, growth, maturity and decline.
Public–private partnership	Joint investment by governmental and private-sector interests, usually in infrastructure.
Pull system	Resupply arrangement whereby replenishment is triggered by customer usage or purchases.
Put-away	Storing incoming material on warehouse shelves.
Responsive order fulfilment	Delivery arrangements that acknowledge customers' wishes and satisfy them because they are adapted to their preferences and lifestyle.
Revenue management	Using the profitability of individual customers and transactions to decide how to respond to and prioritise orders.
Service chain management	Engineering and management of a flow of services (intangible products) and funds so as to maximise customer loyalty. No goods are involved.
Shipment consolidation (deconsolidation)	Aggregation (or disaggregation) of cargo according to its destination (or origin) at a point between the origin and the destination.
Should-cost	Price that the product would cost if all supply chain strategies were properly employed.
Six Sigma	Form of statistical process control designed to ensure the ability of a process to repeatedly deliver output within a prescribed range of tolerance.

SKU rationalisation	Reducing the number of stock-keeping units (SKUs) to minimise the supply chain cost and complexity (for example, inventory carrying, obsolescence and order management costs).
Stock-out (or "out of stock")	Lack of materials, components, or finished goods that are needed.
Stovepipe fashion	Functionally separated into vertical silos with limited communication between each other.
Supplier consolidation	Reducing the number of vendors by offering more attractive economies of scale to improve negotiating leverage and increase supplier commitment and involvement through a deeper relationship with fewer partners.
Supplier _kaizen_	Introducing continuous improvement initiatives into supplier organisations to synchronise supply chain goals and operations between two trading partners.
Supplier pre-packaging	Boxing, labelling and loading by a supplier in the order of delivery or consumption rather than the order of production to facilitate quicker and easier unloading and to eliminate intermediate offloading until the smallest units reach their final customer.
Supply chain	Set of activities involved in moving a product (such as a vehicle) and its associated services (such as service parts) from the ultimate supplier to the ultimate customer.
Supply chain management	The co-ordination of the set of activities involved in moving a product (such as a vehicle) and its associated services (such as service parts) from the ultimate supplier to the ultimate customer so as to maximise economic value added (EVA).

Supply management	The process of getting goods and services from the supplier to the point of production on time and within budget to minimise the total life-cycle cost to the organisation. Includes at a minimum the identification of sources, contracting and purchasing.
Tier-skipping	Voluntary disintermediation by the buyer forwards or backwards in the supply chain to gain the benefits of a more direct relationship with remote supply chain partners by eliminating the profit margins of middlemen and forming a more intimate customer relationship.
Total cost of ownership	The direct and indirect expense associated with owning a product from its purchase until its retirement. This equals the supply chain cost, plus the acquisition cost itself, minus the cost of SCM failure.
Total quality management	The engagement of a workforce in ensuring that quality problems are continuously eradicated through the use of process analysis tools.
Up-selling	Offering a customer or prospective customer a more expensive or higher-margin product or service than what they currently purchase or are interested in purchasing.
Value analysis	The process of decomposing a product or process to its elemental usefulness to the customer, and then eliminating any non-essential steps in designing, producing, or delivering it. Understanding customers' underlying needs based on their preferences.
Value engineering	The redesign of products or processes to optimise the ratio of customer desires to the cost of satisfying them.
Vendor managed inventory	Mode of inventory management in which a supplier monitors the amount of inventory at a customer's location and replenishes it as needed to keep supply and demand in balance.

Warehouse slotting Assigning storage spaces to material coming into a warehouse. Storage spaces can be assigned statically (space is dedicated for specific material) or dynamically (space is allocated to material depending on availability at the time).

Yield pricing Process of adjusting pricing to influence demand and thereby increase sales and margins.

Index

project management 37
promotions 19, 90
prototyping 150, 151, 175, 206
Ptak, Carol 34–5
public-private partnerships 205, 207–9
pull-based demand trigger 96, 98–9
purchasing 25, 43, 183
push supply chain 152

Q
Qatar Fuel 196–7
QEC ("quick engine change") 103
quality 43, 44, 66, 67, 207
quality function deployment 131–3, 132
Quayle, Michael 26
"quick engine change" see QEC

R
R&D 149, 149, 161–2
radio frequency identification see RFID
railways 21, 28, 47–8, 58, 83, 90, 97, 128
BNSF 97–8, 208
rapid replenishment 28, 35, 100
rapid response 37, 126, 142, 207
rationalisation 36, 36, 55, 55, 63, 233, 234
benefits 44, 45, 46, 63–5, 64, 65, 185, 186
and business strategy 54, 54
customer relationship management 179–80
for economic growth 61, 61, 62
elements of strategy 37–40, 38–9, 67–89
fleet rationalisation 207
information systems 171, 172, 173, 174–5, 175, 179, 180, 181, 182
in integrated strategy 56, 57, 58–9, 60, 60
lean approach and 74, 123
metrics 186, 187, 188–9, 192, 194
organisation 155–6, 156, 168, 169

of SKU base 123
and value chain role 53, 53
versus synchronisation 93–4
see also cost leverage factor; low cost
"real options" 141–2
recycling 24, 40, 43, 66, 67
Reid, Dan 32
relationship marketing 143
reliability 34, 35, 36, 53, 90, 94–5, 100
repetitive manufacturing 5–6
replenishment 28, 34, 95, 98–9, 109
kanban cards 95, 100
rapid 28, 35, 100
requests for information see RFI
requests for proposal see RFP
requests for quotation see RFQ
Research in Motion (RIM) 59–60
retailers 9–11, 11
return on assets see ROA
return on capital employed see ROCE
return on net assets see RONA
revenue 46, 185, 186
revenue growth 148–9, 148
revenue management 137–8, 162
reverse auctions 174, 235, 235–6
RFI (requests for information) 200, 234, 235
RFID (radio frequency identification) 43, 103, 127, 145, 164, 202, 203
libraries 178
"smart carts" 134–5
RFP (requests for proposal) 165, 200, 234, 235
RFQ (requests for quotation) 37, 43, 165, 200, 234, 235
eRFQ 70, 170, 171
savings from 45
RFx see RFI; RFP; RFQ
RIM (Research in Motion) 59–60
risk 28–9, 115, 116–20, 180
management 31, 37, 115–16, 120, 189–90
mitigation 96, 115–23